The Personality of Paris

The Personality of Paris

Landscape and Society in the Long-Nineteenth Century

Alan R. H. Baker

BLOOMSBURY ACADEMIC
LONDON • NEW YORK • OXFORD • NEW DELHI • SYDNEY

BLOOMSBURY ACADEMIC
Bloomsbury Publishing Plc
50 Bedford Square, London, WC1B 3DP, UK
1385 Broadway, New York, NY 10018, USA
29 Earlsfort Terrace, Dublin 2, Ireland

BLOOMSBURY, BLOOMSBURY ACADEMIC and the Diana logo are
trademarks of Bloomsbury Publishing Plc

First published in Great Britain 2022
Paperback edition first published 2023

Copyright © Alan R. H. Baker, 2022

Alan R. H. Baker has asserted their right under the Copyright, Designs and
Patents Act, 1988, to be identified as Author of this work.

Cover image: © Fighting at the Hotel de Ville, 28th July 1830, 1833 (oil on canvas)
(Photo by Art Images via Getty Images)

All rights reserved. No part of this publication may be reproduced or transmitted in
any form or by any means, electronic or mechanical, including photocopying,
recording, or any information storage or retrieval system, without prior
permission in writing from the publishers.

Bloomsbury Publishing Plc does not have any control over, or responsibility for, any
third-party websites referred to or in this book. All internet addresses given in this
book were correct at the time of going to press. The author and publisher regret any
inconvenience caused if addresses have changed or sites have ceased to exist, but
can accept no responsibility for any such changes.

Every effort has been made to trace the copyright holders and obtain permission to reproduce the
copyright material. Please do get in touch with any enquiries or any information relating to such
material or the rights holder. We would be pleased to rectify any omissions in subsequent
editions of this publication should they be drawn to our attention.

A catalogue record for this book is available from the British Library.

Library of Congress Cataloging-in-Publication Data
Names: Baker, Alan R. H., author.
Title: The personality of Paris : landscape and society in the
long-nineteenth century / Alan R.H. Baker.
Other titles: Landscape and society in the long-nineteenth century
Description: London ; New York : Bloomsbury Academic, 2022. |
Includes bibliographical references and index.
Identifiers: LCCN 2021036289 (print) | LCCN 2021036290 (ebook) |
ISBN 9781350252646 (hb) | ISBN 9781350252653 (pdf) | ISBN 9781350252660 (ebook)
Subjects: LCSH: Paris (France)–Description and travel. |
Paris (France)–Historical geography. | Paris (France)–History–19th century. |
City planning–France–Paris–History–19th century. |
Paris (France)–Buildings, structures, etc.–History. | Haussmann, Georges
Eugène, baron, 1809–1891.
Classification: LCC DC707 .B294 2022 (print) | LCC DC707 (ebook) | DDC 914.4/36104–dc23
LC record available at https://lccn.loc.gov/2021036289
LC ebook record available at https://lccn.loc.gov/2021036290

ISBN: HB: 978-1-3502-5264-6
PB: 978-1-3502-5263-9
ePDF: 978-1-3502-5265-3
eBook: 978-1-3502-5266-0

Typeset by Newgen KnowledgeWorks Pvt. Ltd., Chennai, India

To find out more about our authors and books visit www.bloomsbury.com
and sign up for our newsletters.

Dedicated to the memory of
Henry Clifford Darby
(1909–1992)
and
Hugh Counsell Prince
(1927–2013)

Contents

List of illustrations		xi
List of plates		xiv
Preface		xv
Prologue		1
1	Beginnings: The founding of Paris and its growth to 1789	9
	The site and situation of early settlement	9
	Medieval Paris	10
	Encircling the growth of Paris	11
	Early modern Paris	13
2	The peopling of Paris: The making of 'Parisians'	19
	On becoming a metropolis	19
	The growth of population 1789–1914	20
	The role of immigration	21
	The making of 'Parisians'	25
	A 'sick' city 1800–50	32
	The emergence of concepts of urbanism and town planning	33
3	Monumentalizing Paris: Commemorating its past	37
	The column in the Place Vendôme 1806–10	38
	The Arc de Triomphe 1806–36	39
	The obelisk in the Place de la Concorde 1836	41
	The July Column in the Place de la Bastille 1840	42
	The statue of Joan of Arc in the Place des Pyramides 1874	43
	The monument to the Republic 1880	45
	The Statue of Liberty 1886	46
	The meanings of monuments	48
	Street names	50
	History and collective memory	52

4	Modernizing Paris: Rebuilding the city	55
	Towards curing a 'sick' city	55
	The context for change	62
	Haussmann's transformation of Paris 1853–70	63
	Critiques of Haussmann's work by his contemporaries	73
	Critiques of Haussmann's work by historians	76
5	Symbolizing Paris: Architectural icons	83
	The Panthéon 1791	83
	The Opéra Garnier 1862–75	86
	The Basilica of the Sacred Heart 1875–1912	88
	The Eiffel Tower 1889	90
	Le Pont Alexandre III 1900	96
	Le Métro 1900	98
6	Projecting Paris: World Fairs 1855–1900	101
	1855 *Exposition universelle de Paris*	102
	1867 *Exposition universelle de Paris*	104
	1878 *Exposition universelle de Paris*	106
	1889 *Exposition universelle de Paris*	107
	1900 *Exposition universelle de Paris*	111
	Five *Expositions universelles*: The whole greater than the sum of its parts?	113
7	Enjoying Paris: Food, fashion and fun	117
	'The right to idleness'	117
	Food: *haute cuisine*	122
	Fashion: *haute couture*	126
	Department stores: *Grands magasins*	129
	Fun in *Gai Paris*	132
	The democratization of leisure?	137
8	Escaping Paris: (Re-)discovering 'Nature' and the provinces	141
	Parks and gardens in Paris before 1850	141
	Parks and gardens in Paris after 1850	145
	Cemeteries	151
	In pursuit of 'Nature' away from Paris	153

9	'Assassinating Paris'?: Revolutions, wars and the twentieth century	159
	Processes of urban renewal	159
	Revolutions and upheavals	160
	Wars	164
	Since 1945	169
Epilogue		181
Chronology		195
Sources		199
Index		215

Illustrations

Figures

1.1	The remains of the Tour Montgomery in the Rue des Jardins-Saint-Paul	12
1.2	Oblique view of Paris in 1615	14
2.1	'*Dire que nous v'là parisiens!*': 'Fancy that, we're Parisians now!'	25
3.1	Column in the Place Vendôme c. 1900	39
3.2	Obelisk in the Place de la Concorde c. 1865	42
3.3	Statue of Joan of Arc in the Place des Pyramides	44
3.4	Monument à la République in the Place de la République c. 1895	45
3.5	Statue of Liberty by Frédéric Bartholdi in the Luxembourg Garden	47
3.6	Le Panthéon 1912	50
3.7	Street sign of Rue Marengo	52
4.1	Rue du Bourdonnais in 1865	56
4.2	Rue Traversine c. 1860	57
4.3	Passage de l'Opéra c. 1909	59
4.4	Rue Rambuteau c. 1890	60
4.5	Demolition of Rue Estienne in 1862	65
4.6	Clearing space for the new Avenue de l'Opéra c. 1855	66
4.7	Boulevard Saint-Michel c. 1860	66
4.8	La Gare du Nord c. 1900	67
4.9	River Bièvre c. 1865	68
4.10	New sewer in 1861	69
4.11	The 'old' Les Halles in 1852	70
4.12	Part of the new Les Halles in 1862	70
4.13	Rue Soufflot's remodelling c. 1860	71
4.14	Rue Soufflot c. 1895	71
5.1	The Panthéon c. 1900	84
5.2	L'Opéra Garnier c. 1900	87
5.3	La Basilique du Sacré-Cœur	89
5.4	The Eiffel Tower 1889	91

5.5	Advertisement for the 1889 Exposition universelle	93
5.6	An Eiffel Tower-shaped perfume bottle	95
5.7	Hitler at the Eiffel Tower on 23 June 1940	96
5.8	Le Pont Alexandre III and the Grand Palais *c.* 1910	97
5.9	Entrance to the Métro station Ménilmontant	99
6.1	Le Palais de l'Industrie 1855	103
6.2	L'Exposition universelle 1867	105
6.3	Rue des Nations 1878	107
6.4	Plan of the Exposition universelle 1889	109
6.5	'History of habitation' by Charles Garnier at the 1889 Exposition universelle	110
6.6	Admission ticket for the Exposition universelle 1900	112
6.7	Le Petit Palais and Le Grand Palais in 1900	114
7.1	Electric lighting on the Champ-de-Mars 1878	118
7.2	Le Café Procope	123
7.3	Café discussion of the Franco-Prussian War 1870	124
7.4	Carte Gastronomique de la France 1809	126
7.5	Fashion Plate from La Mode Illustrée 20 August 1882	129
7.6	Le Bon Marché *c.* 1900	130
7.7	'Le Chahut' 1890 by Georges Seurat	134
8.1	Le Jardin des Plantes 1905	142
8.2	Le Jardin du Luxembourg *c.* 1905	144
8.3	Grand Lac of the Bois de Boulogne *c.* 1860	146
8.4	Bois de Vincennes *c.* 1870	147
8.5	Entry to the Père-Lachaise Cemetery 1865	152
8.6	The artist Jules Le Coeur and his dogs in the forest of Fontainebleau, 1877	155
8.7	The tramway station at Barbizon *c.* 1900	156
8.8	*Une baignade à Asnières* 1884 by Georges Seurat	156
9.1	Barricades in Rue Saint-Maur in the *10ᵉ arrondissement*, 25 June 1848	163
9.2	The burnt-out Hôtel de Ville 1872	167
9.3	La Défense from the Arc de Triomphe	171
9.4	La Tour Zamansky and church of Saint-Étienne-du-Mont	173
9.5	Le Centre Pompidou	174
9.6	La Tour Montparnasse	175
9.7	La Porte d'Italie	176

9.8	La Pyramide du Louvre	177
9.9	L'Opéra Bastille	177
9.10	La Bibliothèque nationale de France site François-Mitterand	178
9.11	No. 175 Boulevard Haussmann in 2020	179

Table

| 6.1 | Expositions universelles in Paris | 102 |

Plates

1	The site and situation of Paris	1
2	The walls of Paris 1190–1845	2
3	The *départements* of France in 1790	3
4	The *arrondissements* of Paris in 1870	4
5	Population of Paris 1801–1911	5
6	Geographical origins of immigrants in Bonnières 1817–46	6
7	Geographical origins of immigrants in Bonnières 1896–1906	7
8	Geographical origins of immigrants living in Paris in 1891	8
9	Foreign, provincial and Parisian origins of residents of the *quartiers* of Paris in 1886	9
10	Auvergnats in Paris in 1911	10
11	New streets in Paris constructed 1850–70	11
12	The geography of 'poverty' and 'wealth' in Paris in 1880	12
13	Principal parks, gardens and cemeteries in Paris 1870	13
14	Plan of Père-Lachaise Cemetery	14

Preface

I visited Paris for the first time in 1958, in the Long Vacation at the end of my first year as a geography undergraduate at University College London. Two fellow students were my companions: we stayed only one night in Paris in cheap and forgettable hostel accommodation, because our main objective was to hitch-hike to Provence – which we achieved. My next trip to Paris was with Sandra, my fiancée, in the summer of 1959, to research at the French Ministry of Agriculture some post-1945 farm consolidation schemes in the Paris Basin for my undergraduate dissertation. My third visit was in August 1960 after graduating and after our wedding: we honeymooned in the Hôtel Cambon, in central Paris. On being appointed Lecturer in Geography at Cambridge in 1966, I renewed my research interests in France. I have pursued some investigations in the Archives Nationales and in libraries in Paris, but my research has focussed on provincial France. My lectures to undergraduates on the geography of France during the nineteenth century encompassed Paris. In the early 1970s, a colleague, Harold Fox, and I delivered a lecture course on the comparative geographies of London and Paris from 1500 to 1914. This present book has, therefore, had a long gestation period and came to term in my retirement and 'shielding' during the Covid-19 pandemic. It is not grounded wholly in original research: instead, it offers a new arrangement of other scholars' flowers, a geographical perspective upon a key period in the history of the landscape and society of Paris.

I am grateful to numerous Cambridge undergraduates, postgraduates and colleagues with whom I have had many fruitful discussions about the 'City of Light'. I have also appreciated warmly the comments of members of the University of the Third Age in Cambridge who attended my courses on the historical geography of France delivered annually since 2012.

I am beholden to three good friends for their willingness to comment on the first draft of my book: Eugene Stevelberg, a retired *lycée* geography and history teacher living in Nice who knows Paris well; Cynthia Clinch, who read French at Oxford and worked in France for some years before retiring to Cambridge; and John Hipkin, a Francophile and Cambridge councillor who became a close friend while we were both serving on the city's Planning Committee. I am also considerably indebted to Roy Doyon, a retired North American professional geographer living in Cambridge, for drawing the colour illustrations. I am also grateful for the helpful comments of three anonymous appraisers of my book proposal, for the anonymous reviewer's constructive critique of my penultimate text and for the editorial guidance of Rhodri Mogford and Laura Reeves at Bloomsbury.

I am deeply grateful to Emmanuel College which has been a stimulating and supportive intellectual environment in which to teach and research the historical geography of France. I thank warmly the Master and Fellows for a grant which has enabled my book to have some colour illustrations.

I am dedicating this book to Professor H. Clifford Darby and Dr Hugh C. Prince, two mentors who awakened me to the joys of historical geography in general and of France in particular.

As always, I owe a deep personal debt to Sandra, my wife, companion, research assistant and critic on our almost-annual *tours de France* spanning more than sixty years.

Emmanuel College Cambridge
CB2 3AP   24 May 2021

Prologue

Each city, each locality, each region, each country, indeed each continent is unique – each individual place might share some characteristics with another while also possessing singular, unique, characteristics. A place may be likened to a person: no matter how two people might look and act alike, each possesses a distinctive personality, shaped by her or his own history and geography. Almost 200 years ago, a French historian, Jules Michelet (1798–1874), claimed in his *Histoire de France* (1833) that '*La France est une personne*'. Michelet argued that 'history is at first entirely geography' but that gradually 'society overcomes nature' and 'history effaces geography'. For Michelet, geography – which at the time of his writing was understood as physical geography – provided a passive stage upon which the French people enacted the drama of their history. The founder of modern geography in France, Paul Vidal de la Blache (1845–1918), applied that concept of personality to France as a place, as a country, as a landscape, in his portrait of its geography published as an introduction to the *Histoire de France* (1903) by Ernest Lavisse (1803–1919), who instructed schoolteachers and their pupils: 'You should love France, because Nature has made it beautiful, and because History has made it great.'

For Vidal de la Blache, the centuries-long struggle of people with their physical environments produced geographical individuality. We would now add to the struggles of people with their physical environments battles for their minds – ideological conflicts (such as clerical against secular and capitalist against socialist) and also struggles by individuals with their own consciences (such as political and philosophical beliefs). Through time, individual places acquire their own historical and geographical personalities so that, as expressed vividly by Vidal de la Blache, each place becomes 'a medal struck in the image of its people'. This concept also underpins, although not explicitly, the magisterial synthesis of the 'identity of France' by Fernand Braudel (1902–1985), one of the leaders of the Annales School of history. But although myriad books about the history and geography – the historical geography – of Paris already exist, the concept of its personality or identity as a place has not been the fundamental principle underpinning any of them. As a historical geographer, I am here offering a distinctive way of looking at Paris in the long-nineteenth century.

The concept of geographical personality as developed by the American geographer Carl Sauer may be applied to a particular part of the earth's surface as an enquiry into the dynamic relationship of land and life. Sauer's essay on the personality of Mexico acknowledged his debt to the English archaeologist Cyril Fox's book on *The Personality of Britain* (1932) and was in turn the inspiration for studies by some of Sauer's students, such as that by Andrew Clark in his essay on the personality of Canada and by Dan Stanislawski in his book on the individuality of Portugal. I discussed the concept in my book exploring the intellectual bridges between *Geography and History* (2003).

The personality of a place is a product of the relationship between land and society through time. Examining that relationship in the case of nineteenth-century Paris is my aim here. Paris features hugely in syntheses by Xavier de Planhol and Jean-Robert Pitte of the historical geography of France as a country. The central role played by Paris in the political, economic and cultural life of France is incontrovertible and well known. But the landscape and society of Paris are rarely given the forensic attention they deserve. There are, undoubtedly, some excellent histories and geographies of Paris, notably 'the biographies' of Paris by historians Colin Jones and Pierre Pinon and the historical atlas of Paris edited by geographer Jean-Robert Pitte. But in such works the landscape of Paris is not their central concern, as mine is here. The nearest approach to my geographically informed study of the landscape and society of Paris in the nineteenth century is the collection of essays edited by a historian, Louis Bergeron's *Paris: Genèse d'un Paysage*, which covers a much longer time span, from prehistory to the late twentieth century: it is an extensive, rather than an intensive, treatment of the landscape history of Paris. Moreover, like most histories of Paris written by historians, it is organized chronologically which mine is not. Also close to my concerns is Michael Marrinan's study of the cultural landscape of Paris from 1800 to 1850. As an art historian, Marrinan analysed representations of the Parisian landscape in art, not only in paintings but also in daguerreotypes, prints, sculptures and architecture, relating their images and symbolic meanings to the intense political struggles witnessed in what he somewhat paradoxically terms 'Romantic Paris' while stressing the city's revolutionary and tumultuous character in the first half of the nineteenth century.

Most tales of Paris by historians are told sequentially, narrating with the flow of time from century to century, from one 'period' to another or from one political regime to another. The most extreme but supremely logical deployment of this chronological approach to the history of Paris are the three outstanding books by social historian Mary McAuliffe on the years 1848–1918: each book covers a distinct period (1848–71, 1871–1900 and 1900–18), but each chapter within these books addresses in turn a single year (or exceptionally two years) within those periods. This rigidly 'horizontal', thin-slicing of Paris's history is both challenging and intriguing, providing a literary 'snapshot' of each year or two years, embracing the city's demographic, economic, political and cultural features year after year. That radical structure is very different from the 'vertical' approach I have adopted, in which each chapter in turn examines one key feature of Paris's personality and traces its development and significance between 1789 and 1914. While there is a chronological tendency within each chapter, my book's overall organizational structure is thematic.

The changing Parisian landscape during the long-nineteenth century is my central aim. Let me address the historical frame of my book, 1789–1914, before elaborating further its geographical perspective. The concept of a 'long' century probably stems from Fernand Braudel's designation of the period from 1450 to 1640 as the 'long-sixteenth century' in his classic study of the Mediterranean and the Mediterranean world in the age of Philip II. But more pertinent to my work is that of the Marxist historian, Eric Hobsbawm, whose three volumes of European history in the 'long-nineteenth century' started with the French Revolution of 1789 and ended with the outbreak of the Great War in 1914. That period, he argued, saw the development of coherent ideas and practices which enabled it to be identified and portrayed as a definable 'century' in history with three distinctive periods: *The Age of Revolution 1789–1848*, *The Age of Capital 1848–1875* and *The Age of Empire 1875–1914*. 'The long-nineteenth century' as a concept embraces the French and Industrial Revolutions and as a term has come to be used in a wide range of history's sub-disciplines. It provides the basic temporal structure for this present study of the landscape of Paris, while requiring an introductory discussion of what the Parisian landscape in 1789 inherited from previous centuries and permitting a concluding consideration of the extent to which the long-nineteenth century's legacy was valued and survived in the century after 1914.

Within that historical framework, my approach is geographical but very different from that of another historical geographer, David Harvey, whose insightful analysis of Paris as the 'Capital of modernity' from 1830 to 1871 sits within the locational discourse of the subject, being concerned centrally with the social and economic representations and materializations of the city, with the construction and use of social spaces within the city. Landscape and society have reciprocal relations. My approach to nineteenth-century Paris is primarily through the former and Harvey's was primarily through the latter. Harvey has provided an intellectually rigorous account of the political, economic and social processes which restructured spatial relations in the city during the middle decades of the nineteenth century. By contrast, my study is situated principally within the landscape discourse of geography but draws also upon its locational discourse when considering spatial relations and the use of space within Paris during the long-nineteenth century. My approach is akin to landscape history and spatial history, with greater emphasis on the former than the latter.

Which ideas and processes produced the distinctive landscape of Paris and how were Parisians affected by the physical and cultural landscape in which they worked and had their lived experiences? Such general questions demand specific and interdisciplinary answers. I am seeking them here from a geographical perspective. This involves an exploration of both the making and the meaning of the changing Parisian landscape. Landscapes are visual and tangible expressions of many, often conflicting, cultural discourses: the built forms of a landscape may be read as materialized discourse. Landscapes are both created and destroyed within an ideological context; moreover, they have meaning and are understood within such a context. Within geography, Dennis Cosgove and Stephen Daniels, among others, have forcefully argued that landscapes need to be read as cultural, symbolic, expressions of the social order that pre-existed them. Deciphering the iconography of landscapes involves recognition that often, but not always intentionally, they send signals that are read – or misread – by those who receive them. A landscape is very complex in its cultural construction and perception. So much so, that reading an historic landscape, like that of Paris, is not an easy task – and for that reason, it is often simplified in order to make it more manageable.

The character of Paris has been encapsulated often in just a few words or 'sound bites'. Paris has been imagined and described in ways which stress its leading, central, historical role in France and also beyond France's frontiers. Some descriptions have emphasized the thematic primacy of Paris as 'Capital of the Nineteenth Century', as 'Capital of Revolution', as 'Capital of Science', as 'Capital of the Modern Self', as 'Capital of Alienation' and as 'Capital of Modernity'. Others have stressed its dominance as the 'Capital of Art', as 'Capital of Gastronomy', as 'Capital of Fashion' and as the 'Capital of Pleasure'. Still others have seen it geopolitically as the 'Capital of Europe', as 'Capital of the World' or more cautiously as 'Capital of the Civilised World' but also more extravagantly as 'Capital of the Universe'. A basic problem with all such terse appellations is that they have been forged in a vacuum, lacking the comparative assessment necessary to establish convincingly the primacy of Paris. In effect, they are often at best unsubstantiated claims and at worst perpetuations of beliefs which might well be closer to myths than to realities. Myths about the past are imaginative simplifications of realities for the benefit of the 'present'. For example, the myth of Paris as *'la vraie Babylone'* ('the true Babylon') dates from its use in a serialized novel by Pierre Ponson du Terrail (1829–1871) published in 1867 as one of his series of *Drames de Paris*. This myth was then fostered by the Catholic Church which preached that an evil spirit was at work in the city.

Paris as a 'modern myth' was the concern of a pioneering paper in 1937 by a young literary critic, Roger Caillois, who was born in Reims in 1913 but migrated to Paris in 1929 to prepare (as it turned out, successfully) for the competitive examination for admission to the École Normale Supérieure. His literary career was centred on Paris; he died there in 1978 and was buried in the Montparnasse cemetery. Caillois argued that myths as imaginative representations of reality are created by and are the property of society collectively rather than of individuals. They become components of a collective *mentalité*. Myths relate to the past but can be powerful influences upon perceptions in the present. Caillois saw myths about Paris as simplifications which tended selectively to emphasize one aspect over all others: they are misrepresentations or distortions of a reality. Myths about Paris are thus multiple. They depict an imagined Paris, they are translations of realities, they are ways of understanding rather than ways of knowing the city. Myths about modern Paris were, Caillois argued, constructed and reconstructed in literature and paintings from the early nineteenth century onwards.

Paris as a city of myths has been analysed at book length and with great acuity by Patrice Higonnet in his *Paris: Capital of the World*. He anatomizes more than a dozen myths, including 'Capital of Revolution', 'Capital of Alienation', 'Capital of Pleasure' and 'Capital of Art' but not – curiously, somewhat perversely – the 'City of Light', arguably the most common myth about Paris. This cascade of representations of Paris has been constructed in arresting 'sound-bites' which make claims for Paris with broad brushstrokes so that the city emerges memorably as being more than the sum of its parts. But in order to understand fully the complex personality of Paris we need to identify and comprehend its key characteristics. Many simplified descriptions of Paris have been made not only by twentieth- and twenty-first-century historians but also by nineteenth-century commentators. As early as 1867, two journalists and writers, Edmond Texier (1815–1887) and Albert Kaempfen (1826–1907), neither born in Paris but both long-time residents and dying there, co-authored a book titled *Paris, Capitale du Monde* (1867). Undoubtedly the most illustrious and frequently used description is of Paris as the 'City of Light'. But there is a surprising degree of ambiguity or even confusion about that appellation, with some employing it literally and others figuratively.

Efforts to bring more light and cleanliness to the city's streets were made in the sixteenth century, funded by a special tax known as the '*Taxe des boues et lanternes*' ('Tax on mud and lights') which dated from 1506. Municipal edicts of 1554 and 1560 prohibited overhanging eaves on buildings, thereby allowing more light and fresh air to reach the streets. Householders were frequently ordered to put lights (tallow candles or oil lamps) in their windows at night to make the streets less hazardous underfoot and to provide greater personal safety for nocturnal pedestrians. In 1588, the Parisian authority decreed that a torch should be installed and lit at each street intersection, and in 1594 the requirement was changed from torches to lanterns. It is sometimes suggested that the origin of the baptism of Paris as '*la Ville lumière*' might relate to the improvement of its street lighting in the seventeenth century ordered by Gabriel Nicolas de La Reynie (1625–1709), the first chief of police in Paris, whose task it was 'to purge the city of disorder and to create abundance for its inhabitants'. Some claim that it is thanks to him that Paris became the cleanest and best-lit town in Europe. The extent to which rules about lighting in Paris were enforced is uncertain. In any event, before the nineteenth century lighting of public places was mainly by oil lanterns and candles. It could not have been very effective. In 1836, Fanny Trollope (1779–1863, mother of the novelist Anthony Trollope) complained about the darkness of Parisian streets, claiming that many small provincial towns in England enjoyed better lighting than did the capital of France.

If Paris seems to have been precocious in introducing tallow candles and lanterns in public places, it was slower to adopt gas and electric lighting. London began to install gas street lights in 1807. The introduction of gas lighting in Paris in the 1820s was an improvement, an early swallow signalling the coming of modernity, but it was only extended slowly. There were perhaps some 13,000 gas street lights illuminating Parisian streets in 1830 and perhaps 56,000 in 1860. But it is difficult to believe that Paris was at this time a 'city of [good] lighting' – or at least, no more so than London. Electric illumination of Parisian streets was introduced in earnest in1878, as it was also in London that year. In 1889 and 1900 electric lighting entered very dramatically into the Parisian landscape, at the World Exhibitions hosted in the city in those years. Electricity certainly excited the imaginations of residents and tourists alike in Paris during the closing decades of the nineteenth century. Electricity was the 'actor' playing the principal part in Camille Pissarro's 1897 impressionist painting *Boulevard Montmartre: Nuit*, one of a series of fourteen views he painted depicting the boulevards under different diurnal and seasonal lighting conditions. The role of illumination in changing the visage of Paris has been addressed at length recently by Hollis Clayson, an art historian, in her 2019 book *Illuminated Paris: Essays on Art and Lighting in the Belle Époque*. While she rightly stresses the dazzling and dramatic impact of first gas and then electric lighting on the streets of Paris, on the night life of the city and on paintings of Parisian scenes by artists (for whom artificial lighting was an engaging extension of their earlier fascination with the significance of the changing character of natural light for their painted subjects, be they people or places). But Clayson refers to Paris as the 'City of Éclairage', as the 'City of Lighting', as the 'City of Illumination', as Paris 'The Illuminated City' – this last being the title of her neoteric and stimulating book. She claims correctly that Paris as the 'City of Light' was linked metaphorically with the Enlightenment of the eighteenth century but mistakenly that it was first called 'La Ville lumière' in that century.

Although new and improved street lighting was an integral component of the modernization of Paris, a literal interpretation of Paris as the 'City of Light' – or of Lighting – is far from convincing. Paris was not commonly referred to as the '*Ville lumière*' until the dusk of the nineteenth century.

Earlier, in 1875, Victor Hugo (1802–1885) had written about Paris as the '*Ville de lumière*' in his essay *La vision de Paris dans l'exil*. Because of his political opposition to Napoléon III, Hugo exiled himself from France from 1851 until 1870, with most of that period being spent in Guernsey and some of the time thinking about Paris, the setting for his two famous novels, *Notre Dame de Paris* (1831) and *Les Misérables* (1862). Hugo reflected upon what he judged to be the darkening ('*assombrissement*') of Europe and even the dimming occultation of France but not an eclipse of Paris, which he considered to be 'the frontier of the future'. Given that Paris was for Hugo as much an idea, a concept, as a material city, it was everywhere ('*Paris, étant une idée autant qu'une ville, a l'ubiquité*'). The future, he suggested, could be found in Paris. If you are searching for progress, he advised, take a look at Paris. There were, he stated categorically, dark towns but Paris was for him 'the city of light' ('*Il y a des villes noires; Paris est la ville de lumière*') – his emphatic use of the definite article was for Hugo, a wordsmith, intentional. Paris for Hugo was not just *a* city of light but *the* city of light. Writing in 1875, Hugo was situating Paris within the dual tradition of the Enlightenment and the French Revolution, no longer being ruled by a king or by an emperor but by an elected president of the only republic in Europe and what he considered to be – or hoped would become – a liberal democracy. For Hugo, Paris personified the future, serving as a progressive beacon shining over the darker, less enlightened, areas of Europe including the provinces of France. For Hugo, Paris was the summit of civilization, the highest expression of all humanity. It encompassed the best and the worst of all civilizations, outshining not only other contemporary cities but also all cities in history. In 1867, in his introduction to a guide to Paris in that year of its second *Exposition universelle*, Hugo asserted that while Rome stood for the idea of might, Athens for art, and Jerusalem for freedom, Paris amalgamated all three concepts. Paris was Hugo's '*Ville de lumière*'.

That description was gradually elided into Paris as 'the City of Light', because by 1900 it had become literally true, exemplified and brilliantly demonstrated at the *Exposition universelle* in 1889 with its startling profusion of electric lighting and its Palais de l'Electricité together with the new, monumental, Eiffel Tower, both itself luxuriously illuminated by electricity and employed as a very tall lamp stand beaming light over the city. By the *Exposition universelle* of 1900, Paris was being described, even marketed, as the '*Ville lumière*', as a modern, progressive and illuminated city. The appellation 'City of Light' was at that time literal and material, no longer a subtle reference to the earlier intellectual Enlightenment. By 1900, Paris as a city of spectacular lights and leisure pursuits had become part of the myth and reality of popular culture.

In the following essays, I analyse the personality of Paris during the long-nineteenth century from 1789 to 1914, when its population grew from about half a million in 1801 to just under 3 million in 1911. That more than fivefold increase was in stark contrast to the city's much slower growth of perhaps half a million in the eighteenth century. The demographic explosion of Paris during the nineteenth century was accompanied by multiple and massive physical and cultural transformations. Studies of the character and identity of Paris have been undertaken from a variety of disciplinary approaches. For example, Christopher Prendergast has revealed what he terms 'the faces of Paris', its 'cityscapes', in nineteenth-century imaginative literature (especially that of Balzac, Baudelaire, Flaubert and Zola) and in guidebooks; Priscilla Ferguson has analysed the idea of Paris as revolution in the novels and other writings of Flaubert, Hugo, Jules Vallès and Zola; Patrice Higonnet and Lisa Weiss have separately examined the literary representations of Paris in the works of Balzac, Baudelaire and Zola. Representations of Paris in paintings have vividly and visually constructed pictures of the city which are imaginative and interpretative while depicting a real Paris. For example, Otto Friedrich and Vivien Perutz have separately situated the modernist painter Édouard Manet (1832–1883) in the Paris of his time, Richard Brettell and Joachim Pissaro have critiqued portrayals of the city in a series of paintings by the Impressionist painter Camille Pissaro (1830–1903) and T. J. Clark has unpacked the character of Paris portrayed in the art of Manet and his followers.

Here, I am approaching nineteenth-century Paris not as a literary or art historian but as a historical geographer. The field of historical geography itself is very broad but one of its main tropes is that of changing landscapes, of landscapes as cultural constructions. To know and to understand the creation of cultural landscapes must, to some extent, be an interdisciplinary enterprise. But I am writing as a geographer working with geographical concepts, applying them to a nineteenth-century city. There have been thousands of books about the history of Paris: the catalogue of Cambridge University Library lists more than 32,000 works with Paris in their titles. Is there room on the library shelves for yet another one? Yes, because the approach to Paris which I employ here is novel: it builds upon works by others while providing a new perspective on the city from 1789 to 1914. My focus is on Paris during that period but understanding it requires not only knowledge of what the city had inherited from earlier centuries but also to what extent its nineteenth-century personality survived in later years.

My opening chapter considers the physical stage upon which the cultural drama of Paris was enacted from its beginnings in the third century BC as a settlement by the Parisii, a small Gallic tribe. I then sketch the morphological and cultural development of Paris through the Roman, medieval and early modern periods to 1789. Succeeding chapters examine the maturation of the personality of Paris through to 1914. I consider, firstly, the peopling of the city and especially the contribution of migrants from the French provinces to its social composition and character. There follows a discussion of the key monuments erected during the nineteenth century to commemorate the city's past and to integrate it into its then 'historic present'. In the next chapter,

I examine the modernization of Paris during the 1850s and 1860s, assessing the aims and achievements of Napoléon III and Baron Haussmann, the Prefect of Paris, as they transitioned Paris from a pre-modern to a modern city. I then discuss the key iconic structures in the built form of Paris, those symbolic of Paris itself but also of France, the nation of which it was very self-consciously the capital. There ensue chapters on the role of a series of World Fairs – *Expositions universelles* – in promoting Paris not only to the rest of France but also to the world; on the acquired reputation of Paris as an international centre of fine food, fashion and leisure; and on the endeavours of the city's residents to escape occasionally and temporarily from its oppressive urbanity, renewing or establishing contacts with rural, less urban, worlds from which many of them originated. In my final chapter, I examine the extent to which the personality of Paris as expressed in its built form was damaged by revolutions and wars in the nineteenth century and in the following century by wars and the hubris of presidents and architects.

1

Beginnings: The founding of Paris and its growth to 1789

The site and situation of early settlement

The earliest human settlement on the site which is today occupied by Paris dates from the third century BCE. Confined to a small island in the river named later as the Seine, it was the capital of a small tribe of Gaul, the Parisii. In 52 BCE, the settlement, occupying no more than 2 ha, was taken over by the Romans and named Lutetia or Lutetia Parisiorum. Both the specific site and the general situation of Paris have influenced its development, its spatial spread, from its beginnings and throughout its history. They have been strong influences on the personality of Paris, with its tripartite structure of the islands and the two topographically contrasting left and right banks (see Plate 1).

Sited on a sweeping northerly bend of the river Seine, the settlement's nucleus lay on an island (later named the Île de la Cité). On the southern, left, bank, a small tributary (the Bièvre) flowed into the Seine upstream from the island. The topography on the south bank was of broken and moderate elevation, with short valleys running down fairly steeply from the plateau 60 m above. From the plateau, a low spur (Mont Sainte-Geneviève) ran down towards the Seine. The Roman settlement, located on an island and on the more spacious but hilly, left, bank, included a temple, baths, a palace and an amphitheatre. The writings of Caesar record that the main island was linked to both the left and right banks by wooden bridges. The northern bank provided a strong topographical contrast with that to the south. The area immediately to the north of the river was a meander plain and included an abandoned meander course. A stream still flowed in its western end but the eastern area was marshland. Beyond lay a low-lying plain offering potential space for urban expansion but the marsh was not drained until the twelfth century: until then, roads from the city going north crossed the marshland by causeways and bridges. Beyond the meander and marshland lay a semicircle of discontinuous heights – notably that of Montmartre, with gaps to its east and west offering communication routes to the north. These three topographic units – the southern heights, the islands and the northern plain – have been key elements which have structured the development of the three key cultural components of Paris: the *université*, *cité* and *ville*, centres, respectively, of learning, of administration and law and of commerce. From a broader geographical perspective, Paris is situated near the centre of a physical basin, a saucer-shaped depression of Tertiary rocks deposited on an older series which emerge as uplands and highlands on the surface at the edge of the saucer: the Ardennes to the northeast, the Vosges to the east, the Massif Central to the south and the uplands of Normandy to the west. These uplands and highlands were cut by river valleys converging upon the Seine, providing easy access to Paris, initially for road and river traffic and later for canals and railways.

Roman Lutetia is estimated to have had a population of between 6,000 and 10,000. At the end of the third century of the Christian era, Franks and Germans (Alamans) crossed the Rhine, invaded Gaul and sacked Lutetia. The settlement contracted to a small defensive site on the Île de la Cité, using debris from the sacking of buildings on the island and on the south bank. The Parisii for the first time surrounded their settlement with defensive walls – which were to become the first of many such structures in later years. Until the fifth century the settlement was known by its Latin name of Parisius, which then became Paris in French.

Medieval Paris

For some centuries, settlement was confined to the Île de la Cité, with not more than 2,000 people huddled inside the walls on just 8 ha, linked by bridges to both banks of the Seine. Its streets were narrow, only 3–5 m wide. In the eastern half of the island, dwellings were clustered around the cathedral whose construction had begun in the mid-twelfth century and continued for about 200 years; in the western section, dwellings were sited around the palace of the Capetian kings. Both religion and commerce promoted urban growth. Christianity was boosted in the mid-thirteenth century by a Papal mission. Churches, monasteries and abbeys sited both within and outside the walls acted as nuclei for clusters of settlements attracting people seeking both spiritual and material protection. Those on the left bank had cultivated land around them and organized fairs and markets. These expansions of the settlement were called *bourgs* in order to distinguish them from the main *cité* on the island. For example, an abbey founded in the sixth century received in the eighth century the mortal remains of Saint Germain, bishop of Paris: it then took the name of the Abbey of Saint-Germain-des-Prés, indicating its location in the countryside. Around it developed a *bourg*. This was not enclosed by a wall but the abbey building itself was strongly fortified and able to serve as a refuge for those who lived and worked nearby. In 1180, this *bourg* had 121 dwellings, suggesting a population of perhaps 600 people and in 1292 it had 201 hearths, suggesting a population of about 1,000. The first record of a market fair being held at Saint-Germain-des-Prés dates from 1176. Further to the east on the left bank, other abbeys were similarly associated with the growth of *bourgs*. For example, that of Saint-Marcel, sited further away from the Seine and the *cité*, retained its separateness for a long time. It originated in an oratory sited along the road from Lyon and then developed into the suburb of Saint-Marcel (today around the Avenue des Gobelins). Saint Marcel, bishop of Paris, was buried there in 436, and the *bourg* was first mentioned in documents in 1158.

The townscape of medieval Paris was dominated by perhaps 300 abbeys, convents and churches, many with spectacular towers. There were twenty-three in the vicinity of Notre-Dame (1160–1345) and the royal Sainte-Chapelle (1238–48). Also notable was Saint-Germain-des-Prés: the earliest part of the basilica was consecrated in 557–9; the bell tower dates from the late tenth century, the nave from the eleventh century and the choir was rebuilt in the mid-twelfth century. But so, too, were some civic buildings – notably the royal palace and the hôtel de ville, seats of the two secular powers. The royal residence was located on the Île de la Cité, as also were many large houses (*hôtels*) of the wealthiest citizens. Most were timber-framed, but some were built in stone.

From the eleventh century onwards, Paris attracted incomers (including foreigners) to its religious schools. The principal school was first located in the *cité*, associated with the then Romanesque cathedral of Notre-Dame and its Gothic replacement, constructed over almost 200 years from 1160 onwards. In 1108, one of the master's aides at the school established on the left bank a small hermitage, near a chapel devoted to Saint Victor at the foot of the Montagne Sainte-Geneviève. In 1113, the chapel's status was changed and it became the Abbey of Saint-Victor with a rigorous ascetic rule of silence and manual labour. At end of the twelfth century, another school was established on the hill, in a barn surrounded by vines. From the early thirteenth century, teachers in the locality formed a syndicate, a *universitas*. Its statutes were formulated in 1210 and its recognition in 1215 by the Pope led to the construction of new buildings for teaching and for lodging students. The most significant school was established in 1257 by Robert de Sorbon, who gave his name to the theological college now known as the Sorbonne, today accommodating a prestigious part of the University of Paris. By end of the fourteenth century, more schools or colleges had been established on and around the hill of Sainte-Geneviève.

There were fewer religious buildings on the right bank. Only one priory, that of Saint-Martin-des-Champs, founded in 1079, saw the growth of a *bourg* and in 1220 the creation of its own church of Saint-Nicolas-des-Champs. From the eleventh century, the right bank saw significant growth of a commercial settlement at the point where the bridge from the *cité* met the river bank. This commercial nucleus grew into a much larger and more economically significant urban development than the one on the left bank, in part because it lay on the routes leading to Flanders, an industrial and densely populated region, while the left bank connected to the mainly agricultural and less densely peopled region of Beauce. Merchant corporations (such as those of butchers and tailors) relocated from the *cité* to the right bank.

Encircling the growth of Paris

The spatial expansion of medieval and early modern Paris was asymmetric. Its main motors of growth – commerce and the royal court – were on the flatter right bank. Here there was an active riverfront, in effect an inland river port, behind which were the busy districts of craftsmen, artisans and financiers. Royal palaces and aristocratic residences (*hôtels*) were served by numerous domestic servants, shopkeepers and artisans. The spatial growth of Paris was contained by a series of encircling walls which have given Paris through the centuries a distinctive but deceptive morphology (see Plate 2). Between 1180 and 1210, a set of fortifications encompassing seventy towers and thirteen gates was erected (Figure 1.1), encircling the three components of Paris: the *ville*, the *cité* and the *université*. The walls enclosed an area of about 300 ha and a population of about 50,000. During the thirteenth and fourteenth centuries, Paris expanded principally on the right bank. In 1358, an attempt by merchants to gain control over the monarch failed and led Charles V to leave the palace on the island of the *cité* and set up a new royal palace on the right bank. Then, in 1370, he had a new wall built, only on the right bank, to encompass that expansion. This wall, incorporating at intervals bastion towers (*bastilles*), followed in its north-western section the course of an abandoned river meander, whose eastern marshy section was gradually drained and converted into market gardens to supply the city. This district,

Figure 1.1 The remains of the Tour Montgomery in the Rue des Jardins-Saint-Paul. Wikimedia Creative Commons (public domain) GNU Public License: Nicolas 555

Le Marais, was eventually built over in the seventeenth century. The newly walled Paris had a population of about 70,000 in 1400, living in an area of about 600 ha. The continuing growth of Paris to the north-west led Louis XIII to have a new set of walls built in the 1630s to embrace that segment of urban expansion.

The population of Paris was probably just under 500,000 in the mid-seventeenth century and only increased slowly thereafter to just over that figure by the end of the eighteenth century. The next set of walls was not built for military reasons or to contain significant spatial urban sprawl. The walls built between 1784 and 1791 were constructed for fiscal reasons: the *Mur des Fermiers généraux* served as a barrier for the collection of *l'octroi*, an indirect tax on certain commodities being brought into Paris. This wall, 3.3 m high and 35 km long, had forty-two gates, barriers and posterns (*portes, barrières, poternes*) as entrances to the city. Portions of the *octroi* wall were to be transformed into boulevards or squares (*places*) after a new set of fortified walls was erected in the early 1840s. These were built around the whole of Paris for military reasons, to provide security against any possible foreign invasion. In 1860, the city of Paris was enlarged administratively by its annexation of the communes which this new wall enclosed. Jean Bastié has calculated that this added 5,100 ha to the area of the city, increasing its total area from 3,402 ha to 8,900 ha. This annexation converted 350,000 people into being 'Parisians', contributing significantly to the city's population increase from 1,174,346 in 1856 to 1,696,141 in 1866.

Early modern Paris

The Hundred Years War with the English (1337–1453) checked the growth of Paris, partly because for much of the war the Royal Court had decamped to the Loire Valley or to Normandy or to Fontainebleau. But in 1528 François I reinstalled royalty in Paris and in 1546 had the twelfth-century fortress (Le Louvre) razed to the ground; he died in 1547, before completion of a new royal palace built (Le Palais du Louvre), to which his son, Henri II, and later monarchs made alterations and additions.

A vivid bird's-eye view of Paris in the late fifteenth century was imagined by Victor Hugo in Book 3, chapter 2 of his 1831 novel *Notre-Dame de Paris*. He describes medieval Paris as having been 'imprisoned' within a circular chain of walls and towers so that the city expanded vertically:

> The houses press upon each other, accumulate, and raise their level in this basin, like water in a reservoir. They begin to deepen; they pile story upon story; they mount each other; they gust forth at the top, like all laterally compressed growth, and there is rivalry as to which shall thrust its head above its neighbours, for the sake of getting a little air.

For Hugo, Paris in the fifteenth century was 'still divided into three wholly distinct and separate towns, each having its own physiognomy, its own specialty, its manners, customs, privileges, and history: the City, the University, the Town'. Hugo argued that from a bird's-eye view each presented 'an inextricable skein of eccentrically tangled streets' but that nonetheless 'the three fragments formed but one body', linked by 'three long parallel streets, unbroken, undisturbed, traversing almost in a straight line, all three cities, from one end to the other, from North to South, perpendicularly to the Seine, which bound them together, mingled them, infused them each in the other, and made one out of three'. For Hugo, Paris in the fifteenth century was 'a handsome city; it was a homogenous city, an architectural and historical product of the Middle Ages, a chronicle in stone'. Gothic Paris had erased Roman Paris and was itself in turn remodelled by Renaissance Paris.

The large-scale plans of Paris which started to be drawn in the sixteenth century provided for the first time clear two-dimensional images of the city's morphology. A wooden engraving of a bird's-eye view of Paris in 1552 in eight sections, measuring 133 cm × 96 cm, offers not an accurate plan but a vivid representation of the city. Its tripartite morphology is clearly identifiable and within them are portrayed its walls and their gates, its churches and other monumental buildings (including the *bastilles*), its streets and their houses. A scrolled banner at the top declaims it as depicting *La Ville-Cité–Université de Paris*, accompanied by the coat of arms of France and of Paris, the former with its three *fleurs-de-lys* and the latter both *fleurs-de-lys* and a sailing ship (signalling the role of Paris as a river port). A more accurate perspective plan of Paris in 1615 was produced by a Swiss engraver, Matthäus Mérian (1593–1650) (Figure 1.2). It depicts clearly the fortifications built in 1370 and the westward extension of the city beyond them. It shows three bridges linking the island *cité* to the left and right banks of the Seine. The stone Pont Neuf had been completed in 1606 and is today

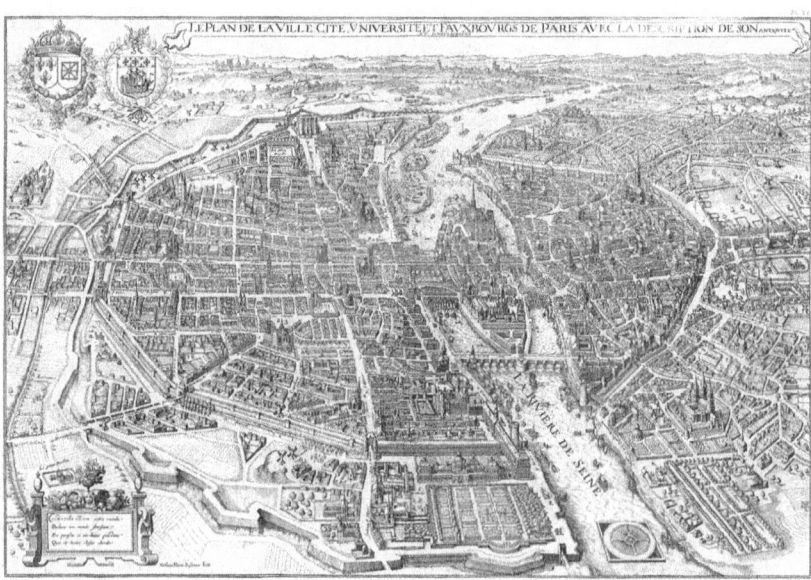

Figure 1.2 Oblique view of Paris in 1615 by the Swiss engraver Matthäus Mérian. Wikimedia Creative Commons (public domain)

the oldest surviving bridge in Paris. Earlier bridges had houses or other buildings on them but none was allowed on the new bridge, so it provided pedestrians with a wider promenade away from the mud and horse manure of the main highway. Also clearly shown on the 1615 plan are the large gardens of the Tuileries, another promenading public space. The Pont Neuf was such a success with the people of Paris that later kings and authority figures sought to enhance their own legacies to the city by building bridges across the Seine. Louis XIII (1638–1715) added five bridges in the seventeenth century; a further nineteen bridges were built between 1815 and 1914. Today, Paris has thirty-seven bridges.

It took twenty years to construct the Pont Marie which was opened in 1635, linking the Île de la Cité and the right bank. Its counterpart (the Pont de la Tournelle) provided a link to the left bank: a wooden bridge built here in 1620 was damaged by ice in 1637 and washed away by flood water in 1651, to be replaced by a stone structure in 1656. These two bridges made possible more intensive and planned development of the Île Saint-Louis for streets, houses, a marketplace, a cemetery and a church (more precisely, a simple chapel dating from 1664). In 1632, a red-painted wooden bridge, the Pont Rouge, was constructed to provide direct access from the Tuileries to the *faubourg* of Saint-Germain, on the left bank, replacing the river ferry which had served this purpose since 1550. This fragile bridge of fifteen arches had to be repaired in 1649, then completely rebuilt two years later; it suffered from fire in 1654 and was carried away by flood water in 1656. It was rebuilt again in wood in 1660 only to have eight of its arches carried away by ice flows during the night of 28–29 February 1684. A replacement bridge in stone, opened in 1689, was financed entirely by Louis XIV and accordingly had its name changed to the Pont Royal.

A plan (rather than perspective view) of Paris in 1652 by Jacques Gomboust (1616–1668), *topographe-ingénieur* to the king, portrayed a small city with buildings set in a sea of cultivated land. From city centre to the edge of the built-up area was in places less than 1 km and everywhere less than 3 km. The area of Paris including its suburbs as shown on this plan was probably about 800 ha, compared with over 8,000 ha in 1914. It retained very clearly its trinity of medieval components: *ville-cité-université*. To us today, Paris in the sixteenth and early seventeenth centuries might have had, as Joan DeJean has expressed it, 'the air of an overgrown village'. But that is a judgement made with historical hindsight and the knowledge that within its bounds there remained vestigial open spaces, including vineyards, orchards, meadows, pastures and gardens. For the perhaps 300,000 Parisians in 1600, and perhaps even more so for provincials nursing exaggerated images of their capital, Paris was a unique city far removed in size and function from the thousands of villages and even from the hundreds of small towns in the French provinces.

During the early modern period, two royal palaces were significant urban features. In 1528, François I decided to make the Palais du Louvre his main residence in Paris and had it reconstructed in the Renaissance style between 1546 and 1578. It was then considerably extended in the seventeenth century. The Château (or Palais) des Tuileries was constructed from 1564 for Catherine de Médicis, the Queen Mother, located just outside the 1370 wall, on the site of three tile-making establishments founded in 1372. Later, during the 1860s, the Palais des Tuileries was integrated with the Palais du

Louvre to form – as desired by Napoléon III – a large and majestic ensemble. Wealthier citizens also made their mark during the late sixteenth century, when they adopted what became the classic design for grand private houses (*hôtels*), with the residential building sited between a garden and a courtyard, so that the residence itself had no facade on the street.

The seventeenth and eighteenth centuries were a period of classic urbanism in Paris. There was to be no foreign power again on French soil until 1814: none being feared or anticipated, the fortifications inherited from previous periods were redundant. The walls no longer defined the boundary of the built-up area, which had spread beyond them. Louis XIV (who reigned from 1643 until 1715) had the walls removed and replaced by tree-lined boulevards some 36 m wide (of which only 10 m were for the road itself, the remainder for pedestrian promenades). The early modern period witnessed the rise of a new concept of urbanism throughout Europe. Paris experienced a period of urban embellishment, partly to increase the prestige of monarchies and partly as a public service. The planned construction of a beautiful townscape was based on rational principles (producing geometrically regular street alignments) and on aesthetic principles (leading to visual perspectives, and stunning architecture and sculptures, and including promenades in parks and gardens).

The cityscape of Paris saw many piecemeal additions and improvements during the seventeenth and eighteenth centuries. For example, 1631 saw completion of the royal Luxembourg Palace, a massive and opulent extension of the house purchased from the Duke of Luxembourg. Attached to it was a typically French formal garden, which was converted into a public park in 1799. Completion in 1666 of the Champs-Elysées created an east-west axis (to balance the older north-south axis). The years 1670–6 saw construction of the Hôtel des Invalides, a hospital and retirement home for war veterans. It had fifteen courtyards and a chapel for the veterans. The domed private royal chapel was completed in 1708 and was at that time, at 103 m, the tallest structure in Paris. Two monumental gates like Roman triumphal arches, Porte Saint-Denis (1672) and Porte Saint-Martin (1674), were added as adornments to the city and as signs of its self-conscious European stature.

A favoured urban improvement during this period was the construction of 'squares' (*places*), exhibiting an imposed, rigid, geometry and often signalling a monarchical control of public space. Five such *places royales* were embellishments to the Parisian cityscape in this period. In 1605–12, Henry IV had constructed the Place Royale with three goals: to adorn Paris architecturally, to provide a distinctive setting for public ceremonies and to proffer Parisians a recreational space. (In 1800, after the Revolution of 1789, it was renamed the Place des Vosges, erasing its monarchical connection and honouring the eastern *département* for having provided the first volunteers to come to the defence of France in its Revolutionary Army.) This was a true square with all house fronts built to the same design of red brick with strips of stone quoins over vaulted arcades that stand on square pillars, and with steeply pitched blue slate roofs with dormers. It was a pioneering architectural project, a planned public recreational space, a prototype of the modern city square. As Joan DeJean has noted, the Place Royale departed from earlier models for city 'squares' which tended to be rectangular and to showcase an individual monument, a church, a city hall or a central statue. There was nothing specifically royal about it until 1639, when a statue of Louis XIII was placed in the centre. DeJean considered that, with the Place Royale, 'Paris had acquired its earliest notable modern architectural monument that, like the Pont Neuf, was neither a cathedral nor a palace'.

The Place Dauphine, at the western end of the Île de la Cité, was created in 1607 and named by Henry IV after his son, the future Louis XIII. Triangular rather than square in shape, this Place was bounded by houses built to a standard design. Access to it was from the recently completed Pont Neuf, the first bridge in Paris built not of wood but of stone and the first to cross the Seine in a single span. It was also the first bridge in Paris without houses lining both sides, having instead raised viewing spaces for pedestrians to ensure their safety from traffic. It was not until much later, in 1781, that such paved walkways for pedestrians were added in a Parisian street (the Rue de l'Odéon). In 1685, the almost circular Place des Victoires was built to provide a framework for a statue of the reigning monarch, Louis XIV. Its houses were designed by the royal architect, Jules Hardouin-Mansart, with sloping slate roofs punctuated by dormer windows (which became the Mansard roof style so widely adopted later in Paris). In 1702, the Place Vendôme was created as a monument to the military victories of Louis XIV. Initially called the Place des Conquêtes, it contained a very large equestrian statue of the king (some 17 m high, the same height as the surrounding houses of the Place) but its name was changed when the conquests proved to be only temporary in duration. In 1772, the Place Louis XV was completed as a vast octagonal space with an equestrian statue of Louis XV.

During the seventeenth and eighteenth centuries, Paris grew both by extension (notably to the west) and by intensification (utilizing many of the remaining open spaces and vacant plots in the city, including areas of ploughed land, meadows and marshes). Such in-filling became almost complete but even today a vineyard survives on the slopes of Montmartre. Streets were narrow: a regulation of 1783 required new streets to be at least 10 m wide and limited the height of houses to 20 m. As Paris grew, so did its environmental problems. It became dirtier and smellier. Most streets were unpaved, sewage disposal was limited and in summer the tributary river Bièvre was often clogged with waste.

In an attempt to curtail the expansion of the city, the royal residence was transferred in 1680 to Versailles by a monarchy aware that its own presence was in considerable measure responsible for the growth of Paris, attracting court followers like moths to a flame. Creating a satellite city - a 'new town' - at Versailles was a deliberate step but it was not totally successful because a substantial part of the apparatus for administering the state remained in Paris. By the end of the seventeenth century, Paris had acquired enough innate momentum to sustain its growth - it had 'taken-off'. Louis-Sébastien Mercier (1740–1818), author of two books on Paris - *Le Tableau de Paris* (1781-8) and *Le Nouveau Paris* (1799) - claimed that in the thirty years 1758–88 some 10,000 houses had been built in the city. Numerous regulations - for example, in 1627, 1633, 1638, 1672, 1728 and 1765 - prohibited further development in the *faubourgs* but they were not enforced (or perhaps not enforceable) and failed to stop urban sprawl. There was particularly vigorous housing construction during the second half of the eighteenth century. The authorities decided to recognize such expansion as a *fait accompli*, doing so not by building a new encircling fortified wall but instead a simple fiscal wall, a *Mur d'octroi*, with entry points to the city where indirect taxes could be collected on goods (such as wine, oil, sugar and coffee) coming into Paris. *La barrière des Fermiers généraux* was initially 24 km long and had forty-seven tax collection offices dotted along it. Building the wall began in 1785. Unsurprisingly, the project was not very popular and work was stopped in 1787 to allow a review of it to be undertaken. Construction work recommenced in 1789. Some of the earliest demonstrations of the Revolution of that year destroyed some of the tax collection offices. To appease the protesters, the *octroi* was suspended but then re-established in 1797.

In sum, while there are identifiable elements of an asymmetrical expansion of Paris from medieval times to the nineteenth century, successive rings and sections of walls give a deceptive impression of a quasi-concentric spatial growth. But the walls and their fortifications were themselves attempts to formalize the uneven nature of the spread of Paris. Much of its development over centuries was extramural despite strenuous but intermittent efforts by its authorities to contain it intramurally. The medieval and early modern growth of Paris took place around multiple nuclei, as well as being related to its specific site and situation. The seventeenth and eighteenth centuries saw some experiments in urbanism inspired by Italian examples. Especially noteworthy were the elegant Place Royale in 1605–12 and the equally charming Place Dauphine in 1607, both initiated by Henry IV, the first of France's monarchs imbued with the spirit of urbanism. Both *places* soon became desirable residences for wealthy Parisians. The Pont Neuf, too, was completed in 1607. The 1670s saw the replacement of no longer needed walls by boulevards. The monumental and classical Place Louis XV, the largest square in Paris, was opened in 1763. Such embellishments of the Parisian landscape, although piecemeal, were significant precursors to the major and more holistic transformation which the fabric of Paris was to undergo during the nineteenth century. They sowed the seeds of a classical urbanism which, it might be argued, were to bear fruit two centuries later. They serve both as a comparator with later developments of the Parisian landscape and a reminder that what was to come – the Haussmannization of the cityscape – was literally and aesthetically building upon precedents in previous centuries.

2

The peopling of Paris: The making of 'Parisians'

On becoming a metropolis

Building on its medieval and early modern foundations, Paris was transformed during the nineteenth century into a modern city with a new and distinctive personality, while retaining some of its earlier features and characteristics. The already commanding role of Paris as the metropolis of France was hugely accentuated between 1789 and 1914: it dominated France not only demographically but also economically, politically, socially, artistically and culturally. The national government in Paris exercised a powerful authority over the provinces through the prefects of the *départements* and the sub-prefects of their *arrondissements*, the new administrative divisions of France established in 1790, an early product of the Revolution (see Plates 3 and 4).

The 'Parisianization' of France was closely associated with the general process of modernization which imposed – or, at least, endeavoured to impose – a new set of universals or norms, both material and intellectual, which contrasted with the traditional, provincial, diversity of regional cultures. A metropolitan modernism and state-sponsored *françization* delivered through programmes of military conscription, schooling and an integrated railway system combined to challenge a provincial traditionalism. The transformation of Paris was a product not only of new technologies (a material transformation) but also of new attitudes and ideologies (a cultural transformation). In the second half of the nineteenth century, Paris moved into a new dimension. It was, as Peter Hall, an urban historical geographer, has described it, 'the city of perpetual public works' between 1850 and 1870. More than being the second largest city in the Western world (following London) and retaining that position until 1900 when it was overtaken by New York, Paris was by far the largest city in France (in 1901 it was more than five times the size of each of the next two largest cities, Lyon and Marseille). As the country's capital, Paris became a place where new social, economic and cultural relations were developed beyond the city itself, and even beyond France. Paris came to exercise its role as a world city. This was in part linked to the construction of a colonial empire but Paris became more than the imperial city of France; it became a cultural metropolis for the world. Metropolitan Paris was a cultural melting pot. It harboured an extremely mobile society, one dominated by immigrants exhibiting great cultural diversity: to be different in Paris in 1900 was to be normal. This both permitted and promoted exceptional liberties of expression. By the end of the nineteenth century, Paris had become an open, diverse society in which postmodern cultural difference was celebrated within a city that had only recently become modern. This is not to deny – indeed it is to accept – that fin-de-siècle Paris harboured many social inequalities and prejudices, grounded, for example, in chauvinism, racism and sexism as well as in the city's long-standing political and religious divisions. By 1900, Paris was a maelstrom of 'isms', among them in addition to modernism were – in content-neutral alphabetical order – absolutism, anti-clericalism, associationism, Bonapartism, capitalism, Catholicism, colonialism, communism, corporatism, expressionism, feminism, idealism, impressionism, individualism, Jacobinism, liberalism, Marxism, mutualism, occultism, opportunism, Protestantism, radicalism, republicanism, socialism, solidarism, syndicalism, surrealism, symbolism and utopianism. Such ideas – and others – were both cherished and demonized, fought out in intellectual arenas of conflict but also sometimes in material street settings. Paris in 1900 contained many 'others' against whom 'selves' could protest.

But who were the Parisians?

The growth of population 1789–1914

How large was the population of Paris? In 1684, the municipal authorities compiled a list of churches, chapels, convents and other religious buildings in Paris and of its *hôtels* and other private houses. This produced a total of 23,086 dwellings. Assuming there were four heads of households to each house and 4.5 people per household, this suggests a total population of 415,548 or approximately 400,000. There might have been more households per house, for contemporary observers noted that houses had five or six storeys, occupied my multiple families. The houses were so tall that it seemed to some as though there were two or three towns on top of each other, but probate inventories (listing the properties and goods of someone deceased) rarely refer to houses of more than four floors. Other calculating methods (using data on baptisms, marriages and burials) suggest for 1700 a population figure closer to 500,000. So, perhaps 450,000 is the best approximation for Paris in 1700.

During the seventeenth and eighteenth centuries, Paris's growth was slow, a product of a small excess of births over deaths and moderate immigration. By contrast, its massive growth in the nineteenth century owed much to huge immigration. Louis Chevalier estimated that 60,000 nobles, priests and bourgeois emigrated from Paris between 1789 and 1792, fleeing from the Revolutionary turbulence of the capital, but he also calculated that 180,000 migrants arrived in Paris during that period. One major effect of the Revolution of 1789 was to bring to Paris a new population coming from the provinces and especially from small towns in northern France. Parisian observers began to comment on the invasion of the city by 'savages'. Census documents provide the following population totals for Paris:

1801	547,756
1846	1,053,897
1876	1,988,806
1901	2,714,066
1911	2,888,110

There had been modest population growth during the eighteenth century, perhaps of between 50,000 and 100,000. Then there followed a demographic explosion in the nineteenth century: a sixfold increase of about 2.5 million, from just over half a million in 1801 to almost 3 million in 1901 (see Plate 5). Especially notable growth from 1851 to 1872 totalled almost 800,000 but the excess of births over deaths in that period was only 120,000, the remainder of the growth (680,000) coming from immigration. In 1841, Paris had a recorded population of 935,261 of whom only 50 per cent had been born in the city; in the fifteen years, 1851–66, some 300,000 immigrants arrived in Paris; and in the late nineteenth century, deaths each year exceeded births by between 6,000 and 9,000. Its startling population growth was principally a result of immigration.

The role of immigration

The geographical mobility of the population in France increased considerably during nineteenth and early twentieth centuries and had some key characteristics. Firstly, mobility doubled. Males aged forty-five living outside the *départements* of their births rose from 21 per cent in 1820 to 38 per cent in 1920; for females, it rose from 19 per cent to 40 per cent. Secondly, most migrants were under forty years of age. Throughout the nineteenth century, most migrants were young, energetic and active. Thirdly, female mobility was lower than male mobility in the early nineteenth century but had exceeded it by the late nineteenth century. Migrants to provincial towns and to Paris were mainly men in the mid-nineteenth century but mainly women at the end of the century. This was related partly to the growth of the secondary (notably, manufacturing and construction) employment sector attracting men before the later massive growth of the tertiary service sector (notably, domestic service and retailing) attracting women.

Richard Cobb's study of ninety-six prostitutes arrested in Paris in 1793 produced an enlightening snapshot of their geographical origins. Except for a minority of native-born Parisiennes, most of the girls and women detained by the police were relatively new arrivals, having been in Paris for at most two years; many claimed to have taken up sex work only recently as a result of unemployment or underemployment, '*pour avoir du pain*'; most were not country girls but had come from provincial towns (to which they might have migrated earlier from rural villages); their average age was twenty-two but their ages ranged from fourteen to forty-four and most had migrated to Paris when they were aged nineteen or twenty. In the June 1848 uprising, 89 per cent of the Parisian residents arrested had not been born in the city. During the 1860s and 1870s, one-third of people living in Paris had not been born there. For the period 1872–1901, 71 per cent of the total population growth of Paris was the result of net migration, which was on average 10,000 persons annually during the late nineteenth century and in some years reached 30,000 or 40,000. In 1911, almost two-thirds (60 per cent) of the French-born population of Paris had not been born in the city but in the provinces.

Patterns detectable in studies of the distances separating the birthplaces of the brides and their grooms reveal that migration was not necessarily a gradual contagious spread but often a leap-frogging movement up the settlement hierarchy – from village to provincial town and then to Paris. A striking example of stepwise, hierarchical, migration is provided at Bonnières, a village on the Seine 66 km downstream from Paris. Evelyn Ackerman revealed that, in the early nineteenth century, two-thirds of its 727 villagers had been born in Bonnières and most of the other Bonnièrois were of local origin; but by the end of the century, native Bonnièrois were only just over half of its population of 1,164 (see Plates 6 and 7). In the early 1840s, the railway line from Rouen to Paris was constructed, with a station at Bonnières. Later years saw the industrialization of the commune, with its acquisition of a sugar beet distillery, a fertilizer factory, a dairying cooperative, a glue factory, a petroleum refinery and a camphor factor. This economic expansion and diversification created a demand for labour that could not be sourced locally. Instead, it was met largely by Breton immigrants, many young men and some young women, moving from areas of chronic unemployment, notably the inland districts of Côtes-du-Nord. Residentially and socially, the Bretons who arrived in Bonnières were largely segregated from other residents: they continued to speak Breton rather than the French of the commune's natives; they tended to marry other Bretons and to have more children, and to be much less literate than the native villagers. Many of them came from the same *pays* (locality) in the Côtes-du-Nord, following each other in the known migration path and becoming members of an identifiable Breton community with a shared *patois* and culture. The Breton immigrants had been pushed by dire poverty in their home villages and pulled by the known and expanding employment opportunities in Bonnières. Immigrants, who arrived both as individuals and as families, were largely responsible for the population increase that Bonnières experienced between 1815 and 1914. Bretons provided the largest cohort of migrants but others came in smaller numbers from throughout northern France. The proximity of Bonnières to Paris and the lure of the capital attracted many of its villagers, both native-born and immigrant. Many moved to the burgeoning industrial, working-class, suburbs on the northern edge of Paris like Clichy and Saint-Denis.

The pull of Paris for provincials was considerable and particularly strong in the mid-nineteenth century. There was massive rural emigration in France during the 1850s and 1860s. More people left rural France between 1851 and 1856 than in any other intercensal five years' period before 1914. Almost 40 per cent of the 772,000 increase in Paris's population between 1851 and 1866 was a product of immigration. This was reflected in the rapid growth of jobs in the service sector (such as banking, insurance, the postal system, retailing, transportation and domestic service), in manufacturing (especially textiles and engineering), in building work and in constructing and operating the new railway network. Expanding employment opportunities were both numerous and widely believed in the provinces to be focussed on the capital.

An Industrial Enquiry of 1847-8 listed 340,000 workers in Paris in a population of slightly over 1 million. One-third of workers were employed in construction. Industrial expansion in the city was not as marked as population growth during the first half of the nineteenth century. The principal advances were in textiles and the building industry. Economic activity was generally small scale: of 64,000 businesses, fewer than 10 per cent employed more than ten workers and as many as 50 per cent employed only one worker or none at all. Much manufacturing was of luxury goods for rich clientele. Heavier industry – such as manufacturing cars and bicycles, machinery and moulds – became a significant source of employment for immigrants during the second half of the nineteenth century, especially in expanding suburbs to which in the 1860s the modernizing Napoléon III relocated polluting city-centre industries such as slaughtering and leather tanning.

Aggregate patterns of migrations were based upon myriad decisions by individuals with their changing levels of knowledge, expectations and aspirations. Public authorities were concerned that rural emigration to towns might undermine agricultural production and threaten food supplies, as well as increasing the number of young and potentially discontented, deracinated, agitators in towns; governmental enquiries in the 1860s sought to probe the reasons for the high levels of emigration. Rural mayors responded along the following lines: 'Those leaving begin not to want to be peasants'; 'new needs, real or imagined, born and exaggerated due to the ease of travelling, take into the towns and out of their sphere of origin, often one after another, all members of a family'; and 'those who emigrate are the young men who have worked on the construction of the railways, who have done military service and have acquired new habits and tastes. They are no longer able to accommodate themselves to the harsh, laborious, frugal life of the fields'.

The regions of massive emigration in the 1850s and 1860s were also regions which had the highest agricultural wages and the highest levels of agricultural productivity, notably the Paris region, the north-east of France and in the south-east close to Marseille. The rural exodus was not simply or even largely a migration of the poorest; indeed, its impact was in some areas to create labour shortages which resulted in higher wages which in turn incentivized the introduction of labour-saving machinery. The 'pull' to Paris was powerful and in some places combined with 'push' factors such as the privatization of common lands, the phylloxera crisis which ravaged the vineyards of France increasingly from the 1860s and the collapse of domestic industries such as textiles in the eastern Paris Basin.

But, on balance, it was the growth of Paris and perceptions of the opportunities, the perceived paradise, on offer in the city which underpinned migration to the capital. Migrants were mainly young adults, who affected the gender balance of the city. Under the Ancien Régime, there were more females than males in Paris (women lived longer than men) and this remained the case until 1817 when Paris had 115 women for every 100 men. Thereafter, substantial migrations of young men to Paris meant that in the 1830s the city had only ninety women for every 100 men.

Decisions to migrate were many and complex. Migration flows did not precisely match economic cycles. Periods of strong migration were not related to, or restricted to, downturns in the economy. There were migrations not only during economic crises ('negative' migrations of the poor) but also during economic booms ('positive' migrations of opportunists, seeking employment and prosperity). Also, we can identify both waves of short-distance migration and patterns of long-distance migration: migration was both linear and hierarchical. Migration from the provinces was not initially caused by the coming of the railways – there was considerable migration in the first half of the nineteenth century but the railway network only developed slowly from the 1840s and its main development was delayed until after 1860. Many of the men who had worked on railway construction, and many who had not, saw the railways as escape routes to new lives in the prestigious capital. Nor can it be argued that migration to Paris was related primarily, or even perhaps significantly, to industrialization. Most manufacturing in Paris until relatively late in the nineteenth century was of high-quality goods produced in small workshops by skilled artisans, not in large factories by unskilled workers. Much migration was related to the construction industry and especially to the rebuilding of the city in the 1850s and 1860s and to its expansion by three-quarters of a million people in just twenty-five years, between 1876 and 1901.

Immigrants made especially significant contributions to the demography of some *quartiers* within Paris. This was the case even, for example, in the central district of Saint-Germain which was in 1869 surprisingly among the least demographically 'Parisian' of the city, with only 25 per cent of its population having been born in the capital. Many who lived in Saint-Germain were nobles, 50 per cent of whom had not been born in Paris; many others were employed by the state in the military or civil services, of whom 66 per cent and 74 per cent respectively had been born in the provinces. Many of the nobility resided for six months in Paris and six months in their provincial homes. Of the working class of Saint-Germain, only 23 per cent had been born in Paris – in part because of the military barracks and religious houses in the *faubourg* and in part because of the high number of domestic servants there, of whom only one in fifty-five or 2 per cent were Paris-born. Among waged employees (e.g. in the department stores – *les grands magasins*), 85 per cent were provincials while among artisans and workers the proportion was 25 per cent.

Twenty-six years of revolution and wars before 1815 had widened the geographical horizons of many provincials. Many young men throughout the nineteenth century were uprooted from their native localities as military conscripts. By 1914, many provincials, men and women, were either pushed away from the countryside and/or pulled to Paris which was seen as offering greater freedom (from the unwelcome control of parents and priests) and employment opportunities (for earning a higher standard of living). An image was constructed of Paris as a value-free centre of excitement, of a place to experience personally or vicariously fame, power, leisure, entertainment and individuality. For many migrants, Paris was a dream – for some, it became a nightmare. Paris attracted migrants from throughout France (see Plate 8). A study of migration flow patterns by Paul White has demonstrated that by 1911 regional migration fields throughout France were overlain by the wider influence of Paris, which had become the dominant lifetime migration destination for migrants from nearly two-thirds of all of the country's *départements* – the demographic magnetic field of Paris reached out across most of the country.

The making of 'Parisians'

People who migrated from the provinces to Paris faced the challenge of merging into its economy and society and of maintaining or abandoning links with their provincial origins (Figure 2.1). To what extent did provincials become Parisians, not just geographically but culturally? There is evidence that the 1850s saw considerable family breakdown and isolation among migrants. In 1855, at a hospital in the central, Right Bank, 2^e arrondissement, 20 per cent of those who died were not claimed by their relatives: they had no supporting families nearby. In 1859, 15 per cent of dead children were unclaimed (partly perhaps because of the funeral and related costs which might be involved and partly because of the fear of infection from cholera or tuberculosis). In 1860, 14 per cent of all of the dead were not claimed, and in 1869 the figure was 11 per cent. There can be little doubt that family life was seriously disrupted for many immigrants who felt alienated from the city while living in it.

Louis Chevalier has argued that cohabitation, what he termed *concubinage*, was a manifestation of working-class culture, a sign of migrants' ill adaptation to the city, a symptom of alienation, of their marginal, deracinated, social status. It has been suggested by Michel Frey that cohabitation also reflected women's particular weakness

Figure 2.1 '*Dire que nous v'là parisiens!*' ['Fancy that, we're Parisians now!']. Lithograph by Honoré Daumier, *Le Charivari*, 23 September 1860

in Parisian society, of their legal, economic and physical vulnerability. Within the popular classes, many couples – perhaps 30–40 per cent – were already living together at the time of their marriage. Another indicator of the problematic nature for immigrants of inserting themselves into Parisian society in the mid-nineteenth century is the relatively late age of marriage of immigrants: Christine Piette and Barrie Ratcliffe found that male immigrants married on average two years and females three years later than did native-born Parisians. Ratcliffe has questioned the explanation offered by Chevalier about the reasons for cohabitation in mid-nineteenth-century Paris, doing so in part because of the paucity of the sources about it and in part because, even when numbers and spatial patterns of cohabitation can be identified, the processes and motives underlying them remain difficult to determine. Ratcliffe accepted Chevalier's suggestion that one in three and perhaps as many as two in five of the popular classes were living together at the time of their marriage. His studies confirm that cohabitation was widespread in mid-nineteenth-century Paris but suggest that underpinning the practice there was more than alienation. There being no firm data on cohabitation, its origins and impacts among the often-illiterate popular classes have to be inferred from observations by members of the articulate and educated elite and from other indirect sources. Ratcliffe, using the archives of private charities which worked to persuade and help members of the popular class to marry, has argued that cohabitation reflected not so much a resistance to marriage *per se* as the existence of perceived and/or real obstacles to the change of status, notably the administrative obstacles and costs involved in providing the necessary documentation (written proofs of civil status and freedom to marry were prerequisites for a marriage as specified by the Civil Code; parental permission for a marriage was required for males younger than twenty-five years old and for females under twenty-one; if there were not a surviving parent, death certificates had to be provided as well as authorizations from grandparents or, if the cohabitees were orphans, from their legal guardians – all such documents had be certified by a notary and paid for). These bureaucratic hindrances to marriage were magnified for migrants who had to obtain the necessary documentation from their place of origin in the provinces. Ratcliffe shows that cohabiting couples often married when their union produced a child. Cohabitation was a 'satisfying' solution until then, when marriage replaced it as an 'optimizing' solution.

Not all migrants sought to be assimilated into the economy and society of the capital. Some selectively sought employment in the capital but rejected its other offerings. Many immigrants endeavoured to maintain social links with their geographical, provincial origins. Many inserted themselves into the city by settling initially in areas where there were already residing people from their own *pays* or region. Such 'villages' within the city were identified by writers even in the early nineteenth century, as noted by Victoria Thompson (2003, p. 530) who cited Louis Prudhomme's stating in 1804 that 'each neighbourhood of this city is inhabited by a group of individuals whose language, style of dress, and lifestyle would make one believe that the immense population of this capital was composed of different peoples'. She also noted Victor-Joseph-Etienne de Jouy's writing in 1813 that 'each neighbourhood is in some sense a separate nation, all of which come together to form the general character of Parisians and the particular physiognomy of this great city'. Similarly, Thompson (2003, p. 531) cited an observer in 1830 who emphasized the distinctive characteristics of each part of the city, where 'each neighbourhood is inhabited by a people that does not in any way resemble that of any other neighbourhood'. Such cultural and geographical clustering was a feature of Paris throughout the nineteenth century.

The first foothold of a migrant arriving in Paris was often a lodging house in which rooms could be rented by the week or even just by the day for those arriving in the city with little or no money. There was a tendency for some migrants from certain provincial regions to cluster and even to create urban 'villages' in Paris, sometimes in the locality of the railway station which had served as their gateway into the capital. A forensic anatomy of these 'villages', almost street by street, by Eric Hazan provides a detailed picture of the significance to 'Parisians' of their place in the city, of their newly created or reproduced *pays* within the capital. Hope Mirrlees (2020, p. 6), in her modernist poem based on a single day and night in 1919 spent exploring and experiencing the city, wrote: 'Paris is a huge home-sick peasant, He carries a thousand villages in his heart.'

A subsequent, intra-urban, migration took many new 'Parisians' to the city's peripheral districts. In 1886, more than one-third (36 per cent) of those living in Paris had not been born there; more than half (56 per cent) had been born in the other *départements*, not in that of Seine in which Paris was located; fewer than a tenth (8 per cent) were foreigners (see Plate 9). The 'true' Parisians – those born in the city – were workers living in the periphery, especially around Belleville in the *20e arrondissement*, in Petit-Montrouge in the *14e arrondissement* and in the adjacent *15^e arrondissement*. There was also a concentration of 'true' Parisians (67 per cent born in the city) in the central *quartier* of the Hôtel de Ville. In 1886, many 'Parisians' born in the provinces were living in central districts, notably in the *faubourg* Saint-Germain (where many aristocrats lived during the social 'season' of winter, retiring to their rural properties for the summer) and the Marais and the adjacent *10e arrondissement*. Foreigners were living around the Champs-Elysées and the Colline de Chaillot as well as the Place Vendôme and the Chaussée-d'Antin in the *9e arrondissement*.

When the Thiers wall was built in the early 1840s, some 24½ miles long with fifty-two gates, it contained inside a 150-m-wide buffer that in 1860 became the Boulevard des Maréchaux. On the outside, the wall projected an artificial 30-m-wide slope and beyond that another physical buffer, a 250-m-wide strip of land that was designated as a *zone non aedificandi* ('not to be built on'). The new walled area included within it a number of villages that would not be incorporated into the administrative city of Paris until 1860 and also – as Luc Sante has expressed it – 'amputated parts of five other villages', including Montmartre and Saint-Denis. The walled area more than doubled the previous size of Paris, its circumference determined by calculating the safest range to protect the 'old' city from enemy artillery fire – but the Prussian army proved in 1871 that that had been a miscalculation. The Zone contained very diverse land uses including fields and vineyards, villages, a few follies and eighteenth-century hunting lodges, railway marshalling yards, gypsy camps, and quite a few *guignettes* (primitive cafés) that had developed just outside the gates of the previous *octroi* wall. The Zone also included neglected land and land of uncertain ownership, which made it attractive for many of the poorest migrants to Paris who took up menial and insecure work, many as *chiffoniers* (ragpickers). As squatters, they erected 'houses' from any construction materials they could find, creating a *bidonville* (shanty town) on the periphery of Paris. The lands beyond the Zone, primarily farmland and villages, as Jean Bastié has demonstrated in fine detail, were to see the development of the new *banlieues* (suburbs) of Paris, a spatial expansion initiated in the late nineteenth century and continued in the twentieth century and responding to demographic and economic pressures – the *banlieues* were developed with a mix of housing styles (from what Luc Sante describes as 'essentially hobo jungles' to villas) and of industrial enterprises (from gasworks and factories to railway marshalling yards and military depots).

In the inner city, the geographical clustering of migrants from the same region in the provinces contributed impressively to the cultural personality of Paris. During at least the first two-thirds of the nineteenth century, immigrant stonemasons from Limousin, on the western side of the Massif Central in the *départements* of Haute Vienne, Creuse and Corrèze, lived in a few districts of central Paris, notably close to the Hôtel de Ville on the Île de la Cité, and on the Left Bank in the Arcis and Saint-Marcel *quartiers* close to the Gare d'Austerlitz, the main line railway destination for migrants from Limousin. The early migrants from Limousin established dormitories (*chambrées*), basically furnished accommodation with a communal kitchen and *réfectoire* (dining room) often run by the wife of one of their compatriots. Such clusters of migrants were, in many ways, villages within the city. Through the community thus established, migrants could obtain their first employment, going with others each morning to work on building sites. Many migrants from the Limousin were in Paris as seasonal rather than permanent migrants, and as such they sought to retain their specific provincial identity and to reject the generalizing pressures of 'Parisianization'. Alain Corbin has argued that it was only by choosing other trades, and as a result integrating into the wider *milieu* of Parisian workers, that children of Limousin stonemasons could achieve not only social mobility but also geographical mobility, moving away from a cluster of fellow Limousines to more dispersed locations throughout Paris.

Migrant workers often settled in *quartiers* where they could speak their own regional language and enjoy their own regional culinary delights and cultural activities such as music-making, singing and dancing. Moving to such locations removed some of the alienating effects of migration and fostered resistance to the assimilating influences they encountered in the city. For example, the Coutant Forges of Ivry, in the south-eastern *13e arrondissement* of Paris, employed almost a thousand workers in the 1870s and until then the ironsmiths were all natives from the Nièvre *département* (some 200 km to the south of Paris) where they had acquired working experience in its iron foundries. They were usually related through blood or marriage, and they formed a closed caste of industrial craftsmen which was only later broken by the company's training program.

In 1900, there were in Paris about 100,000 migrants from Limousin, 75,000 from the Auvergne and 30,000 from Savoy. Many were manual workers who had been attracted by building construction, by work on the *Expositions universelles* of 1889 and 1900 and on the new underground railway which opened in 1900. Migrants from Limousin were mainly stonemasons; those from the Auvergne were often in the service sector, such as carriers of water and coal, collectors of rags and of scrap metal and sellers of umbrellas. Both groups tended to cluster in the south of Paris, around the Gare de Lyon and the Gare d'Austerlitz (see Plate 10). Another case of social clustering is that of Bretons in the district around the Gare Montparnasse, providing an example of immigrant populations from regions of high religious practice maintaining their religion in order to preserve their identity in the large, potentially alienating and definitely secularizing city. A club established in 1897 by Abbé Cduc for Bretons in Montparnasse had 15,000 members by 1907. Provincial cultures imported into the capital have been noted in some cases as limiting the development of class consciousness among immigrants. Breton immigrants provide a good example of provincial workers who resisted assimilation into Parisian ways, at least for a generation. They did not share the anticlericalism developed in the working class of Paris: their traditional, clerical, Breton identity served as a check on their development of a Parisian working-class consciousness.

During much of the nineteenth century, Paris fostered many such urban villages. Migrants came from all over France but some regions of the provinces saw especially large numbers living in the city. For migrants without particular skills or experience, the mushrooming service sector offered jobs with long hours of work as taxi drivers and carters, waiters and cooks, butchers and *charcutiers* (pork butchers). Although such descriptions might be somewhat stereotypical, they contain nonetheless a kernel of truth because even if such clustering were largely mythical it might well have been its image as much as any reality that pulled new immigrants to them as initial, secure, familiar stepping stones into the complexity of Parisian pond life. An image of Paris as including clusters of modest neighbourhoods not unlike villages and inhabited by ordinary working people and focussed around favourite cafés or markets or workplaces was certainly in vogue in the decades around 1900, even in popular songs.

Cultural continuation was also promoted by voluntary associations founded to provide support for migrant groups from specific parts of the provinces. Voluntary associations affirmed cultural identities by arranging social events for groups of people from particular regions of the country: dancing, music-making, singing, drinking and eating together confirmed group allegiance to, or at least common origin from, their shared geographical roots in the provinces. They countered the sense of social alienation and deracination experienced by many new arrivals in the capital. Newspapers were produced for such groups, which had become so distinctive and well known that from the 1870s they were referred to as '*colonies provinciales*'. These cultural groups also organized special train fare deals to 'home' as well as local excursions to the environs of Paris. The first such association, *Les Enfants du Nord*, was founded in 1825. Others were established for migrants, for example, from Savoy (1833), the Vosges (1866), Lozère (1880) and the Auvergne (1886). Such groups cemented their solidarity by meeting in selected cafés to drink and eat, gossip and perhaps make music and dancing.

They also produced 'local' newspapers which provided information about the *pays* and the families and friends migrants had left behind and also about employment opportunities in Paris. For example, *L'Auverngat de Paris* was established in 1882, providing news and gossip about the Auvergne for natives of the *départements* of Cantal, Aveyron and Lozère, and from 1904 organizing two train excursions annually to 'home'. That newspaper is still published but mainly to advertise shops, *brasseries* and restaurants specializing in the Auvergne's food products and culinary dishes. Such voluntary associations were grounded in place and in politics. Their golden age in Paris extended from 1880 to 1914. In 1910, there were some 300 such place-based, provincial, societies in Paris with 140,000 members (about 5 per cent of the population of Paris or about 10 per cent of its population with provincial origins). It was in Paris that many migrants were forcefully reminded of their provincial origins, and it was in Paris that some traditional provincial and regional characteristics were sustained paradoxically longer than in their places of origin. For example, a group from Aquitaine in 1913 'rediscovered' the *madras* (a knotted headscarf) which had been worn in the Bordeaux region until the eighteenth century, while the *bourrée* folk dance, forgotten in its birthplace, was sustained in the *bals* of the Auvergnats of Paris. Provincial traditions were thus reinvented in Paris.

Such provincial communities within Paris were initially of men and boys but not women or girls. It was not until a man had found permanent employment of some kind that his wife joined him, putting an end to the need for seasonal migration intended to restore family bonding. Many migrants retained links with their *pays* of origin, some by being seasonal migrants, some by sending remittances home to extended family members, while some through inheritance enjoyed continuing ownership of (or a share of) a provincial property, in effect a second home. Thus, while becoming Parisians such immigrants did not necessarily stop being provincials: a 'peasant' from the provinces could be both *un paysan* and *un Parisien*.

Confirmation of this is provided by the example of Martin Nadaud, who in due course was to become a *député* (member of parliament) for Creuse, the *département* of his birth. When he was only fourteen years old, Martin undertook a punishing walk in March 1830 with his father to Paris, more than 300 km from his home, as a seasonal migrant stonemason. He complained bitterly in the winter of 1832–3 (after having had to remain in Paris for more than two years because of injuries he had sustained while working) that he was suffering appallingly from homesickness ('*la maladie du pays me gagna*') – his native territory was tugging at his heartstrings. His sentiment was no doubt shared by many of his fellow workers, whatever their ages. Immigrants to Paris also sent messages to other provincials about (the virtues of) the Parisian lifestyle and in so doing encouraged more to join them. For example, at Javel in the *15^e arrondissement* in western Paris, bordering the Seine, the chemical disinfectant industry founded in 1777 attracted migrants especially from Alsace-Lorraine. In 1871, 21 per cent of the population of Javel had been born in Alsace: they arrived with work experience in the chemical industry and a shared language. Paris also attracted foreigners as their temporary or permanent home, especially East European Jews in the clothing industry, Italians and Portuguese as construction workers and Russian *émigrés*, but also American and British ex-patriots, as artists and writers. By 1900, Paris had acquired a reputation as the home of revolutions, or at least of revolutionary thinking, so some political theorists and activists came to the city hoping to learn more about the art and science of revolution. Most notable among them was Karl Marx, who lived in Paris from October 1843 until January 1845: his meeting with the German socialist Friedrich Engels in the Café de la Régence in the Place du Palais-Royal began a lifelong friendship.

For new migrants, integrating into Parisian society was a slow process, achieved gradually by their obtaining more permanent employment and ultimately for some by becoming entrepreneurs (establishing small- and medium-sized enterprises). In 1906, Paris had about 200,000 domestic servants (7 per cent of its total population), most of whom were women. Domestics were in short supply because of the growing demand by an expanding middle class in the late nineteenth century. Relatively few women remained maids (*bonnes*) permanently: for most, a domestic position in service was both a way of obtaining entry into the labour market and of escaping from their provincial origins, from family and priestly constraints and from the perceived mediocrity of village life. Migration to Paris was for some, perhaps for many, an escape into ambiguity and, initially at least, into poverty, not a move into fame and fortune. Many poor young women, unemployed or with only a tenuous hold on the labour market, entered into short-term relationships with students, providing sexual favours and domestic support in return for bed, board and companionship. These *grisettes* (so called because of their cheap grey dresses) were distinguished not by the nature of their employment – they took whatever low-paid work was available, for example, as flower sellers or dressmakers – but by the nature of their relationship with their male partner. Some moved on into more secure work with more stable partners, while some took up prostitution. Migration was a form of liberation: a young woman whose history was not known could reclaim her lost virginity, could accumulate some capital, could contract a marriage. Domestic service offered to many a route to social promotion: it was, as a living-in employee, better rewarded than most other female work. Other employment opportunities for women increased in the expanding service sector (such as shops and offices). By 1906, 40 per cent of those engaged in the service sector in Paris were women. The invention and adoption of the typewriter in the 1870s, like the earlier invention of the sewing machine in the 1820s, created new opportunities for dexterous women. To the early-nineteenth-century image of the young *Parisienne* as dressmaker or hatmaker was added in the late nineteenth century that of shop assistant and then in the early twentieth century that of secretary. One symbol of social advance, of *embourgeoisement*, was the acquisition of a pet. Small dogs in particular could be paraded ostentatiously in public parks, a signal of one's social status, of a settled place in society, and indicative of a personal economic surplus that permitted non-necessitous consumption.

The rapid and massive population growth of Paris during the nineteenth century substantially based on immigration was unsurprisingly accompanied by serious social dislocation and political upheavals, by an exacerbation of social divisions and by an increasing urban awareness and a specifically Parisian consciousness. The deceptive but alluring image of Paris as a powerful beacon attracting provincial and foreign moths ignores the dreadful environmental conditions which many of its residents experienced throughout the nineteenth century but especially before 1850.

A 'sick' city 1800-50

The first half of the nineteenth century saw a doubling of the population of Paris from half a million to 1 million within what was structurally still an essentially medieval and early modern physical framework. During this period, living conditions deteriorated for many of its residents. In 1827, an official report on the city's health admitted that for those coming into Paris 'the sense of smell tells you that you are approaching the first city in the world, before your eyes can see the tips of its monuments'. When cholera struck, it had a disproportionate effect on the poorer communities. The epidemics of 1820 which killed 20,000 Parisians and of 1832, which killed another 18,000, hit poor neighbourhoods first and most severely. Authors like Eugène Sue and Victor Hugo attested to the power of the metaphor of the city as a sick and dangerous organism. Fear of disease was added to a view of the poor as a deracinated and dangerous class whose hostility could erupt onto the streets at any moment. Catherine Kudlick has shown how the 1832 cholera outbreak provoked a noisy and polemical response of the bourgeoisie who tended to blame it on the growing numbers of poor people in Paris (its total population had increased by 40 per cent – some 238,000 – since 1801). A great debate among physicians and administrators, between medical wisdom and central government and between contagionists and anti-contagionists had not been fully resolved by the time of the next cholera outbreak in 1849, although by then there was much greater awareness of the need for cleaner, more hygienic, public places and domestic dwellings.

Gradually, a public discourse developed about how to make Paris a healthier and safer place to live. Overcrowding was a fundamental and worsening problem. Building in Paris during the first half of the nineteenth century did not increase as much as did the population. For example, during the 1820s, the stock of accommodation in Paris was increased by 7 per cent while its population grew by 10 per cent. Many old and large properties of the Church and the aristocracy were acquired by speculators and subdivided into smaller units, intensifying housing densities. Gardens and open spaces were built over, another form of intensification. Overcrowded slums were let for soaring rents, responding to the growing demand for accommodation. In some central districts, population density came to exceed 1,000 per hectare. The critical housing problem was largely ignored by the city council. Public transport was limited and expensive, rendering Paris essentially a pedestrian city for most people. It had a legacy of medieval streets, which were narrow (most less than 6 m wide), with rubbish of many kinds, including horse manure, piling up quickly; streets were dangerous, noisy, dirty and smelly. They were crowded, cobbled and criminalized. An Ordinance of 1788 set the minimum street width at 30 ft (9 m). This was increased in 1820 to 36 ft (11 m) and in 1832 to 40 ft (12 m). There was hardly any system of sewage disposal, with chamber pots being emptied onto streets with '*gardez l'eau*' being shouted from windows, this perhaps being the origin of the English term 'loo'; human excrement was stored in cess pits under each house and only emptied irregularly. It was not unusual to have a polluted water course running down middle of a street. Not until the 1880s did the public authorities decide that the sewers constructed in the 1850s and 1860s should be used to transport both street water and human waste. The project, known as *'tout à l'égout'* (everything to the sewers), proved to be controversial, particularly among cost-aware landlords, and it was not until 1894 that all Parisian houses were instructed to adopt the system, although the regulations did not compel landlords to comply. By 1904, 40 per cent of water closets in Paris disposed of excrement directly into the sewer system, but in the working-class slums of the eastern *11ᵉ arrondissement* the proportion was still only 20 per cent. Rubbish collections were unknown until 1883 when the prefect of the Seine *département*, Eugène Poubelle (who unintentionally gave his name to French dustbins/garbage cans and to the English term 'poo'), required property owners to provide for their occupants three bins: one for putrescible rubbish, a second for papers and rags and a third for glass, crockery and oyster shells. Lighting of public places in the early nineteenth century was mainly by torches and tallow candles. The introduction of gas lights in the 1820s was only extended slowly.

Too little attention was paid to public health before the 1830s. This was a period of peak water pollution; most water for drinking coming from the river Seine (into which was dumped urban waste). Piped water supplies to houses were not installed before 1828 and thereafter added to slowly. Most households relied on purchasing supplies from water carriers (with purchased water being used for cooking and washing, but not for personal consumption, for which there was instead reliance on safer alcoholic drinks like cider, beer, absinthe and rough wines). A multitude of domestic servants laboured to provide the daily basic needs of their employers, spending considerable time and effort fetching water from public fountains and fuel for fires. Migrants provided an abundance of cheap labour, offering themselves as casual labourers at local markets and riverside quays, for engagement hourly, daily or weekly. The poor of Paris were very visible and numerous. Many English visitors to Paris during the first half of the nineteenth century tended, as Claire Hancock has shown, to admire its public architecture – such as the Vendôme Column, the Place de la Concorde, the Arc de Triomphe and the Champs-Élysées – but recognized that its architectural splendour was a deceit, a facade, which hardly hid the miserable dwellings and dirty, narrow streets where many poor Parisians lived. In 1846, two-thirds of households in the city were too poor to pay direct taxes; between 1824 and 1847, 80 per cent of the dead were buried in paupers' graves, 33 per cent of births were illegitimate and one in ten newborn babies were abandoned by their mothers. These figures, combined with a high level of infanticide, reflect the absence of extended family support for many immigrants in Paris during the first half of the nineteenth century.

The emergence of concepts of urbanism and town planning

While the sickness of Paris was becoming increasingly clear, there was only a gradual development of ideas about what should constitute a healthy city. It was not just a matter of how to cope with the needs of a growing population but also of how to go beyond what older cities had historically offered in the way of public services. The

Parisian authorities responded dilatorily to the cholera epidemics of 1820 and 1832. Cholera was predominantly a disease of the poor, of the many jobless and homeless, of the numerous *chiffonniers* (ragpickers) and casual labourers who formed an underclass feared by other Parisians. Crowded living conditions – some dwellings had only between 1 and 3 square metres per person – with poor sanitation and without clean drinking water contributed to the spread of diseases and despondency. Only tardily did hygienists, philanthropists, administrators and property owners come to advocate measures to produce better public health, for example, to eliminate sources of cholera infection. Only gradually was there recognition of the need to tackle poverty by creating jobs, taking care of diseased paupers and ameliorating public hygiene through education and environmental improvements. Congested streets were another problem: Philippe Vigier has noted the increasing number and vehemence of complaints about the difficulty of circulating in Paris during the 1830s and 1840s. Such complaints might have reflected a real increase in traffic, including the beginnings of public transportation, but Pierre Lavedan has argued that traffic in Paris was only mediocre and doubted that its volume was the basis of more complaints. Bernard Marchand has accepted that the growth of the population of Paris and the creation of some public transportation might have led to greater congestion on the streets but he argued that the central districts in these decades saw many wealthy residents decanting to the north-west while the poor moved to the Left Bank. A bourgeois concern about traffic circulation, David Harvey has argued, reflected the growing capitalist mindset of the bourgeoisie with their belief in the rapid movement of people, capital, goods and ideas as the basis of economic growth.

During the first half of the nineteenth century, improvements to the urban fabric were piecemeal and involved mainly the erection of public monuments, the construction of two new bridges and of a few public water fountains. The shock of the cholera epidemic of 1832 which killed 18,000 people, more than 2 per cent of Paris's population of 786,000, engendered more and more rigorous scientific analysis of the social and environmental conditions in which cholera flourished and spread. In the ensuing debate about the urban problem by administrators, politicians and writers, conservatives sought solutions which would produce greater social control while socialists favoured measures which would improve general welfare in the city. In 1833, the newly appointed prefect of Paris, the Burgundian Rambuteau (1781–1869), acknowledged ideas advanced by hygienists about the connection between the insalubrity of Paris's narrow streets and cholera. He set about some environmental improvements, notably construction of a new 13-m-wide and almost 1-km-long street linking the *quartier* of Les Halles with that of Le Marais (the street has carried his name since 1839). During the fifteen years that Rambuteau was prefect (1833–48), he also oversaw the construction of public water fountains, improvements to the city's drains, completion of the Arc de Triomphe, landscaping the Champs-Élysées, completion of La Madeleine and the construction or restoration of a number of churches (including those of Sainte-Chapelle on the Île de la Cité and of Saint-Germain-l'Auxerrois, facing the colonnade of the Louvre). Such environmental improvements were later to be overshadowed by the more comprehensive and more integrated transformations of the landscape of Paris implemented in the 1850s and

1860s by Haussmann – which is why they can and sometimes have been entirely neglected or at least undervalued.

It is the case, however, that it was not until the 1840s that city officials acknowledged that the physical infrastructure of Paris was reaching a crisis which required an overall plan to improve environmental and social conditions and to promote economic activity. The 'urban question' became a debating issue among utopians and social theorists but, as David Harvey has pointed out, many of them retained 'a fierce attachment to the ideal of small, face to face communities' rather than recognition of the new urban community that had seen Paris almost double its population between 1801 and 1846, from 547,756 to 1,053,897. There were then quite a few plans proposed for addressing the city's ills but they generally lacked the holistic vision and the political drive to put them into practice. For example, in 1843, an ambitious plan was put forward by H. Meynadier for a new major road network, slum clearance and embellished public squares and gardens. But his project was seen by the fiscally conservative municipal council as being very expensive and not much of it was implemented. While a number of historians have argued that only piecemeal suggestions for urban improvements before 1850 were adopted because of budgetary constraints, Victoria Thompson has countered that the city's authorities rejected such unifying and comprehensive schemes because they associated them with the authoritarian period of the Terror of the early 1790s. The rejection of any unified vision for the cityscape was most probably both principled and pragmatic.

The condition of Paris astonished many observers in the 1840s, alarmed by its environmental degradation, its rapid growth and its invasion by provincial migrants many of whom fell into poverty and crime. One dramatist Charles Duveyrier (1803–1866) wrote in his *Le Monomane* (1835) that the city had become 'a huge satanic dance, in the midst of which men and women are thrown together any which way, crowded like ants, feet in the mud, breathing a diseased air, trying to walk through encumbered streets and public places'. A novelist Eugène Sue (1804–1857) declared in his *Les Mystères de Paris* (1842–3): 'The barbarians are in our midst.' Such descriptions by imaginative authors of works of fiction were echoed by journalists and other observers of the 'real' Paris. One referred to the 'invasion of barbarians'; another to a 'mob of nomads' – others referred to the 'forest' of Paris and even to the urban 'jungle' where the people were 'wolves' and 'savages'. One observer in 1848 asserted: 'There is not a Parisian society, there are not any Parisians. Paris is no more than a camp of nomads.' Paris was seen by many literate, almost certainly bourgeois, observers as having been invaded by provincials, by rootless savages who were racially different from 'true' Parisians. Such caustic views added to the existing social tensions, to the daily pressures of mass migration on an ill-adapted city. Unrest and the Revolution of 1848 were the unsurprising outcomes. Protests on the streets of Paris in February that year, triggered by plans to close the recently opened National Workshops which provided a basic income for the unemployed, were a precursor to the revolutionary 'June Days' when the imminent closure of the workshops was announced. Street barricades and fighting by insurgents led to perhaps as many as 10,000 protesters and troops of the National Guard being killed or wounded. Among them was the Archbishop of Paris, murdered while endeavouring to negotiate peace. Although some provincial towns like Lyon and

Limoges and many rural areas like the Pyrenees similarly saw social unrest in 1848, Paris was the epicentre of protest which spread in transmuted forms throughout the country. But the tumult of 1848 was essentially an urban and quintessentially a Parisian phenomenon which emphasized the distancing of town from country and particularly of Paris from the provinces. After the Revolution of 1848, the provinces elected Louis Napoléon on a programme to reinstate order in the country and to do so especially in Paris. During 1848 and 1849, a remarkable range of new ideas about the social and economic life of cities emerged. They included socialist theories, propositions for a new economy, a search for new ways of practising fraternity and the emergence of a feminist movement.

3

Monumentalizing Paris: Commemorating its past

Paris in the nineteenth century both inherited old monuments and erected new ones: its cityscape became increasingly monumental. An individual *monument* is a structure or edifice constructed with the explicit intention of commemorating and/ or honouring one or more notable persons, actions or events. Urban structures may be described as being *monumental* when they are massive, conspicuous or historically prominent. In this dual sense, Paris was monumentalized during the long-nineteenth century from 1789 to 1914. The history of Paris has been built and carved in stone and cast in metal (bronze and iron). Its cityscape has been fundamentally transformed by large structures intended to be visually impressive and often designed to commemorate an aspect of the city's history. Constructing monuments was an endeavour to control both the cultural memory of Parisians and the cultural space of Paris. Their meanings derive from both the intentions of their authors and the responses to them by their readers: their meanings are contingent and relational, energized by the times and places of their creators and of their observers. The personality of nineteenth-century Paris was signalled partly in its monuments and their messages interpreted both by its citizens who encountered them in their daily lives and by historical observers employing hindsight.

The built form of Paris at the beginning of the nineteenth century included already quite a few monuments and monumental structures. That they were recognized as such by contemporaries is demonstrated in a board game titled *Jeu des Monuments de Paris*, which dates from around 1820. Of the sixty-three monuments used for the game, most were government buildings, water fountains and churches. But they also included, for example, bridges, city gateways, taxation booths, schools, theatres and water towers. Players of the game began on the square named Porte Saint-Denis and proceeded to the destination, the Arc de Triomphe. In effect, in the early nineteenth century, almost any public building or structure and any large private building might have been regarded by contemporaries as a monument or as monumental. In 1804, Napoléon Bonaparte crowned himself, in the Pope's presence, as emperor in the cathedral of Notre-Dame and went on to promote Paris as a city with monumental structures that would echo the glory of Imperial Rome and endure as historical landmarks and legacies of his rule. Successive political leaders of nineteenth-century France – as well as other influential individuals and groups – similarly stamped Paris with solid representations of their views, of their reverence for the past and of their aspirations for the future.

During the long-nineteenth century, Paris witnessed a significant increase in open spaces – boulevards, squares, parks and promenades – in which public art became part of the city's furniture. Maurice Agulhon has argued that the most numerous were statues of *grands hommes*; a second category were semi-utilitarian monuments like ornamental water fountains; a third category were non-utilitarian but instructive testimonials, notably religious monuments (such as statues of the Virgin Mary) and political monuments (such as representations of the Republic) or historical (and partly political) monuments (such as those commemorating wars or specific battles, or revolutions). Some monuments combined these disparate but related themes. There is space here to consider only a few in rough chronological order (some additional, even more culturally significant, iconic structures will be addressed in a later chapter). Why were these monuments constructed and what messages did they convey to the passing public?

The column in the Place Vendôme 1806–10

In September and October 1805, the French army crossed the Rhine to engage in battle with Austrian forces. On 15 November, Napoléon marched triumphantly through Vienna and the French army then defeated the Russians at Austerlitz, a village north of Vienna. Napoléon decided to publicize and celebrate that French victory: on 1 January 1806 he signed a decree for the construction of a commemorative column in Paris, to be sited in the Place Vendôme (Figure 3.1).

This rectangular *place* had been created in the late seventeenth century with open access on the south side to the Rue Saint-Honoré and surrounded on the others by monumental buildings such as the Royal Library and the Mint and by grand private houses (*hôtels*). In the centre of the square was a bronze statue of Louis XIV on horseback, erected in 1699 but destroyed in 1792 during the Revolution. In its place was erected in 1810 a 44-m-high column: it had a stone core and a veneer of 425 spiralling low-relief bronze plates, made out of Austrian and Russian cannons captured in December 1805 at the Battle of Austerlitz. This casing was decorated with military scenes, imitating Trajan's Column in Rome erected in 113 CE to celebrate the emperor's victory in the Dacian Wars. The original statue mounted on the Vendôme Column was of Napoléon posing as Caesar but in 1814, when Paris was occupied by troops of the European allies, it was replaced by a white (in effect, royalist) *fleur-de-lys*. The bronze of the statue of Napoléon was reused to make the statue of Louis XIII on horseback erected in the Place des Vosges in 1822 and inaugurated in 1825. In 1833, a new statue of Napoléon in military uniform was placed on the top of the Vendôme Column in the presence of Louis Philippe, king of France from 1830 to 1848, who was hoping thereby to appropriate for his own regime some of the imperial glory associated with Napoléon Bonaparte. In 1863, Napoléon III decided that the statue was too small and had it replaced by a copy of the first statue of Napoléon as a Roman emperor. In the 1871 civil war in Paris, the Vendôme Column was demolished by the

Figure 3.1 Column in the Place Vendôme *c.* 1900. Wikimedia Creative Commons (public domain)

Communards, only then to be rebuilt in 1873–5 by the new Third Republic, with the statue of Napoléon restored at its apex. The unstable history of the Vendôme Column is a precise and vivid illustration both of the hubris of those who ruled Paris (and France) and of the political sensitivities of many of those they governed. It demonstrates that historical monuments were expected and required to speak to the 'present' generation of Parisians – a monument could not be expected to retain relevance and meaning in all epochs and for every generation. Times changed and along with them monuments did also.

The Arc de Triomphe 1806–36

After his victory at the Battle of Austerlitz, Napoléon promised his troops that he would return them flamboyantly to France by way of triumphal arches. On 18 February 1806, a decree ruled that 10 per cent of the taxes raised on the marketing of corn would be used to pay for an Arc de Triomphe at the entrance to the Rue Saint-Antoine in eastern Paris, on the route to be taken by the returning French troops. In 1789, however, destruction of the fourteenth-century Bastille (which had been part of the fortifications in the defensive wall built in the late fourteenth century on the instructions of Charles V) had left an urban space ripe for development but which was judged to be too large for a triumphal arch. That vast site needed something even more grand, even more monumental, than an arch. Another possible location was considered at the Place de la Concorde, but that would have put the arch close to the Palais des Tuileries and a large stone arch would have obscured the view of the palace. So, instead, a site was chosen on the Butte de Chaillot, at the tax barrier L'Étoile, at the western extension of the Champs-Élysées, at the point where, at that time, the urban scene gave way to countryside. The new arch was planned hubristically to be twice the size of the Arc de Septime Sévère erected in Rome in 203 CE to glorify the military victories of its emperor. Accordingly, the arch in Paris had to be 50 m high.

The foundation stone was laid on 15 August 1806: completion of the arch would take thirty years. By 1810, the construction had only reached 6 m high. But Napoléon, aged forty and having divorced the Empress Joséphine, wanted his new wife, Marie-Louise of Austria, seventeen years young, to make an impressive entry to Paris on 2 April. In haste, a wooden and linen version of the new arch was erected at the correct height. By 1814, when the Napoleonic era came to an end, the stone arch was still only 20 m high. The occupying Prussian troops surrounding the nascent monument used the timber version as fuel for their camp fires. On coming to power in 1814, Louis XVIII was initially inclined to have the uncompleted arch razed to the ground but instead in 1823 he ordered the arch to be finished as a monument not to celebrate France's imperial glory, as intended by Napoléon, but to celebrate the successful military campaign in Spain of his nephew, the Duke of Angoulême. When Louis XVIII died in 1824, his brother Charles X succeeded him and abandoned the project. It was not until Louis-Philippe came to the throne in 1830 – he was to be the last king of France – that the project was resumed, with its intention changed to being a commemoration of France's expansionist adventures from 1792 until 1815. Sculptured embellishments of the completed arch show the departure and return of French troops, and a long general scene depicts and proclaims 'the glory of the nation'. Stunning stone carvings portray 158 battles and the names of 558 (or possibly 600) French generals of the Revolution and empire. The high reliefs include *La Marseillaise*, a masterpiece by sculptor François Rude. Born the son of blacksmith in Dijon in 1784, Rude had migrated to Paris in 1808 at the age of twenty-four to attend the Imperial École des Beaux-Arts; after Napoléon's defeat at Waterloo and the restoration of the French monarchy, Rude lived in self-imposed exile in Brussels from 1817 until 1827, then returning to Paris where he undertook many commissions for the French state, including that of *La Marseillaise*; he died in 1855 and was buried in the Montparnasse Cemetery.

Building work on the Arc de Triomphe was at last completed in 1836 and the arch inaugurated on 29 July. The intended elaborate, military, parade to mark the occasion was aborted and replaced by a much more subdued inauguration ceremony because the king feared being assassinated in public (there had been an assassination attempt on 15 June). There was, however, in 1840 what amounted to another inauguration with the solemn return through the Arc de Triomphe of Napoléon's mortal remains (he had died in 1821 on the island of Saint Helena, a British-owned volcanic island in the South Atlantic) and then their conveyance to the Hôtel des Invalides (a home and hospital for old and sick or injured soldiers, dating from the seventeenth century). In 1885, the funeral procession of Victor Hugo went from the Arc de Triomphe, covered in black, passing huge crowds of mourners to the Panthéon, travelling from a site of military and patriotic symbolism to one of secular and national significance, a journey reflecting Hugo's personal passage from youthful admiration for a heroic Napoléon to his later heartfelt embrace of the secular republic.

Much later, the historically significant symbolism of the Arc de Triomphe was intensified on 28 January 1921 when the remains of an unknown soldier killed during the Great War were entombed there and then again on 11 November 1923 when an eternal flame was lit in memory of the many nameless dead of that war.

The obelisk in the Place de la Concorde 1836

Following Napoléon's Expedition to Egypt in 1798, which was more a cultural and scientific success than a military one, Muhammed Ali, viceroy of Egypt, drew upon French expertise to modernize the region, to reorganize the army, to build hospitals and to undertake hydrological works. To cement Egypt's links with France, in 1827 Muhammed Ali Pasha, ruler of Ottoman Egypt, offered to Charles X a giraffe. After a month's acclimatisation at Marseille, the giraffe was placed, for visitors to admire, in the Jardin des Plantes (Botanical Garden) on the left bank of the Seine in eastern Paris. But French archaeologists were much more fascinated by Egypt's archaeological remains than by exotic creatures; so, in 1828, Muhammed Ali gave to France an obelisk which had stood before a temple at Luxor, on a bank of the Nile. It was 23 m high and weighed 222 tonnes. It required a vast operation to convey it to France by sea to Le Havre and then up the Seine to Paris – a ship was built at Toulon especially for the purpose, one that could sail on the Nile, the Mediterranean, the Atlantic and the Seine. The ship's journey began from Egypt in August 1832 and ended in Paris in December 1833. It then took almost three years to construct a dry dock and to erect the obelisk on the Place de la Concorde (Figure 3.2). Its official inauguration on 25 October 1836 was watched by a large crowd and by King Louis Philippe from the windows of the eighteenth-century Hôtel de la Marine, originally a furniture store for the Crown but after the Revolution of 1789 it had become the offices of the naval ministry. Putting the obelisk in place took four hours.

The octagonal Place de la Concorde had been constructed between 1755 and 1775. An equestrian statue of Louis XV was installed in the centre of the Place in June 1763; then, in August 1792, the day after the abolition of the monarchy, the bronze statue was removed and sent away to be melted down. The Place, originally called the Place Louis XV, was renamed during successive political regimes as the Place de la Révolution (where a guillotine was installed and used to execute inter alia Louis XVI and Queen Marie-Antoinette), Place de la Concorde, Place Louis XV, Place Louis XVI, Place de la Charte and then in 1830 returned to Place de la Concorde. The centre of the Place was adorned successively by a statue of Louis XV, a Statue de la Liberté, a statue of Louis XVI and finally the Obélisque de Luxor. At each of the eight angles of the Place is a statue representing a major French city: Brest, Rouen, Lyon, Marseille, Bordeaux, Nantes, Lille and Strasbourg. After the Franco-Prussian War of 1870–1, when Alsace was lost to Germany, the Strasbourg statue

Figure 3.2 Obelisk in the Place de la Concorde *c.* 1865. Wikimedia Creative Commons (public domain)

was on state occasions covered in black mourning crape and often decorated with wreaths, a symbolic practice which did not end until France regained the territory as victor in the war of 1914–18. Until then, the symbolic statue of Strasbourg made the Place de la Concorde a rallying point for patriotic demonstrations which were able also to include in their programmes the statue of Joan of Arc in the conveniently nearby Place des Pyramides.

The July Column in the Place de la Bastille 1840

Three days of revolution in 1830 – on 27, 28 and 29th July – led to the abdication of Charles X. The new administration wanted to erect a commemorative monument significantly sited in the Place de la Bastille .

The National Assembly decreed that it should be a column, reflecting the imperial column in the Place Vendôme, and that it would have a crypt for the remains of 504 labourers and artisans who had died in the 'Three Glorious Days' of July 1830. The 50.5-m-high column was constructed from 1835 and inaugurated in 1840. The column replaced the incongruous statue of an elephant which Napoléon in 1808 had wanted to be erected here in eastern Paris to balance the Arc de Triomphe planned for the west of the city. It was to be cast in bronze but never progressed beyond being a plaster version. Always bizarre, the statue became dilapidated and was replaced by the July Column and would probably have been forgotten had it not featured in Victor Hugo's novel *Les Misérables* (1862).

Also placed in the crypt of the column before its completion were some Egyptian mummies that had deteriorated in the humid underground section of the museum where they had been stored. Later, the mortal remains of a further 196 people were placed in the crypt, the remains of those recognized as 'martyrs' who had been killed during the Revolution of 1848. Thus, the July Column was seen as commemorating not one but three revolutions – those of 1789, 1830 and 1848. A staircase of 240 steps provides access to the top of the column for a panoramic view of Paris.

The statue of Joan of Arc in the Place des Pyramides 1874

After France lost the 1870–1 war with Prussia, its new republican administration sought to revive patriotic sentiment in the country by celebrating past times when France had been victorious and had defeated its enemy. It recalled notably the role of Joan of Arc in fighting against the English in 1429–30. Paradoxically, the anticlerical Republican government praised a religious heroine for her role in the Hundred Years War and for her patriotic fervour. In 1803, Joan had been declared by Napoléon to be a national symbol and the French state built on that image – to the chagrin of many in the Catholic Church.

Under the powerful advocacy of the great nineteenth-century French historian, Jules Michelet, Joan of Arc became a contested symbol of French patriotism. The government of the Third Republic ordered that a statue of her should be erected on the site where it was thought she was wounded on 8 September 1429 when leading her liberationist attack on the English forces then besieging the capital. A bronze equestrian statue of Joan by Paris-born Emmanuel Frémiet (1824–1910) was inaugurated on 20 February 1874 in the Place des Pyramides (Figure 3.3). At the ceremony, Catholics and anti-republicans in the crowd came to blows with anticlericalists and republicans about the statue's configuration; the former wanted the statue to have a more religious posture than the militaristic one favoured and decided upon by the Republican government. But the conflict over Joan of Arc had deeper roots. Following the military defeat of 1871, the symbol of Joan was appropriated by the nationalist movement and the Church's anxiety about its loss of public authority led some Catholics to join the glorification of Joan of Arc while others remained unsure, given that she had been burned as a heretic and the debate continued about her claim to having heard 'divine voices'. The campaign begun by some Catholics in 1869 to have Joan canonized succeeded only in having her beatified in 1909; she was not canonized until 1920.

The site of Joan of Arc's statue, in what was originally the Place de Rivoli, had been renamed in 1801 the Place des Pyramides in recognition of Napoléon's victorious 1798 Egyptian campaign. Frémiet took to heart the immediate criticisms of his statue – that Joan of Arc was depicted as a very young and frail woman on a

Figure 3.3 Statue of Joan of Arc in the Place des Pyramides. Wikimedia Creative Commons (public domain) CCO 1.0 Universal Public Domain Dedication

massive Percheron horse – and took the opportunity in 1899, when the statue had to be taken down to permit construction work on the new underground railway, to replace it surreptitiously with a version depicting a more robust Joan and a less muscular horse.

This statue of Joan of Arc in the Place des Pyramides is the sole monument commanded by the state, standing among the 150 or so statues of men and women erected in Paris between 1870 and 1914 by the city's municipal council. In response to the national secular Third Republic's action, in 1891 the municipality of Paris had a statue of Joan of Arc erected on the Boulevard Saint-Marcel, in south-eastern Paris, having been petitioned for one by residents of the *quartie*r known as *la petite Pologne*. Another statue of Joan was erected in 1900, prominently and symbolically placed to affirm her religiosity in front of the Église de Saint-Augustin in the *8ᵉ arrondissement* which had been built between 1860 and 1871 in an eclectic style, incorporating both

Romanesque and Byzantine elements, on the right bank in western Paris to serve the growing population of that district.

The monument to the Republic 1880

In 1879, the municipal council of Paris sought a statue to ornament the Place du Château d'Eau (renamed in that year as the Place de la République). It ran a competition for a sculpture which would personify France. The winning entry was a 9.4-m-high bronze statue of Marianne, the feminine personification of the French Republic, holding aloft an olive branch in her right hand and resting her left on a tablet engraved with '*Droits de l'Homme*' (Figure 3.4).The statue sits atop a monument which is 23 m high.

The plinth on which Marianne proudly stands is surrounded with three statues personifying the Revolutionary trinity of *Liberté*, *Égalité* and *Fraternité*. Also, at the base is a lion guarding a ballot box, an icon of the democratic foundation of the state (even though at this time French women did not have the right to vote and would not be granted that right until 1944). Around the statue are twelve high reliefs depicting some major events in French history between 1789 and 1880, including the first national fête on 14 July 1880. A plaster version of the monument was inaugurated that day and the final bronze cast on 14 July 1883.

Figure 3.4 Monument à la République in the Place de la République *c.* 1895. Photographer unknown.

Another of the entries for this monument's competition was also accepted for erection, not on the Place de la République but further east on the boundary of the 11e and 12e arrondissements, in the Place du Trône, renamed in 1880 as the Place de la Nation. Titled *Le Triomphe de la République*, this is another sculpture erected to mark the centenary of the Revolution, inaugurated at first in plaster in 1889 and then in bronze in 1899. The figure of Marianne, personifying the Republic, stands on a globe in a chariot pulled by two lions and looks westwards along the Rue du Faubourg Saint-Antoine towards the Place de la Bastille. She is surrounded by allegorical figures: *le Génie de la Liberté* guides her chariot; *le Travail* is symbolized by a blacksmith who drives the chariot aided by *la Justice*. Enclosing the whole is an abundance of sculptured fruits, symbolizing the prosperity of the nation. The sculptor was Parisian-born Jules Dalou (1838–1902), who had been an *officier au 83e bataillon des fédérés* in the Commune of 1871 and then for eight years an exile in London.

The Statue of Liberty 1886

From 1865, there developed a public discussion about the suggestion of a donation by the people of France to America of a monument to mark the centenary in 1876 of American independence, a cause which France had forcefully supported. The idea was slow to gain traction because it was a project about American democracy at a time when France was experiencing its Second Empire. There were also financial obstacles, with discussions suggesting that France should pay for the statue and America for its pedestal. After France became a republic in September 1870, the project gained strength and work on a statue – *La Liberté éclairant le monde* or more simply *La Statue de la Liberté* – began in Paris in 1875. The work was not completed until 1885. The following year, the statue was taken in 350 sections to New York, rebuilt and inaugurated there on 28 October 1886. It was astoundingly 92.9 m high, the tallest statue in Paris. Constructed by a French sculptor, Frédéric Auguste Bartholdi, taking advice from a French engineer, Gustave Eiffel, the statue has an internal iron framework which is covered by copper plates. Both Bartholdi and Eiffel were immigrants in Paris. Bartholdi, born in 1834 in Colmar in Alsace, was taken by his mother to live in Paris after the death of his father in 1836; he lived and worked as a sculptor in Paris until his death in 1904 when he was buried in the Montparnasse Cemetery. Eiffel, born in Dijon in 1832, obtained his *baccalauréat* there in 1850 and then migrated to Paris to continue his education which led to his developing an expertise in metallurgy and metal structures. He lived in Clichy, in the north-western suburbs of Paris, just over 6 km from the city's centre; he died in 1923 and was buried in the local Levallois-Perret Cemetery.

There are some replicas of the Statue of Liberty in Paris. The most significant is the 1885 bronze casting of a plaster model made by Bartholdi, given by the Committee of Americans in Paris to the city of Paris. Just over 11 m high, it was sited initially in the Place des États-Unis, in western Paris in the Chaillot *quartier* of the 16e *arrondissement*, the location of an American colony and close to the American embassy. But the statue was soon moved, in July 1889 on the centenary of the French Revolution, to the western point of the Île-aux-Cygnes (a small artificial island created in 1827 to protect the Pont de Grenelle). The statue was sited at the level of this bridge across the Seine. Its architect wanted the sculpture to face west towards America, but this would have meant the official inauguration party would have had to hazard a boat trip on the river. In order to avoid this, the ceremony took place on the bridge, with the statue facing east. Another bronze version, 2.85 m high and cast by Bartholdi in 1889, was placed in the Jardin du Luxembourg in 1906 (Figure 3.5) but in 2012, after its torch had been stolen, it was moved to the entry of the sculpture hall of the Musée d'Orsay and replaced by a copy.

Figure 3.5 Statue of Liberty by Frédéric Bartholdi in the Luxembourg Garden.
Wikimedia Creative Commons Attribution Share Alike 3.0 Yair Hakla

The meanings of monuments

Having considered some individual monuments, each of which was created to make a statement which was then read or misread by people who observed them, what was their overall intent and reception? Maurice Agulhon suggested in 1978 that there was an outbreak of statuomania each time a liberal revolution substituted a secular, optimistic and open-minded regime for one committed to control, tradition and authority: in effect, 1789, 1830 and 1870. Monuments of those periods had clear ideological foundations. Neil McWilliam has highlighted the ideological conflicts which were embedded in some Parisian monuments in the early years of the Third Republic. Catholics and royalists demonstrated around statues commemorating Joan of Arc, while socialists and freethinkers did so around the monument to Étienne Dolet, a humanist freethinker and writer who had been burnt at the stake with his books in 1546. A bronze statue of Dolet was erected in 1889 in the Place Maubert, in the 5e *arrondissement* on the central, intellectual, Left Bank near the Sorbonne challengingly close to the cathedral of Notre-Dame just across the river. This statue was removed in 1942 during the German occupation and never replaced (presumably having been melted down as wartime material). A street named after Dolet in 1879 in Belleville-Ménilmontant, in the eastern working-class 20e *arrondissement*, still serves as a less obvious commemoration of this radical individual. Who were the other 'greats' of France petrified in the landscape of Paris?

In her recent analysis of almost 4,000 statues in France erected between 1804 and 2018, Jaqueline Lalouette excavates their social contexts (the aims of their proponents, their funding, the rituals surrounding their inaugurations, and the controversies and sometimes physical protests surrounding them). What is revealed is a collective biography of statues, tracing their births, their ageing and ultimately their deaths (or in some cases, resurrection). Although some statues predate the Revolution of 1789 and quite a few date from after 1914, it was the long-nineteenth century which saw waves of statue-building – 'statuephilia' or 'statuemania' – reaching their highest level in the Third Republic.

Maurice Agulhon in 1978 drew attention to the neglect of '*statuomanie*' by historians, suggesting that, while erecting statues was at first highly symbolic, a significant militant activity, the frenzy for erecting statues began to lose its political connotations. He asserted that erecting statues quickly became common place, a part of everyday life, and thus lost its sting. Agulhon (1978, p. 148) cited a politician and dramatist, Jean-Pons-Guillaume Viennet (1777–1868), as having exclaimed in his *Journal* in 1842 that '*La manie des statues se propage comme une épidemie*'. Agulhon also claimed that by the end of the nineteenth century, 'the statue that was perceived as a true symbolic object was the exception rather than the rule'. Nonetheless, he judged the early years of the liberal, secular and patriotic Third Republic to have been '*le régime statuomaniaque par excellence*'. Jaqueline Lalouette has recently asserted that in France under the Restoration (1815–30) only three statues were inaugurated annually, under the July Monarchy (1830–48) just six, under the Second Empire (1851–70) ten but during the phase of Republican statuomania between

1879 and 1914 no less than thirty-six. As for their subject matter, most common were statues of politicians, writers and military men, followed by ecclesiastics, artists and philosophers. Only 7 per cent of statues were of women (and their share would be much reduced if one excluded the 124 statues of Joan of Arc). Although Lalouette's work addresses France as a whole, it is reasonable to assume that the general points she makes would apply specifically to Paris. According to Jacques Lanfranchi, twenty-six statues were erected in Paris between 1815 and 1870 and an astounding 150 between 1870 and 1914.

The statuomania which marked the end of the nineteenth and the beginning of the twentieth century may be partly explained not only by that period's heightened interest in art and aesthetics but also by the concerns of both the state and the Church to redeem the damages done to their reputations in preceding decades. With statues, the past was being brought into the service of the present. Monumentalizing great events and great people (but mainly men) in the history of France and of Paris especially provided some solidity for a society seemingly in constant flux and recurrent revolution: while anchoring Paris to its past, the 'open-air Panthéon' (to borrow June Hargrove's collective description of the city's statues) also provided hope for a better future, they were a metaphor for solidity and permanence. During the nineteenth century, the growth of literacy and the expansion of a print and picture culture, eagerly devouring in their new forms both words (in newspapers, magazines and novels) and images (drawings, paintings, advertisements, lithographs and photographs), created a vastly expanded panoply of French 'heroes' who could be commemorated by statues, extending the range from politicians, philosophers and generals to embrace artists, musicians, scientists, explorers and writers. Of the 176 statues inaugurated in Paris between 1815 and 1914, Lanfranchi revealed that almost one in five were literary figures – among them, of course, Balzac, Baudelaire, Dumas *père*, Flaubert, Hugo, Sand, Verne and Zola. The Great War of 1914–18 put an end to statuomania. But it was probably beginning to decline from around 1900, Michael Garval has argued, with a cultural shift in popular sentiment from a monumental and heroic vision of greatness to the ubiquity of a popular culture produced by modern mass media and a market brand of celebrity. There were now so many potential 'heroes' being promoted that fewer individuals stood out in the crowd as being monumental and worthy of being commemorated in stone or metal. By 1914, public art in Paris was to be found throughout the city but far removed in substance from the royalist and religious sentiment which it possessed in 1789.

A major feature of French society during the nineteenth century was its secularization, especially under the Third Republic from 1870 onwards and leading ultimately to the separation of Church and state in 1905. But much earlier, the process of secularization was active in Paris architecturally. At the time of the 1789 Revolution, Paris had an historical legacy of numerous religious buildings which presented secular rationalists with both problems and opportunities. For example, on 19 November 1793, the Lombards' section informed the National Convention that it no longer recognized any divinity other than Reason. Accordingly, the church of Saint-Leu-Saint-Gilles, in central Paris on the Rue de Saint-Denis in the *1er arrondissement* and dating from the thirteenth century, became a salted meat warehouse for the butchers

Figure 3.6 Le Panthéon 1912. Wikimedia Creative Commons Attribution Share Alike 3.0/ Yanterrien

and *charcutiers* of its *quartier*. Much more strikingly, the church of Sainte-Geneviève, built in neoclassical style between 1757 and 1790 on the hill of Sainte-Geneviève to honour the patron saint of Paris, was deconsecrated by the Revolution in 1791 to be transformed into the Panthéon (Figure 3.6) to honour the great men of the Republic, underpinning a monumental cult of personality associated with the Revolution and which permeated French culture during the following two centuries.

Monuments as cultural messages were intended to make strong visual statements. Their meanings were immediate to those who promoted them but perhaps read only slowly if at all by others. Less visually obvious but performing a similar role were the numerous street signs that multiplied in Paris as new roads were built. In addition, some old streets were renamed as a way – it was thought – of erasing history or of promoting newly recognized events and people.

Street names

Street names are often manifestations of a community's collective memory. Until the seventeenth century, streets in many European cities came to acquire names given to them by local people who used them frequently. Thereafter, street naming was increasingly undertaken by public authorities. In Paris, it was not until the 1770s that there was a concerted effort to systematize its street names. Signs bearing street names appeared in 1729 and from 1762 shop signs, which until then had tended to be boards hung vertically at the front but came instead to be placed flat on the facades of shops and other businesses to improve street illumination. Soon afterwards, shop-front windows became common. From the 1780s, cobbled or paved walkways for pedestrians were laid in some of the squares. By the early 1800s, the naming of streets and the numbering of buildings in Paris were well underway.

The Revolution of 1789 banned the use of royalist, religious and aristocratic street names. During the Revolution, both officials and the public became acutely aware of the potential ideological and pedagogical role of street naming. For the revolutionaries, street names were a means of propaganda, less about honouring great men and more about promoting revolutionary ideology. With the Revolution, many street names deemed to be too religious or too monarchist were changed and some of the old stone plaques were defaced (e.g. the Rue de Turenne in eastern central Paris in the 3^e and 4^e arrondissements used to be the Rue Saint-Louis, named after the thirteenth-century king Louis IX who had been canonized by the Church). But it was not until 1889 – the centenary of the French Revolution – that three tiny and until then insignificant and unremarkable streets in a far corner of north-eastern Paris in the 19e arrondissement were named, respectively, *Liberté, Égalité* and *Fraternité*.

Immediately on coming to the throne in 1815, Louis XVIII ordered the restoration of the pre-revolutionary names of forty-nine streets, quays, squares and bridges in Paris. In 1805, when street signs were still a rarity in many parts of the city, its Prefect introduced a standardized system with the names of streets on yellow porcelain plaques with red letters for those that ran parallel to the Seine and black for those that ran away from it – an early Global Positioning System (GPS). Napoléon Bonaparte named many streets after his generals and his successful battles: for example, the Rue Marengo in the 1er *arrondissement* was named after the battle of 1800 in Italy, in which France was victorious over Austrian forces. 1844 saw the introduction by the Prefect of the Seine *département* of new standard street name signs in Paris: they were enamel plaques with white letters on an azure background, familiar to visitors to Paris (and indeed to the French provinces) to this day (Figure 3.7).

The spatial spread of Paris during the nineteenth century involved constructing many new streets and modifying old ones. France at that time possessed the world's second largest empire. Many new streets were given names which recalled its overseas adventures by famous colonial figures and explorers, such as Jacques Cartier (Rue Jacques-Cartier in the *18e arrondissement*, named in 1875) and Jean-François de La Pérouse (Rue La Pérouse in the *16e arrondissement*, named in 1864). So, too, were colonial places such as Martinique (Rue de la Martinique in the *18e arrondissement*, named in 1877) and Saigon in French Indo-China (Rue de Saigon in the *16e arrondissement*, named in 1868). Today, almost 300 Parisian streets out of 5,400 – almost 6 per cent – bear witness to France's colonial past – to its colonies,

Figure 3.7 Street sign of Rue Marengo. Wikimedia Creative Commons Attribution Share Alike 3.9/BrokenSphere

explorers, military conquerors, government personages, writers, scientists and missionaries. There are among them remarkably few names of colonial businessmen or of indigenous peoples or of women.

Analysis by Daniel Milo of the street names in the 1978 *Index-Atlas of France* has revealed that 'Republic' was the most common in a list of the most frequently used names of streets in the plans of ninety-five *préfectures* (administrative centres of *départements)* throughout France. The list includes politicians, military men, scientists, writers, composers and Joan of Arc. Many – even the authors and artists – were political figures, many of whom were connected with the Third Republic between 1882 and 1914: for example, Rue Gustave-Courbet in the *16ᵉ arrondissement*, named in 1885, eight years after his death, and Avenue Émile Zola in the *15ᵉ arrondissement*, named in 1907 two years after his death. Parisian street names emphasized French history and the French nation – they served as powerful and daily reminders to passers-by of the history and glory of France, contributing to its collective cultural memory.

History and collective memory

In sum, from street name plates through statues to massive structures like the Arc de Triomphe, monuments in nineteenth-century Paris provided – and still provide – myriad visual and tangible reminders of the city's and the nation's pasts and were often explicitly intended to promote and enshrine the civic and national histories and the identities and responsibilities of those who viewed them. Indeed, the turbulent histories of many of Paris's monuments and street signs reflect the revolutionary histories of the capital and of France. Each has its own chapter (or at least a paragraph or sentence) to contribute to the eventful historical narrative of Paris and of the nation. Monuments serve to foster a collective memory. But the stormy history of many of them in nineteenth-century Paris demonstrates that monuments are about the historical 'present' and not about the past. They concern memory more than history. They are about the values which, in any given period, societies and/or their leaders wish to celebrate and commemorate.

Underpinning political and personal motives for the monumentalizing of Paris during the long-nineteenth century was the shared desire of many of its 'influencers' to create, in words of Donald Olsen, 'the city as a work of art'. Each generation reads the monuments of its predecessors. There is a certain geographical inertia about monuments. But time and history alter the meanings of monuments. In nineteenth-century Paris, political and social instability meant that its monuments were contested and their fortunes precarious. But toppling monuments and changing street names did not erase history: instead, those processes themselves made history and reflected the kind of past that a society wished to remember or to forget. History cannot be erased; it can only be made.

4

Modernizing Paris: Rebuilding the city

Towards curing a 'sick' city

The eighteenth century saw some ambitious plans for the renewal and extension of Paris but the only large-scale improvement implemented was the creation of the Place Louis XV (renamed the Place de la Concorde, after the Revolution of 1789). This served to link the old city to the new districts to the west. Begun in 1753, it was not completed until 1763. It was a showcase development, with a grandly conceived open crossroad linking the gardens of the Tuileries to the Champs-Élysées. This was a superbly successful piece of city planning on a grand scale the like of which was not to be seen again for another 100 years. It was joined to the Left Bank by a new bridge, the Pont Louis XVI, built between 1787 and 1791.

Another significant addition to Paris's cityscape in the eighteenth century was the École Militaire erected in the 1750s on the less built-up Left Bank and the construction nearby, on vegetable allotments, of a parade and exercise ground, the Champ de Mars, an urban space which could accommodate thousands of the public for spectacles such as military tattoos.

The most fashionable districts of the city were the *faubourg* Saint-Honoré on the Right Bank and that of Saint-Germain on the Left Bank.

The 1760s and 1770s saw a speculative construction boom, with building on the meadows and market gardens of the Chaussée d'Antin *quartier* in the north-west of the city, creating a new residential district of large and elegant houses for wealthier Parisians. Colin Jones has emphasized that ecclesiastical property played a not inconsiderable part in the Parisian building boom from the 1760s, with religious houses owning extensive gardens and grounds seeking to remedy their financial problems, a resultant of mismanagement and a fall in charitable giving, by making property deals using leaseholds, a new financial instrument. Such developments revealed the growing social and spatial gap between rich and poor within the city and provoked discussion about social inequalities and pollution of the city's air, water and streets. A major improvement for the city's centre was the closure in 1780 of the Cemetery of the Innocents, which had served the parishes of Paris since the Middle Ages. Full to bursting and recognized as an environmental hazard, the cemetery's bones were moved in 1786 to subterranean quarries near Montparnasse, creating the catacombs.

Figure 4.1 Rue du Bourdonnais in 1865 in the 1^r *arrondissement*: wide, cobbled, narrow sidewalk, street lamp. Charles Marville

The emptied site was converted into a vegetable market extension to the adjacent Halles.

After the 1789 Revolution, the national appropriation and then sale of properties belonging to the Church and to *émigrés* who had fled Paris involved more than 4,000 houses. Probably more than 10 per cent of the area of Paris came suddenly onto the property market. Much of it was chaotically divided up into small parcels by property speculators. Immigrants piled into furnished lodgings of the already-crowded older districts. The population density in these areas reached 1,000 per hectare in 1846 as compared with just over 300 per hectare for the whole city. Overcrowded slums were characterized by epidemic disease, inadequate sewers, foul odours, crime, violence, prostitution, concubinage and infanticide. By the 1840s, Paris had become a 'sick' city (Figures 4.1 and 4.2) and was recognized as such by both contemporary social observers and by novelists like Honoré de Balzac and Victor Hugo. The 'sickness' of Paris was

Figure 4.2 Rue Traversine c. 1860 in the 5e arrondissement: narrow, cobbled with central drain, doors and gates fronting onto the street. Charles Marville

both environmental and social: to the inadequate housing for many residents were added, for example, problems of water supply, waste disposal, hygiene and circulation around the city, while the social malaise was evident in high levels of crime, suicide, alcoholism, illiteracy, illegitimacy and vagrancy. Louis Chevalier provided a vivid pathology of Paris during the first half of the nineteenth century, dissecting its causes and effects and its perception by contemporaries. A doubling of the population from about half a million at the beginning of the nineteenth century to just over 1 million in mid-century created physical and social problems which outran the ability of the city's authorities to manage them successfully,

Some urban improvements were implemented and they deserve to be acknowledged. Some new structures were devised during the first half of the nineteenth century, such as arcades, new housing 'estates' (*lotissements*), especially on the undeveloped farm lands now incorporated into Paris by the wall of the *Fermiers généraux* (but also on land beyond that wall) and some boulevards. In the centre, arcades or *passages couverts* were built to counter the dirty, noisy, traffic-congested streets. They were covered narrow passages with shops and cafés, catering for the bourgeoisie, providing them with protection from the weather and from hazardous narrow streets with their ever-increasing numbers of pedestrians, handcarts and horse-drawn vehicles, rubbish and horse manure, and from the pestering of street traders and beggars. Some arcades date from before 1800 (the first one was built in 1786, the Galeries de Bois next to the Palais Royal) but most were inaugurated between 1823 and 1831. The first arcade to have a glass roof was the Passage Feydeau, constructed in 1791 and linking the Palais Royal with the Grands Boulevards. Almost 200 arcades existed in 1833, many constructed on the sites of former religious properties and most of them sited on the more commercially minded Right Bank. These passages were modern, new, covered streets, constructed with iron frames and glass roofs as safe spaces reserved for pedestrians for whom they provided quiet, clean and from the 1820s increasingly gas-lit access to boutiques. These novel and modern shopping malls offered new, fashionable, goods, like 'Indian' cottons which had become popular after Napoléon's expedition to Egypt. For example, the Passage du Grand Cerf, which ran from the hostelry Le Grand Cerf onto the Rue Saint-Denis, was constructed in the 1820s with glass roofing panels. Above its shops at ground level, there were two floors, the first for storage and the second for flats. There were boutiques for furniture, candles, jewellery and African art. By way of contrast, the Passage du Caire – at 370 m the longest arcade in Paris – opened in 1799 and named after the victory of French troops in Cairo in July 1798 – comprised mainly outlets providing printing and lithographic services and consequently had little attraction for *flâneurs* (strollers). Even today, this arcade is not for the casual walker or tourist: its activity is focussed on the wholesale trade in fabrics, in ready-to-wear clothing and in supplies for shop windows such as models, stands, decorations and packaging. But its architecture remains of special interest: it has magnificent glass panels and while its overall plan is rectangular its galleries are disposed in the shape of a star. It has six entrances to its galleries.

The arcades of Paris fascinated the German cultural critic, Walter Benjamin (1892–1940), who studied and wrote about those remaining in the early twentieth century. His book *The Arcades Project*, published posthumously in 1982 (and in an English translation in 1999), was based on the extensive notes which he had made between 1927 and 1940. David Harvey acknowledged that Benjamin focused on the arcades in his attempt 'to unravel the myths of modernity', following his 1935 essay on *Paris, Capital of the Nineteenth Century*. For Benjamin, the arcades were significant, modernizing, features – fragments of a greater totality – of Parisian public life from the late-eighteenth century to the mid-nineteenth century until many were surpassed in economic significance by the *grands magasins* (department stores) on the new boulevards in the 1850s and 1860s. In 1925, the outmoded Passage de l'Opéra (Figure 4.3) was demolished: it had been opened in 1822 with three *galeries*, two of which had entrances on the Boulevard des Italiens. It was the arcade which inspired Louis Aragon's *Le Paysan de Paris* (1926), which – in the words of Charles Rearick – 'offered a guidebook-like appreciation of the old arcade's shops, cafés, theatre,

Figure 4.3 Passage de l'Opéra c.1909. Photographer unknown

bathhouse, bookstore and brothel – together with surrealist reveries about everything strange, marvellous and sexual therein'.

The first tentative grand street plans began to be laid out on the Right Bank between 'old' Paris and the new wall of the *Fermiers généraux* . The remains of the old walls of Louis XIII and Charles V were converted into grassed or sand-covered walks for bowling games (*boules*), which some believe to be the origin of the word *boulevard* while others argue that the term comes from the Dutch *bolwerk*, meaning rampart, which would thus respect the military and administrative origins of the old walls. In western and north-western Paris, new *quartiers* were planned and constructed by private companies. The growth of Paris during the 1820s and 1830s saw the conversion of farmland, market gardens and even marshy scrubland into new urban spaces and places. A mosaic of distinct *quartiers* emerged which still characterize that part of Paris today, such as the Quartier de l'Europe constructed on the borders of the 8^e and 9^e *arrondissements*. These areas came to be occupied by better-off Parisians, fleeing from the city's overcrowded centre, in the process becoming bourgeois-dominated, fashionable Paris.

In the early 1840s, the city's authorities began to recognize officially that many wealthier Parisians were moving out of the centre to the north-western and western districts, followed by commercial enterprises and artisanal workshops. So, for the first time, there developed a serious and protracted debate about the fundamentals of urbanism, about the related spatial and social geography of the city. Victoria Thompson has argued that the Revolution of 1830 'changed middle-class perceptions of the urban landscape by making the people of Paris visible in a different way, as the peaceful cohabitation of urban space gave way to insurrection'. A bourgeois west and a working-class east came to be increasingly recognized, social divisions and their spatiality became more visible and more unsettling for contemporary observers. The municipal council implemented some piecemeal improvements to the urban fabric while more holistic ideas were debated but not put into practice. This period saw additional public water fountains, two new bridges and construction of the Rue Rambuteau (1838–9) which involved demolishing some slum properties to create a 13-m-wide street linking Les Halles to La Bastille (Figure 4.4). This was the first time in Paris that old houses were demolished on such a scale to make way for a new thoroughfare bordered by new dwellings, as opposed to their destruction for the construction of public monuments and squares. Histories of Paris often focus on the massively impressive remodelling of Paris by Haussmann from the 1850s, neglecting the more piecemeal improvements that had been made earlier.

Figure 4.4 Rue Rambuteau c.1890. Wikimedia Creative Commons Attribution Share Alike 4.0 International/Hessrick

The year 1843 saw the publication of a plan for Paris as a whole by H. Meynadier in his book *Paris Pittoresque et Monumentale*. His far-reaching proposals included a new major road network, slum clearance in the city centre and the creation of public parks to rival those of London. Such projects were deemed to be prohibitively expensive and implemented only partially. His plans were nonetheless significant because they represented a transition between the urban architecture of the Ancien Régime (principally the embellishment of the capital with individual public squares) and modern urbanism (an overall, interlinked plan) aimed not only at structural improvements but also at improving social conditions and promoting economic activity.

The years 1841–5 saw completion of a new wall, which came to be known as the Thiers Wall, named after the opposition *député*, Adolphe Thiers, whose idea it was and who was to become the president of France from August 1871 to May 1873. The fortified wall and its sixteen forts became the new formal boundary of Paris in 1860, more than doubling the city's area from just under 4,000 ha to just under 9,000 ha, increasing from twelve to twenty the number of its *arrondissements* and the population of Paris from just over 1 million in 1856 to 1.7 million in 1861. This new wall was to provide some protection for Paris during the Prussian siege of the city in 1870–1; much of it was taken down after the end of the Great War in 1918.

Despite improvements to the built form of Paris between 1800 and 1840, Paris remained a city in crisis, a sick city. It had a central core of slums of poorly built housing, lacking light, ventilation and hygienic sewage disposal. From the 1830s, literate middle-class observers complained increasingly about the city's narrow and dirty streets, saying how difficult it was to move through the poorer districts because of their accumulated dirt and rubbish and their surface water. In addition, these districts came to be seen by many of the bourgeoisie as dangerous harbourers of criminality.

It was not until 1850 that a law prohibited the construction of insanitary buildings. The centre had high levels of unemployment and of casual labour. About 20,000 people died in the cholera epidemic of 1820 and about 18,000 in that of 1832 and a similar number in that of 1848–9. There were to be further epidemics in 1853–4, 1865, 1884 and 1892. Movement within the city was difficult. There were some horse-drawn buses but most people travelled on foot encountering many street traders. Not all streets had paved walkways so that pedestrians often faced cobbled or mud surfaces strewn with rubbish and manure, puddles and running water. The 1840s closed with a peak of social unrest culminating in the Revolution of 1848.

Such a sick city was increasingly a cause for concern by local and national authorities. The growth of its population by about half a million between 1800 and the mid-1840s accentuated and made more visible the city's environmental problems, while the concentration of a deracinated proletarian populace in Paris was seen – and rightly so – as bearing the seeds of social discontent and even of revolution. In addition, the scale of provincial, especially rural, migration to Paris was seen by some in authority as a threat not only to the city but also to the countryside and its provisioning of the city with its food supply. By 1850, the many physical and social problems of Paris had become both acute and indisputable. During the following two decades there were ambitious attempts to resolve them and to implement urban planning on a scale and at a pace never witnessed previously in France.

The context for change

Paris in the 1850s and 1860s not only inherited a host of social and infrastructural problems but also witnessed a cluster of developments favourable to urban planning and transformation. The recent growth of banking institutions (such as the Crédit Mobilier and the Crédit Foncier de Paris, both founded in 1852, and the Crédit Lyonnais, established in 1863) had brought together the savings of a multitude of small investors, thereby providing capital for investment in large and expensive undertakings. In its early years, the Second Empire had the authority to be resolute. As a new emperor starting his reign, Napoléon III could dare to sweep aside private interests in favour of what he deemed to be the public good: his newly acquired power could be used to impose his policies for Paris; his newly won authority could hardly be challenged at the outset. Napoléon III was unambiguously ambitious: as the nephew of Napoléon Bonaparte, he aimed to recreate Paris as a personal and enduring memorial in stone. But he was an enlightened despot, influenced, for example, by the socio-economic and egalitarian ideas of Claude-Henri Saint-Simon (1760–1825). Napoléon III aspired to produce a grand and humane capital city in which all social classes would live in harmony, where the poor would have work and the workers would be content rather than restive. Furthermore, he envisaged a Paris whose built form would exhibit a harmony between nature and culture. He selected an experienced team to carry out his plan for modernizing Paris. In 1853, he appointed Georges Haussmann (1809–1891) at the age of forty-four as prefect of the Seine *département*. Born in Paris in 1809 to Protestant parents who had migrated to the capital from Alsace, Haussmann brought to bear on the problems of the capital some twenty years of experience as a sub-prefect and prefect in six provincial *départements* of France. As prefect of the Seine *département*, Haussmann was given wide-ranging powers and enjoyed strong support from Napoléon for more than twelve years before encountering increasing opposition from other quarters. The professional team led by Haussmann included from 1854 Eugène Belgrand (1810–1878), a forty-three-year-old hydrological engineer who was appointed to address the supply of water to Paris as well as the disposal of waste water from the city, and then from 1855 by Adolphe Alphand (1817–1891), a 38-year-old engineer and landscape architect. Haussmann's modernizing team also included the young and very talented Gabriel Davioud (1824–1881), who had been appointed in 1851 at the age of twenty-seven as head of architectural works in Paris. Of the three, only Davioud was a native-born Parisian.

This talented and experienced team were aided by the growing public concern in France about public health. Louis Pasteur (1822–1895) had moved in 1857 from the universities of Strasbourg and Lille to Paris to become the director of scientific studies at the École Normale Supérieure. His research on the causes and prevention of diseases increasingly informed the debate about public health issues. His proof of the existence of microbes contributed to a growing public awareness of the benefit both of sunlight in destroying germs carried by dust and of effective ventilation in dispersing dust. A public discourse had developed about the need to clear the city's slums and a law of 1850 gave public authorities the right to inspect properties and to require buildings considered by the inspectors to be substandard on health grounds to be either improved or demolished.

At the same time, there were growing expectations by the bourgeoisie about their own living standards. Coal-fired stoves for heating and cooking came increasingly into use from the mid-1840s, as did household gas lighting (which in turn permitted the construction of deeper buildings, because there was no longer such a need for daylight). Developments in construction methods lowered building costs: for example, mass-produced nails came to be used instead of chiselled or sawn joints, pine timber instead of more expensive hardwoods and less skilled and cheaper labour. Mechanical cutting of stone permitted its use in large blocks on the more expensive properties, whereas the production of bricks fired by coke rather than charcoal led to tougher and less porous products, making it possible to construct dwellings to a greater height than previously.

This fortuitous cluster of circumstances around 1850 made possible a radical transformation of the built form of Paris. Epidemics and revolutions in the 1830s and 1840s signalled the urgency of the need for change; public debate had identified the main environmental and social problems and suggested some solutions; technical developments made the rebuilding of Paris possible while accumulated capital for investment provided the means of doing so. Such structural changes were necessary but not in themselves sufficient to cure the ills of the sick city. It needed also the motivation and determination of Napoléon III and the commitment and dedication of Haussmann and his team. Both agency and structure underpinned the rebuilding of Paris, its transformation into a modern city.

Haussmann's transformation of Paris 1853–70

Napoléon III is thought to have provided Haussmann with a master plan for Paris, marked in coloured pencils to indicate the level of priority to be given to the construction of new streets. The rebuilding work rested on one old and one new building regulation. That of 1783 limited building height to 18 m and street width to between 10 m and 14 m. New regulations in 1852 and 1859 required both the height of buildings and the width of streets to be 18 m and a regulation of 1864 allowed the facades of buildings to rise up to 20 m in streets which were 20 m or more wide. This control of building height and street width produced the monumental but balanced urban form that became one of the key features of the new Paris. Stephen Clarke has claimed, beguilingly but mistakenly, that it was Haussmann who gave Paris its nickname – '*Ville lumière*' or 'City of Light' – because of the sun's shining through the gaps that he had smashed in the ancient pattern of Parisian streets. Napoléon III and Haussmann recognized that remodelling the city would require the destruction of many buildings inherited from the previous century and even earlier. In 1851, architect Gabriel Davioud was given the task of drawing the facades of the houses which were to be demolished in order to preserve a memory of them. He and his team laboured for three years to produce this architectural record of old Paris. Unfortunately, many of their detailed drawings were lost to posterity in 1871 when the Hôtel de Ville, where they were stored, was deliberately destroyed by fire. Fortunately, many of the projects' *'relevés de terrain'* (land surveys) survived, because Davioud did not put them in the municipal archives until 1877. They have been edited and published in 2012 by an architect and historian, Pierre Pinon. A similar project was also initiated by Napoléon III and Haussmann when in 1862, an official photographer – Charles Marville (1813–1879) – was appointed to compile a record of the streets of 'old' Paris before the city was remodelled. He had been chosen by Napoléon III to photograph his marriage to Eugénie at the cathedral of Notre-Dame in 1853 and the baptism of their son in 1856. Marville published in 1865 his *Album de Vieux Paris*, a visual record of more than 400 photographs of the old city undergoing its transformation.

New streets pierced through the central slums and opened out congested areas (see Plate 11). For example, the Rue Estienne was demolished in 1862 to make way for the new Rue du Pont-Neuf (Figure 4.5); whole areas had to be cleared to allow construction of the new Avenue de l'Opéra (Figure 4.6).

Straight and long boulevards, often with nodal points, linked the city's centre with its suburbs. The overall street plan was very audacious and resulted in visually strong boulevards, such as the Boulevard Saint-Michel (1855–9) (Figure 4.7) and the Boulevard Sébastopol (1858). Haussmann wanted to improve the flow of people and goods within Paris and his new boulevards achieved that, at least for fifty years or so until traffic flows had increased and congestion returned. But there is little evidence to support the belief that Napoléon III's promotion of long and straight boulevards was principally aimed at facilitating movement of the forces of order; nor that the width of the boulevards was intended to complicate and even frustrate the construction of barricades; and there is no evidence for the humourist's claim that wider streets were built in order to accommodate the stylishly expansive dresses of the increasingly fashion-conscious ladies of Paris.

Haussmann's boulevards have been praised by urban historians François Bédarida and Anthony Sutcliffe as the 'apotheosis of the street'. The primary network of new streets was completed with little public opposition: the need for it had become widely accepted and cutting through slums was cheaper than widening existing routes. But the secondary network was not so readily achieved. It was intended to integrate the capital's new railway stations with the city centre. The main railway termini had been placed not (as in case of London) in the city centre but at the 1840s boundary wall, in order to provide Paris with multiple nuclei of activity rather than a single point of focus for all economic and social life. The new railway stations – Saint-Lazare (1837), Montparnasse (1840), Austerlitz (1840), Nord (1846), Est (1849) and Lyon (1849) – were monumental and novel additions to the landscape of Paris, with their often neoclassical styles not only genuflecting to historical architectural precedents in their stone facades but also proudly proclaiming the use of the modern materials of iron and glass especially in their interiors (Figure 4.8). These 'cathedrals of capitalism' intensified the links between the capital and its provinces and for many immigrants they were perceived as their gateways to paradise – or at least to Paris. Connecting these stations, as nuclei of modernity located far from each other, was the intention of the proposed secondary road network in the city but that was not achieved fully.

Figure 4.5 Demolition of Rue Estienne in 1862 to make way for the new Rue du Pont Neuf. Charles Marville

Improvements to the supply of potable water and the disposal of foul water were significant components of the Haussmannization of Paris. Two new reservoirs were built for drinking water brought into the city from springs of the Champagne district, some 1,000 km to the north-east. The length of piped water to buildings was doubled between 1852 and 1869, and sixty-one water fountains were in use by 1870 (most of them with decorative and not just utilitarian designs). In 1850, only 21 per cent of households had piped water on the ground floor but by 1870 the figure was 50 per cent. By 1850, the limited system of drains for removing waste was unable to cope with the volumes produced by the city's growing population. Most waste water reached the river Seine by way of a collector drain. In 1850, only one-fifth of private dwellings were connected to the sewers. Haussmann assumed that his improved drainage system would deal primarily with storm and surface water and that the work of night soil collectors would continue, removing the contents

Figure 4.6 Clearing space for the new Avenue de l'Opéra c. 1855. Charles Marville

Figure 4.7 Boulevard Saint-Michel c. 1860. Charles Marville

Figure 4.8 La Gare du Nord c. 1900. Wikimedia Creative Commons (public domain)

of urban cess pits to sewage farms beyond the city's boundary for conversion into organic fertilizer.

Haussmann constructed a hierarchically nested network of drains or sewers (*égouts*), trebling the system from 160 km to 480 km. The Bièvre river (Figure 4.9) was diverted into them and they joined the Seine downstream from the city. The Bièvre had been receiving polluted water, for example, from the noxious tanneries, starch and dye factories and soap- and candle-making establishments along it. In 1855–62, Félix Nadar took twenty-three photographs of the Paris sewers, taking advantage of the electric lighting that had been installed in some of them (Figure 4.10). The sewers now lost their image as being filthy, dangerous and dark as well as hiding places for criminals, the poor and outcasts and rats. Victor Hugo's novel *Les Misérables* (1862) depicts the sewers in the 1830s as 'the evil in the city's blood'. Under Haussmann, they became instead symbols of progress, of new practices of water usage and personal hygiene and of advances in science and technology. From the *Exposition universelle* of 1867 the municipality of Paris proudly began public tours of the sewers. Haussmann's desire to continue to separate the drainage of storm and surface water from the use of cess pits for human waste was supported by the cesspool cleaning companies that feared a loss of their business and by the collectors of night soil as an organic fertilizer. Property owners opposed higher taxes for yet more sewer construction to cope with both 'clean' and 'dirty' water or for the construction of impermeable cess pools to replace those which allowed their contents to seep into the subsoil. It was not until 1894 that the city was authorized by the national government to compel property owners, at their own expense, to link their properties to the sewage system. By then, growing public aversion to human waste, the increasing use of chemical fertilizers, rising water usage

Figure 4.9 River Bièvre c. 1865 before being covered and diverted into the new system of sewers. Charles Marville

and cholera epidemics in 1884 and 1892 had eliminated the traditional reliance on cess pits. Henceforth, the policy and practice were '*tout à l'égout*'. In 1894, the municipal council undertook to end within five years the dumping of untreated sewage into the Seine: it kept to its undertaking.

Another major problem was the provisioning of Paris with food. This was addressed by replacing the 'old' 1852 stone market (Figure 4.11). When Napoléon III visited the market in 1853 he took exception to the 'old' stone building and decided there should be a new one using modern construction techniques and materials, namely cast iron and glass. The 'old' building was demolished in 1866 and the first of twelve new pavilions, designed by Victor Baltard (a Parisian-born architect) and constructed in iron and glass, opened in 1857, others successively in 1858, 1860 and 1874 (Figure 4.12).

The central, wholesale, food market and its lively *quartier* came to be known as the 'belly of Paris' after the vivid description of it provided by Émile Zola in his 1873 novel *Le Ventre de Paris*. This central market was complemented by numerous smaller, covered, markets built in many *quartiers* throughout the city. On public health grounds, five abattoirs (three on the Right Bank and two on the Left Bank) established in central districts of Paris by Napoléon Bonaparte in the early 1800s, to replace the numerous small slaughterhouses then existing throughout the city, were in their turn replaced by Napoléon III by one large abattoir, built between 1860 and 1867 at La Villette in northeastern Paris, in the *19ᵉ arrondissement*, far removed from the city's centre.

Figure 4.10 New sewer in 1861. Félix Nadar

Napoléon III's Anglomania was reflected in the development of green spaces, which Paris lacked by comparison with London. Haussmann delegated the details of their landscaping to Alphand. Knowing that the emperor admired the English romantic style, Alphand produced parks with winding paths and streams, instead of the rigid geometry of French formal gardens. Green spaces were recognized by Napoléon III and Haussmann as being good for public health and quality of life as well as adding to the national and international prestige of the city. A former royal forest was converted to a public park: the Bois de Boulogne was a monotonous block of poor woodland traversed by straight lines radiating from a point, a crossroad. It was remodelled by Alphand with two lakes joined by a cascading stream, winding paths, floral gardens, kiosks, pavilions and summer houses, producing a 'romantic' effect. His design was greeted as a success by the bourgeoisie of western Paris. In the east, the Bois de Vincennes provided a similar recreational space for its working-class population. To the south, the Parc Montsouris was constructed on old stone quarries and piles of rubble resulting from Haussmann's

Figure 4.11 The 'old' Les Halles in 1852. Charles Marville

Figure 4.12 Part of the new Les Halles in 1862. V. Baltard and F. Callet, *Les Halles centrales de Paris* (Paris 1862)

demolitions in central Paris. In the north-east, the park of Buttes-Chaumont was created on waste land, once the site of public executions and until 1849 the site where the city's sewage was deposited. The park was opened in 1867 and served the growing industrial districts of La Villette and Belleville. This completed Haussmann's attempt to reproduce

Figure 4.13 Rue Soufflot's remodelling, with the Panthéon as its focal point, *c.* 1860. Charles Marville

Figure 4.14 Rue Soufflot *c.* 1895. Wikimedia Creative Commons (public domain)

in Paris the great parks of London. The sinuous designs adopted in the new parks provided a distinct contrast with the straight lines of the newly constructed roads. 'Soft', sinuous, serpentine paths in parks and 'hard' straight, Cartesian, boulevards testify to the duality of the developing personality of Paris.

In sum, Napoléon III and Haussmann's transformation of Paris was achieved dramatically and famously with new or remodelled boulevards (Figures 4.13 and 4.14), sewers, water supplies, green spaces, a central food market, a large abattoir and a new opera house and Hôtel Dieu. But it went beyond those major developments to include more than seventy schools in the area annexed in 1860, fifteen churches and synagogues, two hospitals, nine barracks and seven local markets. In addition, slum clearance of the area between the Louvre and the Tuileries, authorized by the Republican government in 1849, was completed, and the two palaces were joined along the Rue de Rivoli and by two large wings. The gargantuan scale of Haussmann's modernization of Paris was very expensive and raised questions about its financing. The task was at first simplified by expropriating property: a law of 25 December 1852 permitted the expropriation of properties by simple Imperial decree and allowed the city council to sell those fragments of land expropriated but not needed for the new public works, doing so at its new, value-added price (the higher value arising from proximity to the new developments). This measure was objected to by private property owners, so a new law of 1858 required expropriated land not being used for public development to be returned to its former private owner who could then profit from the added development value of his land. Private interest had triumphed over public interest, a decision which created a watershed in the Haussmannization process.

Financing the modernization of Paris became more difficult as a result of a legal decision in 1860 that tenants/leaseholders of expropriated properties should be paid an indemnity as soon as expropriation was announced and not made to wait until people were actually evicted to make way for the new construction (which could be some years after the date of the notice of expropriation). This meant the municipal council had to pay upfront considerable sums well before being able to obtain any return on the investment in a new building. Haussmann responded by financing rebuilding through massive loans for which he had to obtain permission from the national government. The restructuring of Paris from 1858 onwards was founded on deficit financing.

Despite the financing problems, Paris was restructured. Slums were removed on the Île-de-la-Cité around the cathedral of Notre-Dame: this area had some of the oldest houses, narrowest streets and poorest residents in Paris. Slum clearances reduced the population on the Île-de-la-Cité from 15,000 to 5,000. The opportunity was taken to erect some imposing public buildings, notably commercial courts, police headquarters and a hospital. The large-scale clearances meant the facade of Notre-Dame could now be seen unencumbered for the first time since the twelfth century.

Haussmann came increasingly under attack from the Republican opposition, especially for the magnitude of the loans he needed to finance the works and for pushing developments to the legal limits in order to achieve his rebuilding. Haussmann left office in early 1870, only months before the Second Empire collapsed. But he left as his legacy a capital city fundamentally transformed, one that would be cited throughout Europe and beyond as a model of modern urbanism.

Critiques of Haussmann's work by his contemporaries

Criticism of such an ambitious and wholesale transformation was only to be expected. Both the aims and the methods employed to achieve them came under scrutiny from Haussmann's contemporaries. Some argued that the demolition of so many dwellings and streets caused, or at least seriously contributed to, the city's housing crisis. There was indeed a shortage of accommodation in Paris in the1850s, in part because of the time gap that existed between the demolition of the old dwellings and completed construction of the new ones. But the accommodation crisis was produced principally by the city's population explosion from 1.1 million in 1851 to 1.7 in 1861 and 1.9 in 1872. Ironically, much of the increase comprised migrants drawn to the capital by its growing reputation and by its demand for labour to undertake its many construction projects. The reality was that more dwellings were built than were demolished: the period 1852–69 saw 118,000 housing units demolished but also 215,000 newly built. Because of the scale of the disruption – or creative destruction – Haussmann imposed upon 'old Paris', he was scathingly called by some of his critics 'the Alsatian Attila' – he had been born and raised in Paris but his family came originally from Alsace, while Attila was a reputedly ferocious leader of a tribal empire in central and eastern Europe in the fifth century and perceived as a threat to civilization.

Some critics argued that Haussmann's projects encouraged financial speculation and even corruption. It was certainly the case that property prices and rents rose rapidly and sharply during what became a property boom. There is no doubt that speculation was encouraged by the process of expropriation, especially after 1858. But such speculation was mainly in property located in the wealthier, not in the poorer, districts, because returns on investments in the former were almost twice as high as on investments in the latter. Speculators, like Haussmann himself, neglected housing for the poor and the municipal council itself favoured construction of high-quality dwellings. More serious, perhaps, was the criticism that Haussmann's projects aggravated social segregation within Paris, displacing the working class in central districts to cheaper accommodation in the suburbs. The Haussmann decades did see the expansion of shanty settlements on the periphery. The low incomes of their residents did not allow them to move into the new, high-rent, buildings. Haussmann worked with the market forces of his time and it is not surprising that his projects not only accompanied but also accentuated the movement of the wealthier Parisians towards the western and north-western sectors of the city. What Haussmann achieved was less a general modernization of Parisian housing as a whole and more a fundamental but selective transformation of accommodation for the middle class. To be fair, however, Haussmann's works aggravated but did not originate socio-spatial disparities in Paris, those between centre and suburb, between richer *quartiers* of the west and poorer ones of the east, between Right and Left Banks (most public works and major projects were on the Right Bank). From the 1830s, the vertical social segregation of residents of individual dwellings was gradually replaced by a horizontal social and spatial segregation in the city as a whole. This process was also encouraged by architects, for whom it was more economical to design buildings that were essentially the same on all floors (and advertised, e.g., as having the benefit of '*Gaz à tout les étages*' or '*tout-à-l'égout*' ('gas on all floors' or 'connected to the sewers')), so encouraging social homogeneity within individual buildings and social heterogeneity among *quartiers*. In some areas of the city not affected very much by Haussmann's works (such as the Marais), the gardens and courtyards of many former aristocratic dwellings (*hôtels*) were infilled with low-quality accommodation providing shelters for lodging workers. These soon became overcrowded with working families or became workshops of artisans and craftsmen.

Another distinct criticism by some of Haussmann's contemporaries was their belief that his works vandalized 'old Paris'. Haussmann himself estimated that 13 per cent of the city was demolished between 1851 and 1859. For some Parisians, his works represented a violent assault on their city, a traumatic experience with demolitions and constructions creating noise, dust and debris and transforming their familiar cityscape. Some likened the scene to a battlefield. The modernization of Paris by Haussmann provoked a Romantic reaction which favoured the past and attached sentimental value to the 'old' Paris being replaced by the 'new' Paris. Ruth Fiori has highlighted how a discourse about '*vieux Paris*' was grounded in Victor Hugo's depiction of the late medieval city in his 1831 novel *Notre Dame de Paris* which praised its picturesque qualities. Nostalgic histories of '*vieux Paris*' fostered a perception of a city with organic neighbourhoods being destroyed by modernization and nurtured a preservationist discourse.

From 1837, the state had accepted responsibility for the protection of ancient monuments. Its Commission des Monuments Historiques was charged with surveying the state's national monuments and with prioritizing conservation and restoration of those structures in poor condition. In 1851, the Commission initiated a Mission Héliographique and contracted five photographers to travel the provinces and undertake a photographic architectural survey. When two of them, Henri Le Secq (1818–1882) and Édouard Baldus (1813–1889), returned to Paris from their respective missions in northern and eastern France and in south-eastern France, they found a cityscape being transformed and they photographed many individual demolition and construction projects between 1852 and 1864. Their common *modus operandi* was to photograph individual monuments and buildings in empty streets, not as components of lively *quartiers*. Their work was a precursor to that of other Second Empire photographers, notably that of Charles Marville (1813–1879), a Parisian by birth, who was appointed in 1862 as the official photographer of Paris and photographed neighbourhood streets before, during and after their Haussmannization. As Sabrina Hughes has pointed out, many of his photographs portrayed few people and created a deceptive image of an empty Paris when in reality it was more crowded than it had ever been. Another archive of photographs of Parisian buildings and people was created by Eugène Atget (1857–1927) in the late nineteenth and early twentieth centuries. As a documentary photographer, Atget focussed not only on the broad architecture of buildings and streets but also on their detailed ornamentation and on ordinary, taken-for-granted, 'invisible' objects such as door knockers, street railings and shopfronts. As John Fraser has suggested, Atget was concerned with documenting those 'aspects of the city which impinged on someone living in it in an ordinary daily way'. He portrayed Paris 'as a place in which one moves around, consumes things, seeks mental refreshment, and rests'. Atget's Parisian project produced more than 10,000 photographs, some of which were commissioned by the Musée Carnavalet. Documenting old Paris photographically created an historic record of the city's continuously changing landscape and contributed to the emergence of a preservationist movement.

Haussmann's demolitions took in not just individual buildings but whole swathes of the city. If people objected to his destruction of what they deemed to be beautiful buildings and streets he was able to claim that his works were grounded in a new urban aesthetics. There is no doubt that Napoléon III wanted to make Paris the most beautiful city in the world. Moreover, assertions that he and Haussmann were destroying historical evidence about Paris were countered by their arranging for photographs to be taken and drawings to be made of those buildings and streets scheduled for demolition and remodelling. Haussmann also persuaded the city council in 1866 to purchase the Hôtel Carnavalet in the Marais and to convert it into a museum dedicated to the history of Paris. The museum, opened to the public in 1880, was one indicator of Haussmann's hoping to make demolitions more acceptable to the public. Sutcliffe has pointed out that Haussmann, as prefect of Paris, made considerable sums available for research into the history of Paris. Ironically, this strengthened a slowly but steadily growing interest in the preservation of 'old' Paris. As Haussmann's programme of demolitions removed central slums and drove increasingly into middle-class districts, opposition to his works gained support, drawing upon a degree of nostalgia about the disappearance of '*vieux Paris*'. The development of a preservationist movement was retarded by disagreements among antiquarians, architects and scholars about which parts of the built environment should be preserved, conserved or restored. There was in the mid-1860s an abortive attempt to establish a Paris Archaeological and History Society; 1874 saw the successful founding of a Society for the History of Paris and the Île-de-France; the late 1880s and early 1890s saw the creation of local historical societies, such as the Old Montmartre Society (1886), the historical society of the Montagne Sainte-Geneviève (1895) and those established for some *arrondissements*, such as those for the 6e and 14e in 1898 and the 15e in 1903. In 1890 the Society of Parisians was established with membership restricted to people who had been born in the city. These societies, attracting as members mainly the educated middle class, acted as preservationists. Their lobbying led to the prefect's creation in 1897–8 of the *Commission municipale du Vieux Paris* which sought to counter what it viewed as destructive vandalism but its influence was constrained by those city councillors and administrators who preferred development to preservation. Sutcliffe has argued that the city's commercial class came slowly but increasingly to realize that the growing attraction of Paris for foreign tourists, boosted in number by the *Expositions universelles* of 1889 and 1900, was based in large measure on the city's historical inheritance. By 1900, as Fiori points out, the appeal of 'old' Paris was so strong that a pavilion dedicated to the concept was one of the most popular attractions at that year's *Exposition universelle*. The pavilion portrayed three neighbourhoods whose building styles spanned the fourteenth century to the eighteenth, with people dressed in historical costumes selling relevant trinkets.

Sutcliffe (1970, p. 88) contended that 'it was in the late-1880s that a new movement of opinion, more constructive than the nostalgia aroused by old drawings, began to strengthen the growing reaction against what Haussmann had done'. This was the development of a more flexible, artistic approach to the aesthetics of town planning. Preservationists fought campaigns to protect distinctive features of 'old' Paris. The first protests against the degradation of the Marais were made in the early 1900s. An especially strong preservationist movement emerged in relation to Montmartre, as Sutcliffe has highlighted. Street improvements had made Montmartre more accessible and building plots in the lower-lying parts of the city had become rare so that developers began to build 'towering apartment blocks on the slopes of Montmartre, arousing the ire of residents who appreciated the calm and charm of the place'. An organized campaign from 1911 to 1914 to save Montmartre, described nostalgically by the protesters as 'the last hamlet' in Paris, was successful in preserving its two remaining windmills. Sutcliffe has argued that it was in the decade or two before 1914 that the competing movements of preservation/conservation and of modernization reached their apogee. A victory for the former was the decision taken by the city council in 1902 to resist an attempt to modify the building regulations applying to the city centre to allow taller buildings using steel and concrete for their construction. The preservationists had ensured that the building height limit which had been established for central Paris in the late eighteenth century would persist, a decision which protected the cityscape for many decades in the twentieth century. By the end of the nineteenth century, Paris old and new had become a major national and international tourist attraction. From the 1890s, hoteliers increasingly recognized the need to improve their accommodation standards; by 1913, Paris was receiving some 300,000 tourists annually.

Critiques of Haussmann's work by historians

Most historians have been impressed by the immensity of the task to modernize Paris and by its rapid accomplishment (even though some components of the project were not completed until after Haussmann had left the scene in 1870). The scale and the speed of the transformation of Paris were much greater than that seen in London earlier. The generally favourable judgements of historians have, however, been nuanced in detail. Assessments compiled with historical hindsight have been both positive and negative.

Haussmann has been praised for the importance which he attached to public works. Even so, it has to be conceded that London had attended forty years earlier than had Paris to its water supply, its sewage system, its public parks, its street lighting and its public transport. In these fields, Haussmann was not an innovator but the pace at which he modernized Paris was remarkable: his city-wide achievements in seventeen years stand in stark contrast to the thirty years it had taken to construct the striking but singular Arc de Triomphe. Matthew Gandy, a historical geographer, has argued that Haussmann's reconstruction of the sewers of Paris should not be seen as an 'unproblematic epitome of modernity', because his works created further tension – or at least did not resolve all of the existing ones – because of the growing water usage, the persistent threat of disease and changing conceptions of public health policy. Most major urban developments simultaneously create new problems while resolving old ones, attracting both admiration and opposition. In his memoirs, Haussmann admitted to being very proud of the parks he had created in Paris but some historians have claimed that he probably reduced the overall amount of green space in Paris because many private gardens were eliminated and incorporated in new building projects. In 1850, the only municipal parks were along the Champs-Élysées and in the Place des Vosges. The gardens of the Tuileries, the Palais Royal, the Luxembourg Gardens and the Jardin des Plantes were all national properties to which Parisians were admitted but not entitled to use. David Pinkney has calculated that in 1850 Paris had only 19 ha of public parks but 1,821 ha by 1870. In addition, new tree-lined boulevards were significant additional environmental enhancements available for all Parisians to enjoy.

Some have criticized Haussmann for having created *une ville bourgeoise* (a middle-class town). The old Paris had exhibited a sharp contrast between monumental buildings associated with the Crown, the aristocracy and the Church and the mass of buildings lived in by most people. But among Haussmann's achievements was much-improved and architecturally very distinctive housing for the middle class. Part of the modernization process was to have new buildings of the same height – the additional 'noble storey' of the medieval and early modern periods disappeared with the nobility after the Revolution.

The architectural coherence of the new dwellings has been criticized on the grounds that such uniformity brought with it monotony. But others argue that the genius of Haussmann lay in the configured variety of detail and the unity of the whole. Facades had a generally similar design: six storeys, windows of standard proportions and flat walls so that the street seems to be bounded by one immense building rather than by a series of individual, different, constructions. But the decoration of window surrounds, balconies, doors and cornices exhibited an almost infinite variety. The overall picture was one of balance, integrating buildings, streets and gardens. Individual units of different sizes were constructed but designed in relation to each other. A new regulation of 1864 permitted seven storeys where the street width was more than 20 m. The architectural harmony of major streets was achieved by lines of trees which softened an apparently excessive street width. Design principles were applied to the street as a whole, not just to individual units. Every boulevard was to have a vista focussing on a monument or a monumental structure. Haussmann's schemes were driven by a desire to create a visibly wealthier and grander Paris with an expectation that this would in turn lead to the creation of more wealth.

Underneath the broadly supportive assessments of historians lie some detailed objections to Haussmann's projects. It has been argued that they brought Paris near to bankruptcy. But Colin Jones claims that the state bore only 10 per cent of the total costs of the public works undertaken in the 1850s and 1860s. That was, nonetheless, a considerable sum. The estimated overall cost to the public purse was 2,500 million francs, a sum equivalent to the annual budget of France as a nation. But the state's subsidy of the works amounted to only 50 million francs and in due course the state benefited from an increased income of 250 million francs from taxes on the developments. While it is true that taxes on Parisians were increased, the additional burden was certainly not sufficient to pay for the massive public works programme. Until 1858, the modernization programme was financed by reselling expropriated land that was not needed for its implementation. Later, it was financed by loans. The national government became increasingly unwilling to authorize loans, so Haussmann resorted to loans from the municipal authorities and to raising unauthorized loans. Repayment of loans was, of course, a long-term process and effectively delayed until after 1870. In effect, it was Third Republican Parisians from 1870 to 1914 – not those of the Second Empire from 1851 to 1870 – who paid for much of the rebuilding. Colin Jones in his detailed biography of Paris has argued that the rebuilding operations became self-financing, because dilapidated buildings were sold cheaply to urban developers who replaced them with attractive and prestigious properties which could be sold or let as dwellings or businesses – or indeed both. The capital thus accumulated became available for investment in further speculative enterprises. The reconstruction of Paris was dependent on speculation, debt deferral and credit generation, a process which underpinned what Jones terms a 'whirligig of development' employing one-fifth of the Parisian workforce at the height of the rebuilding phenomenon.

Not all of Haussmann's plans were fully implemented before he left office in 1870. His attempt to create better road links among the city's main line railway stations was not completed, but in part this was because not all of the Grand Boulevards planned had been brought into use. They were eventually completed by 1872 when the idea for linking the rail stations by a new underground railway came to be considered. Haussmann's scheme did not include a fully comprehensive sewage system: he was opposed to such because it would lead to all the filth ending up in the Seine. Part of the older system was retained, which meant pumping out individual house privies and having their contents spread out to dry and sold as fertilizer.

Haussmann's works also retained considerable, if mainly *bourgeois*, housing at or near the centre of Paris. They did not set in motion the great commuting flows such as were being developed in London and Brussels. Paris continued to have an active, lived-in centre. Haussmann sought to create a socially harmonious city, one that would not experience the kind of social conflict that Parisians had witnessed earlier in the century. He hoped to achieve this by improving living conditions generally throughout the city and by removing the labouring and 'dangerous classes' from the centre. This was not an explicitly stated policy but an implicit practice. The vast works of destruction and construction attracted thousands of migrants to Paris to work. Eric Fournier in his book *Paris en ruines* (2008) concluded that 'the psychological impact of [Haussmannization] on the population was terrible'. The demolition works certainly removed many Parisians from their homes in the centre and decanted them to the periphery. The rebuilding of Paris in the 1850s and 1860s accentuated its already-existing social spatial segregation. Haussmann removed more than 17,000 families from their homes, and they were mainly the poor who reaped little or no benefit from the massive speculation in land and property that was part and parcel of the capitalist process of creative destruction. Those displaced from the centre could not afford to pay the rents for accommodation in the new tenement blocks; they had to seek cheaper housing away from the centre. To be fair, the asymmetry between poorer eastern and richer western districts was apparent by the 1840s but it became a fundamental and increasingly obvious reality during the 1850s and 1860s. One expression of this was the fact that, of the twenty-four urban squares set out by Napoléon III, only two were located in the eastern, working-class, districts of Paris. Rebuilding the city pushed its poorer residents towards the periphery, creating a ring of working-class suburbs the like of which was not to be seen in any other great metropolis at that time. The hiring fair for day labourers (such as stonemasons from the Creuse) was traditionally at the Place de Grève in front of the Hôtel de Ville (it had been officially renamed the Place de l'Hôtel de Ville in 1803 but the old name continued in popular usage alongside the new one). Many immigrants stayed initially in cheap lodging houses in this central area before moving into the new suburbs to which they were banished by the higher rents of the centre. Haussmann undoubtedly helped to create a distinctive suburban culture which also became in due course a counter-urban culture – and social tension between central and peripheral Paris has been a persistent feature of the city since his time. This social and spatial contrast has been demonstrated for 1880 by mapping the ratio of low-cost to high-cost funerals (see Plate 12).

The rich were living in the old aristocratic districts of Saint-Germain and Saint-Honoré and in the *quartiers* constructed during the 1830s and 1840s in the 8e, 9e and 10e *arrondissements* and in the west and south-west of the city; the poorest were located in the eastern and south-eastern districts.

Such clear social and spatial segregation was a potential threat to public order and a miscalculation by Napoléon III and Haussmann who sought to prevent a recurrence of the social unrest and revolutions of earlier decades. In fact, the barricades erected during the street fighting of May1871 were in many cases at the same locations as those built in the Revolution of 1848 – which shows both that works of Napoléon III and Haussmann had changed the social geography of Paris less than has sometimes been argued but that, viewed just through the optic of social order, they had failed or at the very least not been wholly successful.

The new boulevards did at first make circulation of people and commodities within Paris easier and quicker. But an increased volume of traffic and new modes of transport soon filled the extra space. In 1880, the city had about 80,000 horses but the number declined to about 55,000 by 1912. There were 10,000 horse-drawn taxis in 1896 but none by 1922. They were increasingly replaced from 1906 by internal-combustion-engined taxi cars and then by buses.

In sum, Napoléon III's most enduring and most impressive achievement domestically was the rebuilding and modernization of Paris. He promoted and undertook a very ambitious urban remodelling project in the 1850s and 1860s which largely created the city – or rather the popular image or myth of the city – as many know it today. The straight and wide boulevards reflected Enlightenment rationality: they promoted connectivity among Parisians; they incidentally facilitated military movements and as an unintended consequence made the erection of barricades more difficult than had been the case in the narrower streets of 'old' Paris in 1789, 1830 and 1848. But a boulevard also reflected aesthetic principles of landscape design, opening up a long and tree-lined vista to a monument or monumental building. Away from the boulevards and in the new or remodelled parks and gardens, Napoléon III allowed his Anglomania full rein, putting into practice in sinuous pathways, lakes and streams the Romantic tenet that 'Nature abhors a straight line'.

A major transformation of the city's built form was intentionally achieved. Material living standards for many – but not all – Parisians were markedly improved during the nineteenth century. Less intended was the geographical reworking of its social structure, with wealthier people focussed on its central and western areas and the poor on the periphery, especially in the eastern districts. Nonetheless, Napoléon and Haussmann left an architectural legacy which has helped to make France today the most visited country in the world. The crucial role played by Napoléon III and Haussmann in the rebuilding of Paris is beyond doubt, although it was challenged and debated by their contemporaries and subsequently by historians. Nonetheless, two reservations deserve emphasis.

First, Paris witnessed significant changes to its landscape and society in the half-century *before* 1850. Haussmann's predecessors as prefects of Paris – Gilbert-Joseph-Gaspard Chabrol (1812–30), Claude-Philippe-Berthelot de Rambuteau (1833–48) and Jean-Jacques Berger (1848–52) – all had plans to straighten, widen and lengthen streets, in part to give greater prominence to visually isolated monuments. But their works were not undertaken comprehensively and have tended to be overshadowed by the impressive geographical scale and remarkable historical speed of the developments during the 1850s and 1860s. Light has been increasingly thrown on the modernization of Paris in the five decades before Napoléon III and Haussmann took over the Parisian stage and redesigned its scenery and redirected its cast of players. In 1969, Pierre Lavedan's study of the growth of Paris in the 1840s made it clear that 'modern' theories and practices about urbanism were being actively discussed and partially implemented in advance of Haussmann's ideas and achievements. Quite a few authors – among them François Loyer and David Van Zanten, as well as Lavedan again in a second volume on Parisian urbanism, and more recently Nicholas Papayanis in his *Planning Paris before Haussmann* (2004) – have emphasized that the achievements of Haussmann were not as innovative as has often been claimed. Haussmann, it needs to be acknowledged, was building – intellectually and materially – on the ideas and practices of social theorists, engineers and architects who, in the late eighteenth and early nineteenth centuries, had debated a new way of thinking about the city, described by Papayanis as a shift from seeing the city as a work of art towards viewing it as spaces of utility benefiting the largest number of people. Urban awareness moved from a focus on aesthetics to utility and from individual buildings to urban spaces as a whole. Many others had laid the intellectual foundations on which Haussmann was to build his new Paris.

The second reservation about the pæan sung so often about Haussmann for his creation of a 'new' Paris is that the city's remodelling continued after he left his post in January 1870. Some new streets remained to be finished, notably the Avenue de l'Opéra (1877), the Boulevard Saint-Germain (1877), Avenue de la République (1889), the Rue du Louvre (1906), the Boulevard Raspail (1907) and the Boulevard Haussmann (1926). The Opéra Garnier was only completed in 1875. But Haussmannization involved not merely products, such as new built forms and green spaces; it was also a process, which saw property as a social product, a commodity. That in itself was not innovative. Speculative building for profit, for investment, was an integral part of Paris's history before 1850. Property was seen as a secure investment in part because housing provision lagged behind the growth of population: the number of dwellings in Paris increased by 15 per cent between 1817 and 1851 but the population grew by 48 per cent. The rate of return on rents in the 1820s was about twice that on state debt. Daumard has shown that, while all sections of the bourgeoisie saw property as a way of storing and accumulating wealth, so too in the 1840s did shopkeepers, artisans and people in the liberal professions. By 1880, a new picture had emerged, with property owning dominated by people who simply called themselves landowners (*rentiers*), overshadowing all other categories. Central Paris came to be dominated by an *haute bourgeoisie* of landlords and companies, while the lower middle class and *petite bourgeoisie* were displaced to the periphery. As David Harvey has stressed, 'the mobilisation of capital flow to transform the built environment of Paris during the Second Empire was a spectacular affair'. Haussmannization unleashed a massive, speculative, property market which – after being checked by the Prussian siege and the Commune – continued after Haussmann's dismissal from office in 1870.

Alexia Yates has drawn attention to the complex social and economic networks which powered the profit-driven construction of multitudinous apartment buildings in fin-de-siècle Paris. She has calculated that between 1879 and 1885 about 13,500 such buildings were erected, while the population of Paris increased by about 300,000. This time around, the building boom was much more fragmented than the centrally driven, top-down, boom of the Second Empire. The tangled skein of the property market embroiled architects and urban planners, lawyers, speculators, individual owners, individual financiers and financing companies and a new breed of estate agents, as well as city councillors and officials. Given their significance, Yates's focus on apartment buildings in changing the face of Paris is understandable but it neglects the construction also of individual mansions (*hôtels particuliers*) in the wealthier districts and of small houses along with factories and warehouses in working-class areas. But it must be admitted that the focus on apartment buildings could be justified because – following the example of Haussmannization – they contributed more to the personality of Paris than did other building types.

Notwithstanding these two reservations – the degrees of 'Haussmannization' both before and after the Second Empire – it remains the case that remodelling of Paris during the 1850s and 1860s produced an image of the city which persisted for at least a century. David Pinkney, writing in 1958, made the key point that 'except for a few landmarks like the Church of the Sacré-Cœur and the Eiffel Tower, the new buildings erected since 1870 have not fundamentally altered the characteristic appearance' of the city. Judges of Haussmann, both his contemporaries and later (including today's) critics, agree that he was instrumental in influencing the physiognomy – the personality – of Paris in the long-nineteenth century and gave it an identity that became famous not only nationally but internationally. But the extent to which changes to the landscape of Paris during the last sixty years have obsolesced Pinkney's judgment deserves consideration – and will receive it here in due course.

5

Symbolizing Paris: Architectural icons

Townscapes are cultural texts to be read and interpreted, codes to be deciphered. They are often intentionally charged with skilfully articulated social meaning. The built form of Paris, together with its green spaces, was increasingly used during the nineteenth century to convey a sense of social order and a confident belief in its historical destiny. Its structures reflected a developing urban consciousness on the part of its authorities which was in turn relayed to its residents. Monuments were erected to celebrate the history of Paris specifically and of France generally. Additionally, notably fine buildings were offered as models of social order itself, of an anchored society with a positive future. Components of the built form of Paris variously transmitted civic, national and universal messages.

The Revolution of 1789 had remarkably little impact on the Parisian cityscape and there are very few outstanding buildings in Paris dated from the period 1790 to 1850. One exception was La Madeleine, the construction of which as a royal church was begun in 1763 but suspended during the Revolution when the purpose of the building was debated. In 1805 Napoléon decreed that it should be completed but as a temple to the glory of France's army. Work proceeded slowly and was stopped in 1811 on cost grounds. In 1812, following his failed Russian campaign, Napoléon declared that the building should revert to its original intended use as a church. The building in neo-Classical style was finally consecrated as a church in 1842.

That new constructions in Paris during the nineteenth century were deliberately erected as iconic structures is proved by the debates which surrounded many of them. Six key examples will be considered here.

The Panthéon 1791

Before 1789, iconic buildings were mainly associated with royalty or the Church: they were palaces and a variety of religious buildings. During the Revolution, many of the royal statues which adorned the public places of Paris were vandalized. Properties owned by the clergy were appropriated by the state. Some were demolished, some were sold, others were reassigned to new uses. A notable example of the last process was the conversion of a church built to honour God to being instead a secular memorial for the great men of France: on 4 April 1791, the church of Sainte-Geneviève in the Latin Quarter was deprived of its religious function and became the Panthéon (Figure 5.1).

In 1744, Louis XV had become seriously ill and promised to God that if he survived he would build a church devoted to Sainte Geneviève: he did survive and accordingly ordered the construction of a church on the site of the Abbey of Sainte-Geneviève, which lay in ruins. Several architects submitted plans for a new church and the project was allocated to Jacques-Germain Soufflot (1713–1780), a Burgundian who had studied in Italy and practised as an architect in Lyon before moving to Paris in 1755. His design reflected Classical and Gothic styles but with both Byzantine and Greco-Roman influences: Soufflot's was an eclectic style. Construction of the new church began in 1757 and Louis XV laid the ceremonial foundation stone on 6 September 1764. Critical voices raised about technical matters during construction delayed completion of the building until 1790. By then, following the Revolution of 1789, the National Assembly had decided that the church – which had not yet been consecrated – should be transformed into a necropolis or mausoleum for the mortal remains of exceptional men who had contributed to the greatness of France. The National Assembly saw the new building as a Temple of the Nation and approved a text over the entrance: 'Aux grands hommes la patrie reconnaissante' ('A grateful nation honours its great men'). Celebrating so monumentally the great personalities of France signalled a significant cultural mutation from an old age of faith-based religion to a new age of secular reason.

Between 1791and 1793, the building was modified for its new purpose. It became a Panthéon, with its facade modelled on the Panthéon in Rome built in the first century BCE but with an added dome modelled on those of sixteenth-century Italian churches.

Figure 5.1 The Panthéon *c.* 1900. Wikimedia Creative Commons (public domain)

As stressed by François Loyer, the modifications were considerable: towers were pulled down, the halo on the pediment was removed as were also many embellishments deemed to be superfluous (sculpted bouquets, palms, cherubs' heads, medallions and garlands and other religious ornaments) and a host of sculpted patriarchs and Church Fathers who crowded the four naves. Two architectural languages considered appropriate to the cult of great men – those of light and of sanctuary – spoke to the modifications. The church's thirty-nine windows provided variable light whereas meditation upon immortality required constancy. Indirect lighting was deemed to be necessary in order to create an effect of the sublime. This was achieved by bricking up the existing windows and equipping the cupola with skylights of frosted glass. The Panthéon was thus to be not a church, not a cemetery, not a museum, not a garden of remembrance. It was instead a mausoleum, a contained space, enclosed, severe and grandiose, animated only by its statuary. The Panthéon was and remains an impressive icon of French national greatness. But it can hardly be read as an icon of national unanimity because there have been heated debates about which great men should be housed in it. No great pre-Revolution figures other than Voltaire (1694–1798) and Rousseau (1712–1778) were awarded the honour of a permanent place, nor were any first-rank figures of the Revolution itself, although some second-rank figures were, like Condorcet (1743–1794), the Abbé Grégoire (1750–1831) and Gaspard Monge (1746–1818). But the Panthéon does today store the remains of some great nineteenth-century Frenchmen, including Louis Braille (1809–1852), Émile Zola (1840–1902) and Pierre Curie (1859–1906), and one naturalized French woman, Marie Curie (1867–1934).

On the top of the dome of the secular Panthéon today sits somewhat incongruously a Christian cross. There is a rich story behind this one small icon. In 1790, a cross was installed temporarily while awaiting a statue of Sainte Geneviève; in 1791 it was decided to change the church building into a mausoleum, replacing the cross by statue of a woman blowing a trumpet (to herald the great men whose mortal remains were or would be entombed in the building). In 1806, Napoléon Bonaparte returned the building to being a church but left the statue where it was; in 1822, the statue was replaced by a gilded bronze cross; in 1830, Louis-Philippe reinstated the building as a Panthéon and had the cross replaced by a flag; in 1851, Napoléon III reinstated the building as a church and a gilded bronze cross was placed on the dome; in 1871, the Communards sawed off the two side branches of the cross and flew a red flag from its stem; in 1873, the new Republican government of 'moral order' installed a stone cross; finally, in 1885, when the remains of Victor Hugo were transferred to the building, the Third Republic had it restored as a Panthéon but deemed it unnecessary to replace the cross.

The unstable history of the Panthéon's cross reflected the volatile nature of the relations between Church and state in nineteenth-century France and demonstrates the acute awareness on the part of the authorities and of people on both sides of the conflict that the debate could be played out in iconic architecture. Not only the cross but the whole building had an eventful history during the nineteenth century. In 1801, Napoléon Bonaparte signed a concordat with the Pope and agreed to restore former church properties, including the Panthéon. From 1806, it was both a mausoleum and a church, with the crypt continuing in use as an official resting place for designated heroes of France. In 1816, during the Bourbon Restoration which followed the fall of Napoléon, Louis XVIII returned the entire Panthéon, including the crypt, to the Catholic Church. The building was at last officially consecrated in the presence of the king, a ceremony which had not been undertaken during the Revolution of 1789. The next Revolution, that of 1830, put Louis Philippe on the throne. Sharing some of the views of the revolutionaries, in August 1830 he returned the church into being a mausoleum – but the crypt was closed and no new remains were added. In 1848, Louis Philippe was ousted, his regime replaced by the Second Republic. The new government revived the Panthéon as a 'Temple of Humanity' but admitted no newcomers into it. In 1848, Louis Napoléon was elected as president of the Second Republic and then in 1851 staged a coup d'état and appointed himself as emperor. One of his earliest acts was to return the Panthéon to the Catholic Church as a 'National Basilica'. Its return to exclusive use as a mausoleum was decreed in 1881 by the National Assembly of the Third Republic; in 1885 it received the mortal remains of Victor Hugo, the first such reception in more than fifty years.

The unsettled, conflicted, history of the Panthéon justifies Mona Ozouf's claim that although it was conceived as a quasi-religious showcase of French national unity, it has been in reality a focal point of internal division. It is an icon not of a single national memory but of the multiple political memories available to the French. As of 2018, the remains of seventy-eight people were accommodated in the Panthéon, among them five women. But more than half of the *panthéonisations* had been made under Napoléon Bonaparte's rule during the First Empire (1804–14). Contrasting with the variable symbolism of the Panthéon is the more stable iconography of the new Opera House.

The Opéra Garnier 1862–75

Construction of the Opera House began in 1862 and it was inaugurated in 1875 (Figure 5.2). Architecturally, it was a grand and arresting building, amalgamating quite different Byzantine, Italian and French styles: it was an effective distillation of Second Empire aesthetics. Designed by its Parisian-born architect Charles Garnier (1825–98) as an expression of its time, the Second Empire, it is a monumental building whose political and cultural symbolism has been forensically decoded by Penelope Woolf. The Opera House was designed with the modernization project for Paris being implemented by Napoléon III and Georges Haussmann very much in mind. It was intended to inspire a sense of pride and achievement, testifying to social progress under the Second Empire; it was to be spectacular, providing an architectural link to the spectacle (involving music, dancing and paintings) that would be staged within it; it was to embrace, like opera itself, both tradition and novelty, thereby establishing a radical modernity as the cultural orthodoxy of its age, holding on to the past while simultaneously looking forward to the future; and finally it was to be an indicator of opulence and prosperity, like the new railway stations, market halls and banks, in the modernizing landscape of Paris. The facade of the Opera House was lavishly ornamented and ornately decorated, incorporating sculptures of great composers and

Figure 5.2 L'Opéra Garnier *c.* 1900. Wikimedia Creative Commons CCO 1.0 Universal Public Domain

others representing poetry, instrumental music, dance and lyrical drama. The interior exuded wealth and extravagance. A grand theatrical staircase in differently coloured marbles divides into two flights of stairs leading to the Grand Foyer, where Parisian society could mingle, to be seen and to see. The horseshoe-shaped auditorium could seat almost 2,000 opera goers in luxurious comfort and surroundings, including a great bronze and crystal chandelier.

The Opera House was a powerful statement about French society and especially about Parisian society of the 1860s and 1870s. It was intentionally symbolic and interpreted as such by its contemporaries: its iconic role is not a simple matter of interpretation with the benefit of hindsight by modern historians. For Napoléon III and Haussmann, the Opera House had to be, as a symbol of national prestige, the largest such building in Europe, thereby affirming Paris as the cultural centre of Europe. It had also to be centrally located within Paris, emphasizing its role as a centre for its society: by locating the Opera House on the Right Bank at the centre of the district that was itself the heart of Paris, just as Paris was claiming to be the artistic capital of Europe (and even of the Western world), the imaginative power of the monument rested on layers of symbolic meaning collectively proclaiming it to be the cultural epicentre of Paris and of Europe. Furthermore, in design and construction materials, the Opera House had to be characteristic of the nineteenth century as one of progress.

These were the views held by contemporaries. They became components of the idea of Paris as the capital of pleasure, of Paris itself as a vast open-air theatre, of Paris as spectacle, indeed of Paris as performance and as opera (complete with sounds of street musicians, singers and traders).

That the reality of the Opera House was different from its perception by contemporaries has been convincingly argued by Woolf. She has stressed that the Opera House attributed an aura of wealth and prosperity to the city when most Parisians were not able to share in those riches. The Opera House was a bourgeois, exclusive, statement, a facade whose symbolic meaning was comprehended only by a few not the many. In reality, the Opera House emphasized the social differences embedded within Paris, contrasts of which the authorities were very aware. In 1864, Napoléon III wrote to the municipal council to urge that the new hospital (*Hôtel Dieu*) under construction should be completed before the Opera House because of the adverse publicity that the government would suffer if a prestigious cultural venue for the benefit of wealthier Parisians were seen to take precedence over a building for the sick and the poor. His wish was not granted in full. Construction of the Hôtel Dieu began in 1867, it came into use in July 1877, it was officially inaugurated in September 1877 and its construction was finally completed in 1879. For the Opera House, construction began in 1862 and was completed in 1875. Such monumental projects took many years to bring to fruition and completion to a scheduled programme of works could not be assured. This was also the case with another Parisian icon, the Basilica of the Sacred Heart.

The Basilica of the Sacred Heart 1875–1912

Sited atop the Butte Montmartre, the Basilica of the Sacred Heart is a political and cultural monument to Catholicism and to nationalism (Figure 5.3). It was constructed in the aftermath of France's defeat in the Franco-Prussian War and the horror of the 1871 civil war in Paris. The need for such a monument was recognized by the Catholic Church as a response to the perceived decadence of the Second Empire and as a check on the growth of left-wing Republicanism. Construction began in 1875 but was not completed until 1912; use of the building began in 1891 but it was not consecrated until 1919.

The Basilica was built prominently on the heights of Montmartre, at an altitude of 130 m and to which its central dome added a further 84 m. It is a stunning building in the Romano-Byzantine style in a commanding position, visible from great distances throughout Paris. Its dramatic visual impact is emphasized by its having been built not, like most of the city's earlier churches and public buildings, from local limestone (*pierre de Paris*) and plaster of Paris from nearby quarries but from stone from Château-Landon and Souppes-sur-Loing, in Seine-et-Marne, almost 100 km to the south of Paris. Only one other Parisian monument, the Arc de Triomphe, was built using this stone which is much whiter than the commonly used beige-coloured limestone, enhancing the Basilica's considerable topographical visibility.

The Archbishop of Paris, Joseph-Hippolyte Guibert, wanted to have in the city a sanctuary for 'refugees' from the decadent Babylon that he considered Paris to have

Figure 5.3 La Basilique du Sacré-Cœur. © Alan R. H. Baker

become. A large church was needed to achieve what he sought, a revival of the national soul after France's defeat by the Prussians in 1871. The basilica was intended, as a national church, to promote in France both a Catholic and a political revival, to lead to a national renaissance through a renewed Christianization of public life. It was a symbol of Catholic royalism, a monumental atonement for what were perceived as the sins of Revolutionary France. It embodied both spiritual and national aims. The vow to build such a church in Paris was made in January 1871, before the declaration of the Commune later that year. It was envisioned not as an ordinary place of worship – Montmartre already had its own parish church – but as a place of pilgrimage. The winning design, in an open competition which attracted some seventy entrants, was inspired by Romano-Byzantine architecture, with its ovoid domes and cupolas. It was, as François Loyer has described it, 'an artificial foreign body' imposed on the landscape of Paris. Construction costs of 45 million francs were met entirely from private collections and donations, not from public funds, which might have moderated criticism of the Basilica but did not arrest it entirely. The Basilica was embroiled in the prolonged conflict between Church and state, between Catholics and Republicans.

The Basilica's hill-top site and its startling architecture combine to proclaim its domination of the city below Montmartre. It was a semiotic clericalist endeavour to signal the role of Catholic law and order and respect for its authority, most especially to the profane 'Red Belt' of the city's suburbs below the hill in eastern Paris. But, as David Harvey has emphasized, the Basilica was built not to commemorate the thousands of Parisians who had died in the civil war of 1871 but partly to honour just two generals of the French national army who had been caught by the Communards and executed by a firing squad on the hill of Montmartre. The Basilica was built by the Catholic Church partly to commemorate those two generals whom it regarded as 'martyrs of yesterday who died in order to defend and save Christian society'. The Basilica is thus a Catholic monument and a national monument, not a narrowly Parisian monument. It stands as witness to the fundamental schism in French society during the nineteenth century: even while it was being constructed, Church and state were constitutionally separated in 1905. Loyer judges the Basilica to be 'more an edifice of reconquest than of reconciliation. ... a permanent insult, a defiance of republican political power throughout the Third Republic'. It symbolizes the political and social fragmentation of France. This dazzling, white, massive and architecturally arresting edifice loomed over Paris from its hill-top site, competing for attention with the secular riverside Eiffel Tower, these two monumental structures materializing the ideological debate within French society.

The Eiffel Tower 1889

The ending of the nineteenth century marked the culmination of the two revolutions that in combination transformed not just France but most of Europe: the French Revolution which proclaimed 'Liberty, Equality and Fraternity', providing the seminal political and social ideology for the Western world; and the Industrial Revolution which it was thought would furnish the material means to attain those ideological objectives. In France, confidence in material progress and in human perfectibility perhaps peaked in the last quarter of the nineteenth century, reflecting the perceived achievements of those two revolutions and marked by the optimism generated by the celebratory *Expositions universelles* in Paris in 1889 and 1900.

The year 1889 marked the centenary of the French Revolution and the government decided that it should be celebrated and symbolized in the capital by a radical feat of engineering: an iron tower 300 m (996 ft) high, the nearest metric equivalent to 1000 ft (Figure 5.4). The design competition for the tower was won by Gustave Eiffel (1832-1923), a civil engineer and architect, France's master builder in metal who had been designing and building bridges and other metal structures for thirty years, both in France and abroad. Building the tower was an ambitious project: it spread over more than two years, from 26 January 1887 until 31 March 1889; it engaged more than 250 workers who rivetted together in Eiffel's factory more than 18,000 metal pieces, creating structures that were then assembled on

Figure 5.4 The Eiffel Tower 1889. Wikimedia Creative Commons PDM 1.0

site. The Eiffel Tower was by far the world's tallest built structure, much higher than the Washington Monument at 555 ft (169 m) and it remained the tallest building in the world until 1929, when New York's 319-m (1,046-ft)-high Chrysler Building was constructed.

The Tower was a triumph of engineering and immediately recognized as such. It also carried a heavy semiotic burden. As Joseph Harris (1976, p. 20) has stressed, the Eiffel Tower's immediate and intentionally symbolic importance was spelled out by Alfred Picard (1844–1913), an engineer and the Tower's official historian:

> This colossal work was to constitute a brilliant manifestation of the industrial strength of our country, attest to the immense progress realised in the art of metal structures, celebrate the unprecedented progress of civil engineering during the course of this century, attract a multitude of visitors, and contribute largely to the success of the great peaceful commemoration of the centenary of 1789.

It was, in effect, a self-assured expression of modernity and came to be seen as a symbol of the French revolutionary ideals of 'Liberty, Equality and Fraternity'.

There were many contemporary critics of the project. It was divisive because it was a republican and metal structure celebrating the Revolution of 1789 and the skill of engineering technology. There were many sensitive pegs on which criticism could be hung. Deemed a dramatic sign of French progress by some, the Tower was considered by others to be aesthetically, politically and religiously repugnant. In 1887, some fifty intellectuals, including the writers Alexandre Dumas *fils* and Guy de Maupassant, architect Charles Garnier and composers Charles Gounod and Jules Massenet, signed a petition which complained that the proposal was for a 'vertiginously ridiculous tower dominating Paris like a gigantic black factory chimney, crushing by its barbarous massive scale Notre-Dame, the Sainte-Chapelle, the Louvre, the dome of the Invalides and the Arc de Triomphe, humiliating all our monuments'. Gustave Eiffel's response was that the Tower, like the pyramids of Egypt, transcended rather than transgressed both artistic canons and historical precedent. For many clergy, the Tower was a sacrilege, while for many aesthetes it was an ugly horror. Like the statues of Joan of Arc, the Eiffel Tower reflected the ideological rift in Parisian society. Republican newspapers praised it, while the Catholic press lambasted it. For some, it was a symbol of national pride based on technological prowess, for others it was a sacrilege that a president of the French Republic had visited the construction site on a Sunday and that three months later the Tower was inaugurated by the prime minister, also on a Sunday – while architects and builders of glorious medieval churches and cathedrals like Notre-Dame had eschewed their construction sites on Sundays.

Nonetheless, the Eiffel Tower, completed after two years' work, became the most popular feature of the *Exposition universelle* of 1889 (Figure 5.5). By the closure of the Exhibition, 1,968,287 people (on average, 11,800 per day between 15 May and 6 November) had visited the Tower, which could accommodate 10,000 visitors at a time, on its interior and exterior (first floor) galleries, in its four restaurants, on its second platform and on its top platform and on its lifts and staircases. Electricity, which had gradually since the late 1870s been replacing melancholy gas lights along Parisian streets, made the 1889 Exhibition the first world exhibition to remain open in the evenings. The Tower itself was illuminated by thousands of electric light bulbs, effectively converting night into day. According to Henri Loyrette, a biographer of Eiffel, the Tower fulfilled the nineteenth century's obsessive need for a beacon to guide and illuminate. It was not only a republican and secular symbol but also an unavoidable sight: it could be seen from almost anywhere in Paris. Loyrette suggests that the Tower unified the twenty *arrondissements* of the city, 'turning a patchwork of neighbourhoods into a single capital'. The Tower generated a sense of community, of being 'Parisian', be it permanently as a resident or fleetingly as a visitor. Eiffel himself, immensely proud of the Tower as an engineered structure, endorsed the imaginative symbolism of his edifice. A distinctive interpretation of the Eiffel Tower was produced by the engraver, Henri Rivière, in his *Trente-six vues de la Tour Eiffel* published in 1902: inspired by the thirty-six views of Mount Fuji by the Japanese artist Hokusai, Rivière imagined a Japanese interpretation of the Eiffel Tower from varied angles in his engaging coloured lithographs.

Figure 5.5 Advertisement for the 1889 *Exposition universelle*.

The Tower rapidly became the world's best-known landmark and boosted both the national and the international reputation of Paris. By the end of 1989, its centenary year, the Tower had had an accumulated total of some 15 million visitors. It was seen variously, for example, as a totem pole, a maypole and as a 1,000-foot flagstaff. One critic called it 'a hollow chandelier'. Its heavenward trajectory was, for some, an arrow of progress breaking into the clouds. It was the subject of a painting by Seurat in 1889, by Signac in 1890, and in subsequent years by other artists, including Chagall, Utrillo and Dufy. The Tower featured in poetry before 1914 and played a dominant role in Jean Cocteau's play, *Les Mariés de la Tour Eiffel*, first performed in 1920.

While the Tower was a startling demonstration of the power of science, technology and engineering, it was also a symbol of French republicanism and French nationalism, a powerful symbol of national recovery after the country's defeat by the Prussians in 1870–1. Miriam Levin has argued that the Eiffel Tower was promoted as a conscious and programmatic artistic expression of the Republican ideal – it consisted of a multitude of small parts each clearly articulated, efficient and interlocked with the others to form an integrated, controlled and dynamic system – it was thus, she claimed, a paradigm of a liberal democratic society. Over time, the Tower became a symbol of Paris as capital of pleasure: a symbol not only of people's mastery of their fate and their environment but also of their uninhibited creativity and unbridled enjoyment of life. It was an outstanding tourist attraction. The Tower, as well as providing exciting panoramic views of the city and even some of the countryside beyond it, offered dining and wining in the sky in four restaurants, each of which could accommodate 400 covers. Maupassant often lunched at a restaurant in the Tower, not because he rated highly its cuisine, but, he proclaimed, 'It's the only place in Paris where I don't have to see it.' There were also dining and wining facilities on the ground adjacent to the Tower. Here was held a banquet for mayors of France: hosted by the government, it was enjoyed by almost 16,000 of them.

The Tower as symbol has borne many interpretations. For example, its form has been likened to a church spire reaching toward heaven which would allow it to be in conformity with the other historical towering structures in the landscape. But, as William Thompson has pointed out, the Tower's 'religion' is not Christianity but 'Modernity'. It plays to the religion of science and technology, in effect to material progress. Another interpretation insists on the Tower's phallic form, paradoxically in a city whose femininity is often proclaimed. Roland Barthes suggested that there are so many and diverse readings of the Tower because each person wishes to appropriate its meaning to her/his own purposes. The Tower is a symbol but acting within not one but many theatres of thought. Thompson says that the Tower's many symbolic connotations are too numerous to list but then proceeds to roll call their diversity: 'The Tower has been proclaimed the symbol of industrial and artistic progress, the métro, electric lights, elevators, telephones, military power, centralisation, the union of workers and engineers, mathematical energy, technical utopianism, modern Paris, practical science, superhuman exaltation, the marriage of skill and imagination, and architectural eclecticism.' The numerous descriptions of the Tower include a tragic lamppost, a lighthouse of industry and capital, a giraffe and a modern Tower of Babel. While the Tower is self-evidently monumental, it is not a monument to any actual person(s) or historical event(s). Perhaps because of this, the Tower was soon adopted as an icon of Paris and subsequently of France. Souvenirs of the Tower were produced in their thousands from 1888 onwards, ranging from replicas as lollipops through candlesticks and bedside lights to perfume bottles (Figure 5.6). Taking such a souvenir home was offered as 'proof' of having visited the Tower in particular and Paris in general.

The symbolic national significance of the Tower was to be demonstrated doubly during the Second World War. When Paris was occupied by German forces in 1940, they discovered the Tower's lifts had been sabotaged by the French Resistance, forcing them to climb the 1,665 steps to fly a Swastika flag from the Tower's top. Throughout the war, the French Resistance made sure that the lifts could not be operated. And in the early morning of 24 June 1940, Adolf Hitler undertook a victory tour of Paris in an open-topped car, taking in the church of the Madeleine, the Opera, the Place de la Concorde and the Arc de Triomphe before having himself

Figure 5.6 An Eiffel Tower-shaped perfume bottle in a provincial shop window at Bourbon (Allier) in 2007. © Alan R. H. Baker

photographed in front of the Eiffel Tower (Figure 5.7). The Tower remains a major tourist attraction despite the fact, as Barthes has emphasized, that there is in no interior into which tourists can penetrate. There is nothing for visitors to see inside the Tower, which is empty except for catering outlets. Tourists ascend the Tower in order to say that they have done so and to admire not the Tower itself but Paris laid out below and before them. The Tower is a major feature of the skyline of Paris for observers on the ground. But the principal benefit, for visitors ascending it, is the panoramic view which it provides of the whole of Paris through 360 degrees. The role of the river Seine and its bridges in shaping people's experiences of the city is spread out on the ground like a patterned carpet. Monumental Paris is observable in miniature.

However it is viewed, interpreted and understood by individuals, each experiences the Eiffel Tower personally. Its meanings are multiple but specific. Barthes consider

Figure 5.7 Hitler at the Eiffel Tower on, 23 June 1940. Wikimedia Creative Commons Public Domain photo of the National Archives at College Park, United States

it to be a 'pure sign', 'a limitless metaphor', open to the untrammelled imaginations of those who observe it. To this day, the Tower remains a powerful, physical, experience for Parisians and a symbol of France throughout the world. Historian Graham Robb stresses the unique iconic quality of the Tower: 'It was the only monument that gave Paris a character of its own: all the others might have been found in any city.'

Le Pont Alexandre III 1900

The Pont Alexandre III is the most ornate, most ostentatious, bridge in Paris (Figure 5.8). Plans were being made in the1890s for the *Exposition universelle* to be held in Paris in 1900. The Palais de l'Industrie, which had extended along the length of the

Figure 5.8 Le Pont Alexandre III and the Grand Palais *c.* 1910. Wikimedia Creative Commons Attribution Share Alike 4.0 International/Philippe Alès

Champs-Élysées since the *Exposition universelle* of 1855, was torn down. A new road was planned from the Champs-Élysées to open up a view across the Seine to the Hôtel des Invalides. The new avenue, with the Grand Palais on one side and the Petit Palais on the other, was to be called – after the Russian emperor – the Avenue de Nicolas II, while the new bridge across the river would be named after his father, Alexandre III. Nicholas II laid the foundation stone for the bridge in 1896: it was a physical expression of the political friendship between Russia and France, between an empire and what was then the only republic in Europe. Construction was completed in 1900.

The bridge is magnificent. It was, daringly, a 6-m-high single metal arch of 107 m, with two tall stone pillars surmounted by gilt-bronze statues at each end of the bridge which linked the Right and Left Banks. This stone and iron bridge effectively linked the seventeenth-century stone Hôtel de Invalides of Louis XIV with the new metal and glass republican Grand Palais. The bronze statues are of the *Quatres Renommées*: those of the sciences, of the arts, of commerce and of industry. At their bases are the four Frances: Contemporary France, France of Charlemagne, France of the Renaissance and France of Louis XIV. Nymph reliefs, at the centres of the arches over the Seine, are memorials to the Franco-Russian Alliance. The *Nymphs of the Seine* has a relief of the arms of Paris and faces the Nymphs of the Neva with the arms of Imperial Russia. Both of these have been executed in hammered copper. This bridge is an elaborate, spectacular, enhancement of the cityscape, much more than simply functioning as a link between the two banks of the Seine. Improving links within the city while adding to its splendour also lay behind the construction of the underground train network of Paris.

Le Métro 1900

The Métro of Paris was named after London's Metropolitan underground line, the world's first underground railway, opened on 10 January 1863 with gas-lit wooden carriages hauled at first by steam locomotives but from 1890 by electrically powered engines. Émile Zola's novel about the provisioning of Paris, *Le Ventre de Paris* (1873), was set in the 1860s and includes reference to a project for an underground railway network linking the main line stations in Paris. In reality, such a project for Paris only began to be discussed by its municipal council in 1871. It wanted to have a network which would serve the needs of its citizens but the national government and the railway companies sought a network which would link together the main-line railway stations. There ensued a prolonged public debate in France during the closing decades of the nineteenth century about the need for and the nature of an underground railway for Paris.

Those opposed to such a project argued that it would involve tearing up the fabric of the city once again, too soon after the disruptions that had been suffered during Haussmannization. They also asserted that travelling underground would be dangerous and some revived the fear of 'miasmic' infection associated with what were assumed to be unhealthy emanations underground. By contrast, proponents argued that the project would be an unambiguous symbol of the modernity of Paris and a key development in the production of a fully rationalized city. Both the extension of the overground system of transport and construction of an underground system were seen by their advocates as components of a comprehensive project to improve circulation in the city, to produce a clearly ordered and efficiently functioning capital city.

In the mid-1890s, it was increasingly argued that Paris should have an underground train network completed in time for the *Exposition universelle* scheduled to be held in 1900. In 1895, the national government granted the city of Paris the right to install such a network. Its construction was indicative of the tension between Paris and the provinces represented in the national government. The municipal council went ahead and built a system with tunnels which were purposely too small for standard-sized railway carriages so that the overground system could not have direct access to and connection with the underground system, and the municipality could thus retain full control of the Métro. Partly for the same political reasons, the network was not extended underground beyond the main gateways into Paris in the encircling wall built in the 1840s, but with the additional strategic consideration of ensuring that the network could not be used by any 'enemy forces' to gain entry to the city.

The Métro's first line (Vincennes-Maillot, with eight stations) was opened on 19 July 1900 with no publicity and with no inaugural ceremony because that undoubtedly historic event was nonetheless overshadowed by the *Exposition universelle* which had been opened by President Émile Loubet on 14 April. The Métro gradually replaced the river boats and horse-drawn trams and omnibuses as public transport.

The technological achievement of the Métro was matched by an artistic achievement above ground. The street entrances to the underground platforms were decorated by the *art nouveau* work of Hector Guimard (1867–1942). These embellished the streetscape, their cast iron plant stems soaring skyward towards a drooping flower that embraced an electric light bulb (Figure 5.9). They represented a rebellion against 'academism', the neo-Classical and Romantic style of the French Académie des Beaux Arts. They were offered as an expression of 'art for the people', confirming the Métro's contribution to the democratization of circulation within Paris.

In sum, during the nineteenth century Paris acquired a suite of architectural icons which demonstrated its developing personality, adding complexity to the capital's character which had been shaped by monumentalism and Haussmannization. Paris was in many ways a model for other European capital cities. Göran Therborn has suggested that such cities had four key iconographic elements: first, a set of buildings for central, national, state institutions, in particular, the legislative body, the judiciary and the executive ministries; second, a layout of elegant streets for commerce, promenading and parading; third, a set of institutions of national high culture, such as museums,

Figure 5.9 Entrance to the Métro station Ménilmontant. Wikimedia Creative Commons Attribution Share Alike 4.0/JLPC

art galleries, theatres and opera houses situated in buildings which signalled a shared national identity; and fourth, a determined politicization and monumentalization of urban space. Therborn showed that these four elements were to be found, to varying degrees, in the nineteenth-century European capital cities of Berlin, Brussels, London, Madrid, Rome, St Petersburg/Moscow and Vienna – but par excellence in Paris. Therborn widened the geographical scope of Donald Olsen's earlier but much more detailed comparison of London, Paris and Vienna as works of art, as architectural monuments materializing social histories.

In many ways, Paris was iconographically the model for European capital cities in the long-nineteenth century. Its constellation of iconic buildings, in addition to those already discussed, included within Therborn's fourfold classification the following examples: the Élysée Palace (built in 1722 for Henri de la Tour d'Auvergne but from 1848 used as the office of the French president) and the Luxembourg Palace (built in the early seventeenth century for the Regent Marie de Médicis but after the Revolution converted into a legislative building); the Grands Boulevards which around 1700 replaced former fortifications; the boulevards created later by Haussmann; the Institut de France, a learned society founded in 1795, grouping five academies, accommodated in a seventeenth-century building, and the Sorbonne, a university with origins in the thirteenth century and buildings dating from the seventeenth century; and fourthly, the products of the 'statuomania' already discussed. Clearly, quite a few of nineteenth-century Paris's significant icons were legacies from earlier periods. But the scale and scope of icons created in its cityscape between 1789 and 1914 added both complexity and uniqueness to its personality.

The outstanding icon – literally and metaphorically – in Paris was, of course, the Eiffel Tower, today recognized worldwide as representing not only Paris specifically but also France generally. It connected the ideals of the French Revolution with the practices and achievements of the Industrial Revolution. Small-scale replicas of it were and are universally available as souvenirs, ornaments and toys and as commercial logos to indicate a Francophile connection. In addition, there are even large-scale replicas of the Tower in other countries, notably those in such different cultural settings as Las Vegas in the United States and Tianducheng in China. The Tower has projected the image of Paris and of France globally. It did so originally as part of the *Exposition universelle* of 1889. That and other such exhibitions cultivated an image – but a changing image – of Paris.

6

Projecting Paris: World Fairs 1855–1900

Markets and fairs for selling products have deep historical roots in many European countries, including France. But in the early eighteenth century a new kind of exhibition came into being in Paris: a public art show sponsored by the king and staged by his Academy of Fine Arts. These salons evolved into annual events by the end of the century. They were public exhibitions of paintings and sculptures, aiming to improve public tastes about art, to increase competition and promote excellence among artists, and to strengthen France's international reputation for artistic creativity. Almost incidentally, they also served to promote sales for artists. Towards 1800 and for similar purposes, there were also promotional displays of industrial products. From 1798 and then during the first half of the nineteenth century, a series of national exhibitions were mounted in Paris at roughly five-yearly intervals. These exhibitions of, for example, agricultural tools and equipment, manufactured goods, ceramics and musical instruments were organized by the state. Each exhibition aimed to surpass its immediate predecessor in order to maintain an atmosphere of innovation and progress.

The last national exhibition was held in 1849. The next one, scheduled for 1854, was postponed until 1855 because Napoléon III proclaimed that the next exhibition would be an international one, a world fair, to surpass Britain's Great Exhibition of 1851 in the Crystal Palace. The 1855 Exhibition in Paris was officially called 'The Great Exhibition of the Works of Industry of all Nations'. It was international in the sense that different countries exhibited their own achievements in varied fields of human endeavour, such as industry, science, commerce and the arts. The 1855 Exhibition and its successor in 1867 enabled Napoléon III to advance the cause of internationalism while also promoting France's prestige and material interests: they were admirable examples of 'soft power'. Those two exhibitions and three which succeeded them in 1878, 1889 and 1900 attracted increasing volumes of visitors – their number increased tenfold while the population of Paris grew just over twofold. For the Exhibition of 1900, the number of visitors (51 million) for the first time exceeded the total population of France (40 million): there must have been very many foreign visitors, adding to the exhibition's justifiable claim to be an international event (Table 6.1).

Table 6.1 Expositions universelles in Paris

	Visitors (millions)	Population of Paris (millions)
1855	5.1	1.2 (in 1856)
1867	6.8	1.8 (1866)
1878	16.1	2.0 (1876)
1889	28.1	2.4 (1891)
1900	50.8	2.7 (1900)

Sources: Mandell (1967); Greenhalgh (1988); Allwood (2001); Gaillard (2003); official census data.

1855 *Exposition universelle de Paris*

The 1855 Exhibition was the first such world event to be held in Paris and the second in the world. It was as much a political as a cultural event, held on the Champs-Élysées from 15 May until 15 November. Twenty-five countries and their colonies participated, especially notable among them being the British and Dutch exhibits. Visitors were attracted to this and the following 1867 Exhibition mainly because of the novelty of fine arts and industrial products on display. The latter were housed in the Palais de l'Industrie (Figure 6.1), a building 208 m long and constructed using for the first time in Paris beams of wrought iron on columns of cast iron, with stone casings around the columns to give the building a solidity which bare iron appeared to lack. The entrance to the Palace of Industry was a monumental Arc de Triomphe with a corniche decorated with a sculpted allegorical group representing *La France distribuant des couronnes au Commerce et à l'Industrie*. All four sides of the building had a double row of glass windows with the names of great and famous men engraved on the stonework between the two rows. The building, large as it was, could not accommodate the 234,000 exhibits, so an annex was added. The Paris municipal council itself exhibited a novel map of the city under the ground, indicating its quarries, caves, rivers and *catacombes* (ossuaries). There was a section on horticulture and agriculture, which included exhibits demonstrating improved ways of draining and irrigating soils, and of mechanizing farming (including McCormick's threshing machine). The Palace of Industry had more than 4 million visitors, while the fine arts exhibition attracted just under 1 million.

The Palais des Beaux Arts was an architectural contrast: a Renaissance-style building in the form of a horseshoe. Twenty-eight nations exhibited 4,979 works of art by 2,176 artists. Their displays included works by Delacroix, Millet, Courbet, Pissarro, Degas and Sisley. Napoléon III and his government were keen to have displays not only of industrial and commercial progress but also of the fine arts. They featured hugely in the 1855 Exhibition, and this practice was emulated in all major international exhibitions around the world afterwards. An emphasis on the fine arts reflected a strong nationalist and imperialist sentiment. The 1855 Exhibition aimed to show that France was producing finest-quality works in, for example, painting, sculpture, ceramics, architecture, textiles, graphics, food and drink and music.

Medals were awarded to companies and to individuals for outstanding exhibits as determined in some cases by Napoléon III and in others by appointed juries. At the award ceremony held on 15 November 1855, some 40,000 spectators crowded into in the main hall of the Palais de l'Industrie. The ceremony was concluded with an orchestral performance of works by Mozart, Beethoven, Gluck and Rossini conducted by Hector Berlioz who used for the first time in France an electric metronome.

The 1855 and two succeeding exhibitions were paid for out of public funds (subsidies from the State and the city council) and from public subscriptions, with the intention of recouping the balance of the outlay from entrance fees. There is hardly any physical legacy of the 1855 Exhibition surviving in Paris today. The only vestiges are the sculptures which ornamented the entrance to the Palais de l'Industrie: they were moved in 1900 to the Parc de Saint-Cloud, on a hill about 10 km to the west of Paris, overlooking the Seine. The park had been set up in the late sixteenth century by Catharine de Médicis because it contained a spring of drinking water which she wanted to have piped to the Palais des Tuileries. The Château de Saint-Cloud, expanded in the sixteenth century from a *hôtel* and owned by families of nobles, was bought in 1785 by Louis XVI for Marie Antoinette. In the aftermath of the Revolution of 1789, the château was declared to be state property and it was here that Napoléon Bonaparte was proclaimed as emperor of France and Napoléon III invested himself in December 1852 as emperor of the French. Queen Victoria visited the 1855 Exhibition and expressed her strong liking for French furniture.

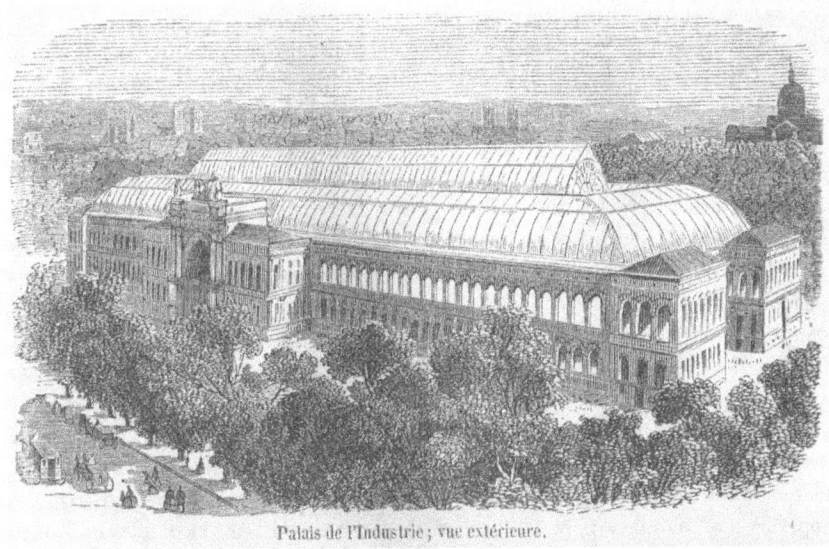

Figure 6.1 Le Palais de l'Industrie 1855. Wikimedia Creative Commons (public domain)

1867 Exposition universelle de Paris

Napoléon III decided in 1864 that the next *Exposition universelle* should be held in 1867, on a site of 50 ha on the Champ-de-Mars, a large open space on the Left Bank of the Seine adjacent to the former military training ground next to the eighteenth-century École Militaire (Figure 6.2).

Preparing for the exhibition involved the construction of an oval-shaped building 490 m × 380m surrounded by a designed garden. This stone and iron building took two years to construct employing 26,000 workers. It provided six thematic concentric galleries and a radial passage for exhibits by different nations, with a garden at its centre and a museum portraying the history of labour from prehistoric to modern times. Gustave Eiffel, then in his early thirties, was involved in the construction of the Galerie des Machines. On this occasion, scientific and technological exhibits were dominant with minimal space devoted to the fine arts. Walking from the entrance, visitors passed through massive exhibitions of agricultural and industrial products, before arriving at a small section devoted to the visual arts. Visitors saw the new, light and strong metal – aluminium. The American section included a display by Charles and Norton Otis of their lift, soon to be an essential component of new apartment buildings being constructed in Paris. While the managers of the exhibition wanted only a small showing of what it deemed the best paintings of France, artists themselves wanted some of their recent work on show. The strongest protest came from Gustave Courbet, who had also clashed earlier with the jury of the 1855 Exhibition who had accepted eleven of his paintings but refused space for three, his *A Burial at Ornans* (1849–50), *The Painter's Studio* (1854) and his portrait of Champfleury (1854), the writer and art critic who approved of Courbet's realistic work. Exasperated, Courbet set up his own exhibition at a site alongside the official *Exposition universelle* where he displayed forty of his pictures and four of his drawings. In 1867, Courbet again showed his level of dissatisfaction with officialdom, which had agreed to include just five of his paintings among the 684 works exhibited, by having his own private pavilion built close to the official exhibition as an alternative venue for a display of more than a hundred of his paintings gathered from museums and private collectors. During the winter of 1866–7, he painted a huge canvas *The Death of the Stag*, which portrays a lone animal against a larger contingent of men, horses and dogs – an image of the whip hand of power bringing the stag (figuratively representing Courbet himself) to bay. Another artist excluded from the *Exposition universelle* of 1867 was Édouard Manet who by then had already painted what were to become recognized later as masterpieces, such as *Music in the Tuileries* (1862), *Olympia* (1863) and *The Fifer* or *The Young Flautist* (1866). Like Courbet, Manet set up his own one-man show alongside the official exhibition.

The 1867 *Exposition* had almost 7 million visitors (among them the Queen of Portugal, the King of Belgium, the Tsar of Russia Alexandre II, the Prince of Wales and a large official Japanese delegation). It had more than 50,000 exhibitors with a marked imperial and colonial emphasis: the French displays stressed its colonies of Tunisia, Morocco and Algeria. The exhibition included an amusement park and fairground,

Palais de l'Exposition universelle de 1867, vu à vol d'oiseau.

Figure 6.2 L'Exposition universelle 1867. Wikimedia Creative Commons (public domain)

in order to widen its public appeal, and was the first *Exposition universelle* in Paris to include (native) people as exhibits: an Egyptian Bazaar had craftspeople and vendors of their artefacts as well as camels with their Arab keepers; an authentic Tunisian barber's shop; and various North African cafés with imported and authentic waiters and chefs. There were thus displays not only of material progress but also of people, especially colonial people. This exhibition was a physical statement about French national character and its world impact: it was a public proclamation of France's self-declared civilizing mission overseas.

Furthermore, the 1867 Exhibition was concerned not only with innovation and design style and with colonial impacts but also with improving the living conditions of the poor. One section was devoted to 'dwellings for the poor, constructed on sanitary principles and at small cost, and articles exhibited with the special object of improving the physical and moral condition of the people'. France erected six model dwellings, and there was also one by Prussia and one by Austria. This exhibition was significant in moving public debate away from design and architecture towards social and moral issues – themes which would be pursued further in later exhibitions.

These two exhibitions in 1855 and 1867 together attracted almost 12 million visitors. They were products in part of Napoléon III's wish to show proudly to the world the new imperial grandeur of Paris that he and Haussmann were creating. Under the Second Empire, the enhanced national and international reputation of Paris launched it into becoming a major tourist attraction – not only for French provincials but also for foreigners, among the latter in 1867 were some 12,000 English visitors brought from London by the enterprising travel company of Thomas Cook.

1878 *Exposition universelle de Paris*

The 1878 Exhibition was held on a 75-ha site on the Champ-de-Mars and in a purpose-built Palais de Trocadéro (also known as the Palais de Pierre), a vast concert hall where meetings of international organizations could be held during the exhibition. Large statues in its garden included one of a rhinoceros and another of an elephant. The Palais de Trocadéro was demolished in 1937 to make way for that year's *Exposition universelle*. In addition, the Palais de l'Exposition (also known as the Palais de Fer or the Palais du Champ-de-Mars) was a large rectangular building with an arcade running north-south. On one side were the exhibitions of different nations (Germany was the only major country not exhibiting, Prussia's defeat of France in 1871 being too recent in national memories), embracing examples of their domestic architectures (Figure 6.3). On the other side were exhibitions of France and its colonies. There was also a Galerie du Travail displaying the diversity of human labour. When the exhibition ended, various sections of the buildings were taken down and recycled by setting them up elsewhere in Paris and in the provinces. A novelty at this exhibition was a tethered balloon which took forty to fifty passengers up to a height of 500 m. A dozen flights daily provided visitors with startling views of the exhibition's footprint and of Paris generally.

This 1878 Exhibition was intended to show that France had recovered from its defeat by Prussia in 1870–1. In order to achieve its aim, it had to be grander than its predecessors. France was on show as a country of wealth and importance, clearly signalled in the Palais du Trocadéro on the crest of the Chaillot Hill facing the Champ-de-Mars. The building's elaborate and flamboyant design is judged by design historian Paul Greenhalgh to have reflected the splendour of French baroque architecture, thereby recalling a previous age of French power and confidence.

To project France as a major cultural centre of Europe (even, more ambitiously, of the world), much attention was given to architecture and the fine arts. One detailed example of this was the exhibition of some of Charles Marville's photographs of 'old' Paris alongside his images of the 'new' Haussmannized city, demonstrating the improvements that had been made to the cityscape since the 1850s. But the decisions taken about which paintings would be included were more political than artistic. This *Exposition* came only seven years after the Paris Commune in which prominent artists had been involved – including Courbet, who had self-exiled in Switzerland in May 1873 and died there on 31 December 1877, five months before the 1878 Exhibition opened, with just one of his paintings, a seascape *La Vague* (1870). Jean-François Millet, in the 1870s regarded by the establishment – mistakenly, some art historians have argued – as a negative social commentator because of his realist paintings of rural lives and landscapes, was completely excluded from the 1878 Exhibition having had ten of his paintings displayed in that of 1867. Among his paintings excluded were *L'Angélus* (1857–9) and *Les Glaneuses* (1857) both of which were to become highly appreciated by art collectors and endlessly copied for a popular market. The 1878 Exhibition – and the next two – had a substantial impact in broadcasting Orientalism in fine art and displaying Oriental lifestyles. Displays about colonies provided entertainment rather

Figure 6.3 Rue des Nations 1878. Wikimedia Creative Commons public domain photo in the Gallica Digital Library

than education. These imperial displays were located in facilities on the Chaillot Hill leading up to the Palais du Trocadéro. The French colonies occupied half the space, with other nations filling the rest. Many displays of imperial life included people from the colonies: for example, there was an Algerian bazaar, a Cairo Street with shops, a bazaar and many North Africans.

Like the two previous *Expositions universelles*, this one was funded by the national government and the Paris city council and by entrance fees. Among the 16 million visitors were 400,000 who had travelled from England under the aegis of the enterprising agency of Thomas Cook & Son. Even so, this exhibition made a heavy loss and the funding system was changed for subsequent exhibitions. Nonetheless, the 1878 Exhibition was hugely successful in boosting morale within France as well as its international standing.

1889 *Exposition universelle de Paris*

The 1889 Exhibition was unsurprisingly intended to mark the centenary of the French Revolution (Figure 6.4). But it proved to be controversial from its planning stage in the early 1880s. Neither the monarchist right nor the socialist left could be expected to support the Revolution wholeheartedly or to support a Republican-sponsored exhibition. Furthermore, France was now a republic surrounded by monarchies, so some doubted whether it was sensible for France to celebrate so ostentatiously its anti-monarchist character. Some thought it might be better to hold the next exhibition in 1900, to celebrate peace and to symbolize the material progress of the Industrial Revolution. Although invitations to participate in the exhibition had been issued in April 1887, only four nations had accepted them by 1 January 1888. By the end of that year, twenty-nine nations had accepted, four (including Germany) had declined completely and fourteen others (including Great Britain, Russia, Italy and Spain) eventually participated unofficially through private commissions. Queen Victoria recalled the British ambassador from Paris to London so that there could be no representative of the British government in Paris on the exhibition's inauguration day.

Organizers of the 1889 Exhibition stressed its apolitical character, excluding exhibits with political overtones. French socialists were denied their requests for their own special section and a purely workers' exhibit. They were denied because the organizers wanted to stress scientific and industrial progress more than controversial social developments. Exhibits with revolutionary references were prohibited: for example, a proposal to erect on the Champ-de-Mars a model of the Bastille sacked in 1789 was rejected but, as a compromise, it was permitted at a location just outside the official grounds of the exhibition.

Similarly, displays of French paintings reflected traditional, reactionary, Beaux Art taste and played down the development of the new art of the Impressionists and post-Impressionists (such as Camille Pissarro's paintings of Paris and Paul Gauguin's of Brittany). But the 1889 Exhibition, as also those of 1878 and 1900, brought thousands of examples of Oriental and North African art to Paris.

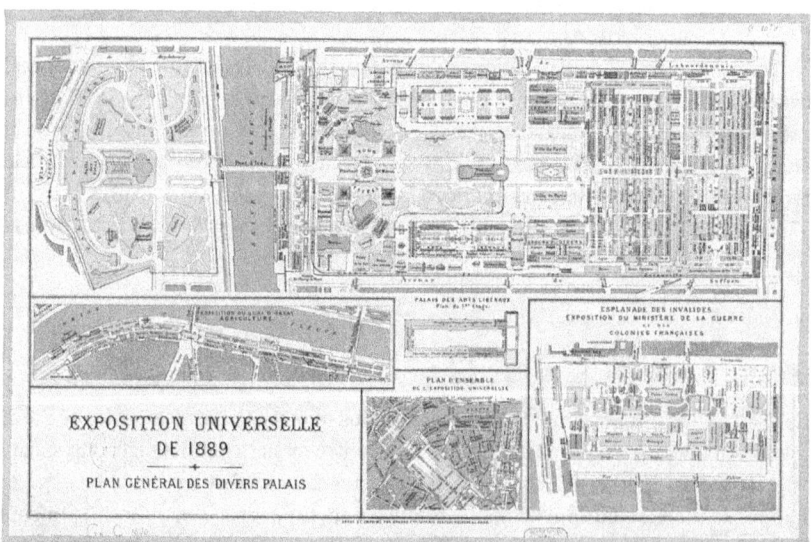

Figure 6.4 Plan of the Exposition universelle 1889. Wikimedia Creative Commons public domain photo in the Gallica Digital Library

Undoubtedly, the central attraction in 1889 was the Eiffel Tower. Funded one-fifth by the government and four-fifths by Gustave Eiffel's mortgaging his own company, this was a controversial project. It was both praised and hated by contemporaries. Eiffel said he wanted the opinions not of artists but of engineers and scientists. It became the triumphal arch of the exhibition and the international symbol of Paris and of France. The Tower could hold 10,000 people at once and when it first opened it had 20,000 visitors daily.

The largest building created at the 1889 Exhibition was the Galerie des Machines, at the opposite end of the Champ-de-Mars. This was a rectangular building covering 6 ha and its apex was 45 m high. Strongly influenced by the new technology introduced by Eiffel in bridge structures, the architects of the Galerie des Machines spanned the building with an unprecedented 115-m beam with a gigantic glazed roof balanced on twenty arches without immediately obvious support. Inside, an electrically driven raised platform carried 200 visitors at a time the length of the building, allowing a bird's-eye view of the gears, tie rods and whirligigs, the mechanical marvels of the age. Some thought this the most beautiful building of the exhibition, regarding it as 'a cathedral of the nineteenth century'. It was the last great engineering experiment to appear at *Expositions universelles* and was demolished in 1909 in order to open up the view towards the Champ-de-Mars.

Less spectacular were the Palais des Beaux Arts et des Arts Libéraux and the Palais des Industries. There were also about fifty restaurants, bars and cafés. Visitors could enjoy the view from the Champ-de-Mars across the Seine to the Trocadéro Palace with its horticultural exhibits around its central fountains. In the gardens, more than forty small but highly detailed constructions depicted the history of human habitation (Figure 6.5). There were also agricultural pavilions exhibiting food products from across the world.

The idea of progress underpinned this exhibition. Ten thousand of Edison's latest invention, the incandescent electric bulb, highlighted this concept. Using electricity allowed the exhibition to be open at night and provided spectacular illuminations of the Eiffel Tower and of the fountains in the garden. The exhibition was fundamentally a spectacle but it included also aural surprises. Musical entertainment was provided in a familiar way by bands serenading passers-by from bandstands; much less familiar but also pleasurable was cultural and dance music played by performers from foreign countries, such as Romania and Java; but most different and novel was the opportunity to listen to music played on Edison's phonograph in the Galerie des Machines and strangest and most exciting of all was the sound of live musical performances in Paris that could be listened to in the pavilion of the private Société générale des téléphones on the recently invented telephone system.

Many visitors must have been thrilled by the spectacle. One expressed his joy passionately, declaring: 'This is not a Parisian place but a fairyland that transports you to Arabia, the Far East, and the banks of the mysterious Congo in one day.' France's colonial empire was presented in huts, bazaars and cafés attended by hundreds of native people demonstrating their various crafts and skills as well as offering folk music, singing and dancing. The contributions of France and its colonies, forming the core of the exhibition, sprawled in pavilions sited on 40 ha between the Champ-de-Mars and the Trocadéro. They brought to Paris the sounds, sights, tastes and smells of the different cultures to be found in the French empire and beyond. A massive display of native villages was erected on the Chaillot Hill: the most popular were the Senegalese, the Congolese, New Caledonians and Gabonese, and settlements from Cochin-China and Java. The international flavour of the 1889 Exhibition was highlighted in its official guide which informed visitors that, while Jules Verne had imagined in his 1872 novel travelling around the world in eighty days, visitors could do this on the Champ-de-Mars in six hours.

The exhibition included some astonishing features – astonishing to us today but probably even more so to its visitors. One such was a human zoo – *'le village nègre'* – of forty native colonial people not brought to serve as exotic demonstrators of craft goods or as waiters or servants but, instead, simply to be observed as exotic specimens of humanity, as a human zoo. Their presence reflected the rise of anthropology and geography as academic disciplines in the closing decades of the nineteenth century.

Then there was also Buffalo Bill's Wild West Show, with Annie Oakley and her gun. And included among exhibits was the first modern *brassière* – in effect, a corset cut into two – invented by Herminie Cadolle. Born in Beaugency in the Loire Valley in 1842 and migrating in the 1860s to Paris with her husband and young child to work as a corset maker, she died in 1926 at Saint-Cloud to the west of Paris. She was an activist during the Paris Commune of 1871, promoting the feminist *Union des Femmes pour la défense de Paris et les soins aux blessées*. She experimented with corset design during the Commune, to find a way of making women more comfortable when fighting on the barricades.

For the duration of the 1889 Exhibition, from 5 May until 31 October, Paris exhibited a carnival spirit, contributing to the post-war regeneration of France. It had approaching

Figure 6.5 'History of habitation' by Charles Garnier at the 1889 Exposition universelle. The dwellings shown are (from left to right) Scandinavian, Romanian and Renaissance. Photographer unknown

30 million visitors when the population of Paris itself was just over 2 million. Many visitors came from other countries but the exhibition was undoubtedly very popular with French provincials keen to see and experience the capital, a sentiment which pleased the central government as an antidote to the increasingly outspoken advocates of regional separatism. At a banquet in mid-August for over 13,000 French officials and mayors, President Carnot referred to the exhibition as the centennial celebration of political liberty and social justice.

Thirty-five countries participated in the 1889 Exhibition. It cost 42 million francs but achieved an income of 50 million francs. The national government contributed 17 million francs, the municipal authority of Paris 8 million francs, while the balance was guaranteed by the banks which recouped their investments by selling books of admissions tickets (Figure 6.6) which as an additional incentive doubled as lottery tickets for draws projected as far forward as 1964! The colonies were asked by the French government to contribute and there was also some income from rents paid for space given over to private pavilions. Subsequent exhibitions followed the successful funding model employed in 1889.

This exhibition was proudly used to reaffirm France as a nation both to its own citizens and to the world. It was a celebration of science and art and an affirmation of the belief in material progress and its ability to alleviate suffering. One visitor's verdict was that 1889 gave to the poor the enjoyments of luxury and to the ignorant something of the dazzlements of science. The 1889 Exhibition marked the zenith of nineteenth-century optimism in Paris and in France – but this celebratory mood was dampened in 1891 by a major influenza epidemic which killed about 1 million people worldwide, then in 1891–3 by the Panama financial scandal which damaged some 80,000 French investors, and from 1894 by the socially divisive Dreyfus Affair with its toxic combination of a miscarriage of justice and anti-Semitism.

1900 *Exposition universelle de Paris*

Planning for the 1900 Exhibition began eight years earlier. It was opened by the French president, Émile Loubet, on 14 April and closed on 12 November. During seven months, it had more than 50 million visitors (when the total population of France was 41 million). Thomas Cook & Son claimed to have taken 1,000 people a day from England, with many of them staying in hotels specially erected for the company's excursionists. The 1900 Exhibition was a page-turning event, a celebration of the closing of the nineteenth century and the opening of a new one. Countries around the world were invited to exhibit their achievements and lifestyles, enabling visitors to compare their similarities and differences. The 112-ha site of the exhibition was located mainly on the Esplanade des Invalides, the Chaillot Hill and the Champ-de-Mars, on both the Left and the Right Banks. Additionally, there was in the Bois de Vincennes in eastern Paris an overflow site for agricultural exhibits, workers' housing and events of the world's Second Olympic Games. Ultimately, forty countries displayed 83,000 exhibits, with France accounting for almost half of them. The French government maintained control over the official French exhibits but not over those from other countries. This led to dissatisfaction by some French manufacturers who therefore set up some private exhibitions (e.g. by Mouët and Chandon to publicize its champagne and by the Printemps and the Bon Marché department stores to promote their extensive ranges of merchandise).

Many visitors to the 1900 Exhibition came by train, using the newly opened Gare d'Orsay line from Orléans to Paris built specifically to serve the exhibition. Two bicycle parks totalling 1,000 m^2 were provided, reflecting the vigorous adoption of cycling in France during the closing decades of the nineteenth century. The year 1900 also saw the first line of the Métro opened in July, from Porte de Vincennes in the east of Paris to Porte Maillot in the west, designed to service the world's Second Olympic Games in the Bois de Vincennes. Attractions at the exhibition included a 3-km moving footpath (with two lanes at different speeds, of 4.2 and 8.5 km/h) and a cinema of the Lumière brothers, with a giant screen 21 m × 16 m.

The pavilions of foreign countries were set up as the Rue des Nations: they were built only to last for the duration of the exhibition and so were constructed using jute fibre, plaster of Paris and cement. Two much more substantial and enduring new buildings for exhibits were Le Petit Palais and Le Grand Palais built on the site of the 1855 Palais de l'Industrie and des Beaux Arts. These two exhibition halls focused on the history of art from its origins to 1900 and included not only paintings but also ivory carvings, tapestry, metal work, jewellery, porcelain and furniture. The selection of paintings for display was undertaken by the relatively progressive art critic Roger

Figure 6.6 Admission Ticket for the Exposition universelle 1900. Wikimedia Creative Commons (public domain)

Marx (1859–1913). As Greenhalgh (1988, p. 206) has emphasized, 'his selection traced the struggle between romanticism and classicism, the rise of realism and naturalism and the subsequent development of impressionism and post-impressionism'. The display included works by Manet, Monet, Renoir, Pissarro, Sisley, Seurat, Gaugin and Cézanne. With this rich selection from the immediate past, Greenhalgh (1988, p. 206) argued, 'Marx introduced the avant-garde into the Exposition in an historical context outside the immediate control of the Beaux Arts. Modernism had crept in, as it were, when the academy was not looking.'

The Petit Palais, built between October 1897 and April 1900, drew on seventeenth- and eighteenth-century architectural styles (Figure 6.7). The Petit Palais stands today, housing the Musée des Beaux Arts de la Ville de Paris (complemented by the Musée nationale de l'Orangerie, on a terrace the Tuileries Gardens, in the building which Napoléon had built in 1852 to overwinter the citrus trees from the gardens and which today accommodates Impressionist and post-Impressionist paintings). The Grand Palais was also constructed from 1897 to 1900, after demolition of the 1855 Palais de l'Industrie. In the Beaux-Arts architectural style as taught by the École des Beaux-Arts of Paris, it featured ornate decoration of its stone facades. The building had a roof of iron and glass and a wrought-iron frame surrounded by masonry (including the novel use of reinforced concrete). The Grand Palais provoked controversy, some seeing it as an unhappy compromise of old and new styles. Its exterior was a Classical stone facade with lots of *art nouveau* ironwork and sculptures. Some likened it to the railway stations built earlier in the century in Paris. The Grand Palais represented two contrasting views of the world: one by traditional architects and one by new engineers. In addition to displaying art in its various forms, it was used during the exhibition to demonstrate innovation and modernity, for example, in aviation, automobiles and household appliances. Today, there is a central police station in the basement while the main building is used for major art exhibitions and varied other purposes, such as fencing competitions, and in 2017 the Tour de France went through it en route to the Champs-Elysées in the final stage to promote Paris's bid for the 2024 Summer Olympics.

Following precedent set in earlier *Expositions universelles*, that of 1900 included a gigantic banquet to which were invited all the 36,172 mayors of France. Held in the gardens of the Tuileries, the 20,777 mayors who attended enjoyed a meal of eight courses (*Hors d'Oeuvres, Darnes de saumon glacées Parisienne, Filet de boeuf en Belleville, Pains de caneton de Rouen, Poulardes de Bresses rôties, Ballotines de faisans Saint-Hubert, Salade Potel, Glaces Succès-Condés* and *Dessert*) washed down with four wines (*Preignac en carafes* or *Saint Julien en carafes, Haut-Sauternes, Beaune-Margaux J. Calvet 1887* and *Champagne Montebello*).

Five *Expositions universelles*: The whole greater than the sum of its parts?

State policies dominated the first five *Expositions universelles*. The first two were stamped with Napoléon III's determination to boost France into becoming a progressive industrial state, like England. The third (1878) lacked such confidence and idealism: it struggled to show both foreigners and the French themselves that national recovery from the humiliating 1870–1 Prussian defeat and from the horror of the Commune of 1871 was complete. Napoléon III had used the exhibitions of 1855 and 1867 to court the feared and 'dangerous' working class. For the 1867 Exhibition, free travel by train to Paris was provided for visitors from the provinces nominated by their mayors and commune councils. Free lodgings were provided for 67,000 people on the site during the seven months of the exhibition. There was a consequential flood of provincials into Paris, in many cases of people with little travelling experience and who would never otherwise have travelled to Paris.

Like the two previous exhibitions, that of 1878 was paid for by the national government and the Paris city council and by entrance fees. But that of 1878 made a heavy financial loss, so the funding model was changed for subsequent exhibitions. The first two exhibitions, those of 1855 and 1867, attracted visitors because of their sheer novelty but for later ones additional attractions were provided as popular entertainment. They encouraged social and cultural mixing: fine arts, opera and *haute couture* were on offer but so also were fairground stalls, joy rides, trinket sellers, popular sports, bandstands, music halls and buskers.

In sum, the five exhibitions attracted over 100 million visitors. Alain Corbin suggests that in an era fascinated by exploration – and, one could add, empire – a trip to the exhibitions in Paris was for many akin to a world tour. The exhibitions educated visitors but also entertained them: visitors were regarded both as citizens and as consumers, with the emphasis shifting from the former in the earlier exhibitions to the latter in later ones. The second most visited exhibit in 1900 was the Palace of Fashion and the entrance to the exhibition was dominated by *La Parisienne*, a 5-m-tall model of a woman wearing the latest creations of Parisian *haute couture*. From 1855 onwards, there was a gradual drift in the exhibitions towards entertainment so that by 1900 the emphasis was more on pleasure than on education. The later exhibitions offered fairground rides and stalls, musical and comic troupes, sellers of food and of souvenir trinkets, becoming reminiscent of medieval and early modern markets and festivals. The exhibitions recalled France's national heritage but added new features

Figure 6.7 Le Petit Palais and Le Grand Palais in 1900, looking towards the Pont Alexandre III. Wikimedia Creative Commons (public domain)

reflecting new technologies (e.g. brass band concerts and joy rides) and new countries (such as native villages from all parts of the French empire) and also some displaying groups of people housed in 'colonial' surroundings where they lived for six months, preparing their own meals, performing cultural rituals and demonstrating their native arts and crafts.

From that of 1867 onwards, exhibitions included these 'human zoos' as *tableaux-vivants*, transforming human beings into objects: visitors paid to observe them as exotic creatures who provided unfamiliar sights, sounds and smells of Asian and African cultures.

By 1900, the entertainment aspects of exhibitions had become so considerable that those of education, commerce and national propaganda were disguised as pleasurable activities; otherwise, it was thought the targeted masses might pay them little attention. The 1889 and 1900 Exhibitions in particular offered respite from the many social, economic and political anxieties that were pervasive in France during the closing decades of the nineteenth century. They moved Paris towards acceptance of the idea of pleasure and leisure, even of hedonism, preparing the way for a cultural laissez-faire period which Dominique Halifa has described as 'a privileged moment in French history', marked by peace, scientific and economic progress, prestigious cultural achievements but also – and perhaps above all – by the triumph of a certain lifestyle, characterized by *'la gaieté et l'insouciance autant que par l'esprit'* of the decades around 1900 now termed the Belle Époque. Halifa's search for what he calls the 'true history' of the Belle Époque confirms that the appellation was applied retrospectively in the 1930s, by looking with hindsight from that standpoint and comparing the two decades on either side of 1900 with those which had witnessed the Great War and the Great Depression.

These exhibitions offered for many visitors a chimerical escape from their quotidian realities. Until the 1880s, the exhibitions stressed material progress and technological innovation as the highway to the dream of a better life. Thereafter, their emphasis was less on reality and more on fantasy. The Paris Exhibition of 1900 was the most developed example of an exhibition as an imagined paradise: it made spectacular use of electricity in conjunction with water cascades, mirrors and glass to create arresting landscapes. Architectural styles and devices were used to astonish visitors (e.g. India had a princely palace packed with opulent produce and exotically dressed Indians as serving attendants). The aims of the exhibitions were to provide surprises, to educate visitors and to promote understanding of France as a new-style imperial country. But their aim also became increasingly to entertain. These World Fairs incrementally became colossal funfairs while showcasing Paris as the capital of France and even perhaps of the world. The self-referential official theme of the 1900 Exhibition was 'Paris, Capital of the Civilised World'.

Most of these five exhibitions left long-lasting or permanent architectural legacies: for example, the Palais de l'Industrie (1855–1900); the Palais de Trocadéro (1878–1937); the Eiffel Tower (1889–); the Galerie des Machines (1889–1910); the Grand Palais and the Petit Palais, and the first Métro stations (1900–). But perhaps the longest-lasting and most significant legacy of these five *Expositions universelles* was their underscoring of the developing image of Paris by 1914 as a multifaceted world city, as a city of modernity and innovation, and as a city of pleasure and leisure.

From the mid-nineteenth century to the start of the Great War, France was the leading nation in organizing World Fairs: France held five, the United States (1876, 1893, 1898, 1904) and Belgium (1897, 1905, 1910, 1913) each held four, Great Britain (1851, 1862) two, and Austria (1873), Australia (1880), Spain (1888) and Italy (1906) each held one. Both Imperial and Republican regimes in France shared the conviction that the country was and should be the world's leader in many or most or even all fields of human endeavour. Nineteenth-century Paris was undoubtedly the most exhibitionist of the world's cities. A recent collection of essays edited by Hollis Clayson exploring the representations of Paris between 1850 and 1950 in a broad range of media, including painting, printmaking and photography, has argued that it was the capacity of Paris to put itself on display that was the foundation of the city's global reputation and mythic power. That self-proclaimed image was reinforced by foreign observers and made Paris the epicentre of modernity internationally.

7

Enjoying Paris: Food, fashion and fun

'The right to idleness'

The titanic transformation of the built form of Paris from the 1850s attracted both admiration and antipathy, from Parisians themselves, from provincial and foreign tourists and from professional urbanists worldwide. The changing landscape of the city was a physical spectacle. The development of artificial lighting meant that the theatrical spectacle of day-time street life continued into the night. Gas lighting was introduced to Paris in 1823, in galleries of the Palais-Royal, and was then gradually installed in other public squares and streets. Gas eclipsed oil lighting gradually during the 1830s and 1840s but by the1850s thousands of street lamps had been installed. It was, according to Hollis Clayson (2019, p. 4), the 1850s and 1860s that made a great impact, ushering in 'arresting and abundant gaslight, whose practical and symbolic benefits were much remarked and generally well liked'. In the 1840s, Paris experimented with artificial electric lighting: in 1840–4, the Place de la Concorde saw the introduction of arc lights which produced a glaring white light which contrasted with the darker, softer, light of fluttering, orange, gas lights. But it was not until the 1870s that electric arc lighting was generally adopted, providing the public squares and streets of Paris with effective nocturnal illumination (Figure 7.1).The provision of more and better lighting in public places was one of Haussmann's cherished ambitions, an integral part of his project to transform a dark and dangerous old Paris into a fully spectacularized and functionally efficient and safe capital. The public face of Paris – its cityscape – was altered almost beyond recognition, supplying both a promise of exciting social entertainment and a reassurance of personal safety and security. More light meant more nocturnal activity and, it was hoped, less crime. Symbolically, the provision of public lighting represented a triumph over social and cultural 'darkness'. Clayson, in her recent book *Illuminated Paris* – with an introduction tellingly titled 'Paris, City of Éclairage' rather than 'Paris, City of Light' – has shown how the continuing improvement in the lighting of public places, both outdoors and indoors, during the course of the nineteenth century promoted a lively nocturnal culture and a fresh artistic response to the city. One of Clayson's (2019, p. 182) central arguments is 'that qualities of urban lighting, and a related sensitivity to contrasts of dark and lightness, shaped the definition of the tell-tale visual and social qualities of the French capital on the part of a number of

Figure 7.1 Electric lighting on the Champ-de-Mars 1878. Charles Marville

innovative artists oriented toward modern life between about 1860 and 1890' – both French artists like Édouard Manet and Edgar Degas and American artists like John Singer Sargent and Charles Courtney Curran painted the vivacious nightlife of the city in strong colours and contrasts under the new lighting conditions, as did also Henri de Toulouse-Lautrec in his lithographed posters. Themes of leisure and entertainment dominated the great years of Impressionist painting between 1865 and 1885: cafés, opera houses, theatres, racing tracks, parks and riversides were, as Robert Herbert has stressed, frequently depicted by artists, thereby capturing for posterity the leisure activities and festivities of late-nineteenth-century Parisians. Paintings and posters, novels and magazines have been meticulously mined by Charles Rearick to produce a colourfully illustrated account of the gamut of Parisian pleasures in the Belle Époque.

The evolving townscape of Paris served as a stage for a continuously changing human spectacle. This is depicted vividly in paintings of the city by Camille Pissarro which highlight traffic, motion, work, transport, exchange, unloading, loading, buying, selling and walking. The activities of hundreds of people dominate his Parisian scenes, with architecture and urban spaces serving as physical frames for human pageants. Similar portrayals of urban commotion are portrayed in many works of literature set in nineteenth-century Paris. Some depict specifically the *flâneur* and the practice of *flânerie* – of strolling, just observing and enjoying the ever-changing visual parade of people, and doing so at leisure and for pleasure, relishing its diversity, its perpetual motion and the opportunity it provided for chance encounters.

This was the city as spectacle, open to a mobile, mainly male, bourgeois gaze. Idealized depictions of *flâneurs* are presented in two illustrations in Louis Huart's *Physiologie du flâneur* (1841): each portrays a lone bourgeois man with a top hat, waistcoat, coat and cane standing in a controlled, leisured, satisfied and almost dream-like pose and comfortable in gazing at his surroundings – and, in some cases, especially at women. A poet Charles Baudelaire (1821–1867) was the quintessential *flâneur*: a bohemian, he spent years strolling in the Latin Quarter on the Left Bank and, drawing on that experience, wrote two works of poetry: *Les Fleurs du Mal* (1857) and *Le Spleen de Paris* (1869). Nancy Forgione has argued that the practice of *flânerie* involved a coherent intertwining of body, mind and soul, a combination which artists and photographers endeavoured to capture in their portrayals of strolling in late-nineteenth-century Paris. Priscella Ferguson has suggested that *flâneurs* emerged on the streets and in the narratives of Paris in the early nineteenth century but began to decline from mid-century with the increasing commodification and rationalization of urban space: Ferguson (1994, p. 112) has contended that 'a democratised *flânerie* opened the city to anyone with a bit of leisure time at his (and now also her) disposal'. Idle inactivity unredeemed by creativity of any sort was no longer the prerogative of bourgeois males.

For long, historians focused on the role of *flâneurs* but increasingly have turned their attention to *flâneuses* and their distinctive reading of the city both in literature and paintings and in reality on the streets and in the parks. Single women did not enjoy the social freedom that men had to move about the city, observing and being observed, but never interacting with others. In 1831, when the novelist and journalist George Sand (1804–1876), born in Paris but brought up by her grandmother in provincial Berry on the north-western margins of the Massif Central, sought to widen her horizons by experiencing life in Paris and connecting with the intellectual and artistic culture of the capital: she dressed as a young man in order to claim the ambulant freedom she knew young women did not have in Paris. It was not acceptable for women to stroll alone in the city. Janet Wolff has argued that, unlike the *flâneur*, the *flâneuse* was invisible in the literature of modernity which recognized lone women as prostitutes, widows, old ladies, lesbians or murder victims. Some have suggested that department stores from the 1850s allowed women to become *flâneuses*, browsing among their displays but not necessarily making purchases – the pretence of shopping provided a socially sanctioned cover for respectable women to browse and gaze in public. If, as Ferguson argued, the native Parisian *flâneur* or *flâneuse* became virtually extinct by the end of the nineteenth century, some twentieth- and twenty-first-century guidebooks for foreign tourists in Paris – such as Edmund White's *The Flâneur: A Stroll through the Paradoxes of Paris* (2008) – are grounded in the belief that Paris (especially classic Paris in the parallelogram defined by the Arc de Triomphe and the Eiffel Tower to the west and the Place de la Bastille and the Panthéon in the east) is a world meant to be seen by idlers, for only a strolling pace permits the rich details of Paris and Parisians to be appreciated.

Paris as spectacle was foregrounded on the 14 July 1880 which saw the first modern Bastille Day commemorative celebration of the Revolution of 1789. Following the loss of the Franco-Prussian War of 1870–1, the ensuing civil war of 1871, the economic slump from 1876 to 1879 and the *Exposition universelle* of 1878, the national Republican government decided the time had come to boost people's morale. An immediate opportunity to do so was provided by the approaching centenary of the 1789 Revolution. There was to be a new secular and republican celebration in the summer, in contrast to traditional religious and royalist celebrations which largely avoided the summer harvesting season. It was an anticlerical weapon in the deep-seated culture war in France which gathered momentum in the 1880s and 1890s. Festivities on 14 July 1880 ushered in two decades of jubilant celebration and joyful recreation – labelled as *le fin de siècle* by contemporaries but renamed with hindsight in the more austere 1920s and 1930s as *la Belle Époque*. These sentiments underpinned the *Expositions universelles* held in 1889 and 1900. From the 1860s onwards, and especially from the 1880s, there was a burgeoning of choral societies, of brass bands and of sports clubs in Paris and in many parts of provincial France. The expansion of leisure and recreation progressed as working hours were reduced and as standards of living improved. Until the 1890s, most industries and craft enterprises had working days of eleven or twelve hours but by the turn of the century a ten-hour day had become common. But most workers also spent considerable time each day travelling – mostly walking – between home and workplace. In addition, many workers were employed only by the day or for short periods of time rather than permanently. 'Leisure time' was essentially a bourgeois concept about which many of the working class in the nineteenth century could only dream. In 1880, the anticlerical Republican government abolished legal sanctions which specified the seventh day of the week as a time of rest from work; instead, Sunday was to be a day like any other, so the demand for more leisurely entertainments encouraged an increase in its supply during the closing decades of the nineteenth century. Before the normalization of Sunday as a working day, some workers had in any event preferred to have what they called 'Saint Monday' as their one non-working weekday, not least because it required fewer formalities like attending church services and wearing Sunday-best clothes. For some, it had become a day of 'idleness' to recover from the exertions and excesses of the previous days.

Some leisure activities were simple and cheap, like sauntering along the parapets of the *quais* of the Seine idly examining the cases of the *bouqinistes et bouquineurs* (second-hand booksellers and lovers of old books). The growing demand for more *liberté* was fed by the greater commercialization of leisure. Free time and recreation came gradually to be claimed as practical expressions of the revolutionary principles of liberty, equality and fraternity. The right to idleness was first asserted in 1880 by Paul Lafargue (1842–1911), a Cuban-born Marxist doctor, journalist and writer (and Marx's son-in-law, having married his second daughter, Laura), who was brought at the age of nine by his parents to live in France. Following his secondary schooling at

Bordeaux (his father's birthplace), he moved to Paris to study medicine. *Le Droit à la paresse* (1880) was the title of his powerful attack on the work ethic and the social inequalities of leisure. More leisure time gained from shorter working hours gradually opened more doors to commercial entertainments and private pleasures. From the 1860s onwards, many guidebooks to Paris commodified the city as 'the capital of pleasure'. H. A. de Conty's 1863 pocket guide to Paris for the stranger dubbed it 'the city of pleasure and pleasures *par excellence*'. Richard Davis, an American, in his book *About Paris* (1895), wrote: 'Americans go to London for social triumph or to float railroad shares, to Rome for art's sake, but they go to Paris to enjoy themselves.'

Some pleasures of nineteenth-century Parisians were simply observing some of the city's singularities and surprises. Public tours of the new sewers – of *'un second Paris souterrain'* – were offered during the *Exposition universelle* of 1867. Visitors descended into the sewers on an elegant iron spiral staircase and then travelled on luxury versions of the vehicles used to cleanse the sewers. Guidebooks assured ladies that they could take the tour of forty-five minutes or so 'without fatigue or fear of anything not clean', while a writer in *Harper's Weekly*, an American political magazine, in April 1893 reported that ladies dressed fashionably on the tour 'in stylish costumes, light bonnets, and high heels'. Another extraordinary subterranean experience, available for organized public groups from 1807, was a visit to the underground ossuary of Paris: the *catacombes*, dating from the late eighteenth century, provided an unusual venue for private events such as concerts and from 1874 were opened to visits by individual members of the public. Old underground quarries of building stone and gypsum in the *14ᵉ arrondissement* were used to store and display millions of bones removed from churchyards and cemeteries closed on public health grounds.

Another popular visiting place was the new morgue, a neo-Greek mausoleum built in 1804, sited on the Île de la Cité on the Quai du Marché-Neuf at the corner of the Pont Saint-Michel, not far from the Notre-Dame cathedral. This building stood in the way of Haussmann's project to widen the route from the Boulevard Sébastopol across the Île de la Cité to the Place Saint-Michel. So, in 1864, the 1804 building was demolished and a new and larger morgue, in design resembling a Greek temple, was constructed on the point behind Notre-Dame on the Quai de l'Archevêché. It flew a *tricolore* flag from its roof and its stonework was inscribed, like so many public buildings, *Liberté, Égalité, Fraternité*. A plaque on its wall invited visitors to enter free of charge. Its serious purpose was to display cadavers behind a glass panel to enable visitors to identify them. At the end of the nineteenth century, the morgue was attracting many curious visitors, mainly French but also some foreign tourists: each year from the mid-1860s to the late 1870s the morgue received between 565 and 786 visitors. In 1907, free admission was ended as a measure of 'moral hygiene' – thereafter, prior authorization had to be obtained by those wishing to visit.

Another singularity for those possessing the necessary curiosity as well as leisure time were the Abattoirs de la Villette. Constructed in the 1860s, their site including the meat market occupied 39 ha and was served by two branch-line train stations. Its market shared with Les Halles a key role in the provisioning of Paris. According to Edward Lucas, author of *A Wanderer in Paris* (1911), the Paris *Daily Mail* was 'diurnally anxious' that its English and American readers should make a tour of these abattoirs. Karl Baedeker's handbook for travellers to *Paris and its Environs* (fifteenth revised edition, 1904) noted that visitors were freely admitted to the market, 'a busy scene' of three large pavilions, the central one capable of containing 5,080 oxen, the one on the right about 2,000 calves and 5,800 pigs and that on the left 31,000 sheep. The abattoirs were on the other side of the Canal de l'Ourcq: 'Although they are not public', reported Baedeker (1904, p. 236), 'strangers are normally permitted to walk around. The busiest time here is in the morning, but the scene is not one which will attract many visitors.'

Practising the right to idleness, to leisure, to enjoyment in Paris will now be viewed here selectively, through the three complementary optics of food, fashion and fun.

Food: *haute cuisine*

Coffee houses flourished in Paris during the eighteenth century but after the 1789 Revolution many new cafés opened offering the excitingly novel 'colonial' drinks of coffee, tea and chocolate, and also ice creams and sorbets, but not yet food. The most renowned café in the early nineteenth century was *Le Procope*, established in 1674 by an Italian, Francesco Procopio, on the Rue du Tournon; it moved in 1684 to the Rue de l'Ancienne-Comédie. This was the first café in Paris: it closed in1890 but reopened in the 1920s as a restaurant and welcomes customers to this day (Figure 7.2), maximizing its historical context to attract them – it was frequented by intellectuals like Voltaire and Rousseau and by revolutionaries like Danton and Robespierre.

In 1800, cafés were indoor venues where people met to relax and to socialize. Different cafés tended to become meeting places for specific social groups or professions. From the 1850s, the café became an increasingly important social institution, commanding loyalty of its clients and becoming associated with particular sets of views (political, occupational or recreational – there were, e.g., cafés where the clientele was dominantly anticlerical or construction workers or members of cycling clubs or musical societies). Cafés were, of course, drinking places but as important was gossiping, discussing and socializing with like-minded people (Figure 7.3).

Many cafés provided entertainment intermittently, such as ballad singers, accordionists, dancers, conjurors, puppet shows, song birds, caricaturists (*grimaciers*) and flower sellers. With the creation of the boulevards from the 1850s, cafés came out onto the sidewalk. By the late 1840s, Paris had 4,500 cafés; by 1870, 22,000 – their number peaked probably in 1885 when there were more than 40,000; by 1900, the number was down to about 27,000. While many customers frequented cafés for recreational, non-necessitous, drinking, it was also the case that many, probably most, workers in nineteenth-century Paris spent a considerable time walking from home to and from their place of work and relied on cafés for nourishment stops. Café culture enriched the social lives of many working Parisians.

Towards the end of the eighteenth and the start of the nineteenth centuries, some *restaurants* (literally 'restoring places') were opened by cooks from no-longer existing

Figure 7.2 Le Café Procope. Wikimedia Creative Commons Attribution Share Alike 3.0/ ich selbst

noble and aristocratic households which had fled from revolutionary Paris to the provinces or abroad. This marked the birth of the restaurant as a public place to sit down for a meal, at that time a European novelty. In low-cost restaurants, customers seated themselves at the single guest table, joining other customers already seated, while at more expensive restaurants customers were guided by a waiter to separate tables with laundered table cloths and napkins. The first named restaurant in Paris was opened near to the Louvre in 1765, by a Mr Baker (M. Boulanger) who invited people to his establishment with the following entreaty on his signboard: *Venite ad me omnes qui stomacho laboratis et ego vos restaurabo* (Come to me all who are hungry and I will restore you). He served his guests different meat soups and was taken to court for doing so by *charcutiers* (pork butchers) for breaking what they regarded as their monopoly. The *charcutiers* lost their case and consequently the number of restaurants multiplied in the centre of Paris, in the commercial *quartiers* near the Halles and the Palais-Royal.

The first restaurants to provide *à la carte* menus were those patronized by *députés* (politicians) of the National Assembly. In 1789, there were perhaps a hundred such restaurants in the locality of the Palais-Royal and Les Halles and by 1820 perhaps 3,000 throughout Paris. Two farming brothers from Lorraine – *les frères Véry* – opened a restaurant in 1790 in the arcades of the Palais-Royal. Jean-Robert Pitte has used a rare printed menu from that year to indicate the wide range of foods and wines offered in this expensive restaurant. It listed eleven soups, six fish *entrées*, thirty-four hot meat dishes, ten cold meat salads, twenty vegetable dishes, eleven desserts, fourteen wines (most of which had been brought to Paris by river boats from Burgundy) and eleven liqueurs.

In the early nineteenth century, most restaurants were located in the cultural heart of Paris, around the Palais-Royal. They then spread to the boulevards to the west and in the 1850s and 1860s to Haussmann's new boulevards. A survey of restaurants in 1850 listed forty-five on the Right Bank and only five on the Left Bank; of the former, most were concentrated in the triangle delimited by the Palais-Royal, the Opéra and the Boulevard Poissonnière. From the 1870s, the number of restaurants expanded with more offering an *à la carte* menu and/or one that was *prix fixe:* menus to suit differing tastes and differing abilities to pay. In 1900, in its chapter on 'Paris la nuit', *Le Guide de Paris* encouraged visitors to the *Exposition universelle* to enjoy not only the city's many theatres, music halls and cabarets but also one or more of the sixty-seven restaurants

Figure 7.3 Café discussion of the Franco-Prussian War 1870. Illustrated London News of 17 September 1870.

in its list. By 1900, Paris had about 1,500 restaurants and about 27,000 cafés and wine shops: Michael Marrus has calculated that in 1900 Paris had more places for drinking (many of them for what he terms 'non-necessitous', social, drinking not accompanied by meals) than any other major city in the world – one for every 100 residents. For Theodore Zeldin, the cafés were to the late nineteenth century what the salons had been to the eighteenth century, but a democratization of them: an opportunity for relaxed socialization.

When the Revolution of 1789 annulled the monopoly of brewers for selling beer, *brasseries* offering beer and food emerged to compete with cafés. Many offered luxurious surroundings and artistic decors: solid oak tables replaced the marbled tables of cafés and were complemented by massive wood carvings, ancient *tapisseries* on the walls, ceramic tile decorations and coloured glass ornamentations. Some reflected the impact of the *art nouveau* movement, with its floral, vegetal and curving designs. All of which created a refined experience, with German beers providing an additional *caché*. The 1855 and 1867 *Expositions universelles* promoted foreign products, including German beers, while that of 1867 introduced a new concept, that of a *brasserie* with only female staff, a novelty soon adopted throughout Paris. After the war with Prussia in 1870–1, a new wave of Alsatian-style *brasseries* swept into Paris to counter the loss of Alsace and taking advantage of the railway opened in 1854 from Strasbourg to the capital to import beer – to be accompanied by the 'classic' Alsatian dish, *la choucroute*.

The service offered in the early restaurants in Paris followed that of the French nobility: *le service à la française* (with different dishes all served simultaneously). But that gave way during the nineteenth century to *le service à la russe* (with different dishes served sequentially), this having been introduced by Prince Alexandre Kourakine, the Russian ambassador to France in Paris from 1808 to 1812. This Russian style of service became fashionable and spread throughout France and indeed much of Europe, with the rise of gastronomy.

The word *gastronomie* seems to have been used for the first time in 1801 in a poem. The first guide to Parisian restaurants was published in 1803 by Alexandre Grimod de la Reynière: his *L'Almanach des Gourmets* went through eight printings by 1812, leading to the publication of the first 'gastronomy maps' of France (Figure 7.4). Guides to Paris for tourists published during the nineteenth century listed recommended restaurants. Then in 1900, *Le Guide Michelin*, intended for cyclists and motorists touring France, provided information about hotels, garages and places of interest and from the early 1920s included information about restaurants and from 1926 rated their quality by awarding stars. During the nineteenth century, Parisian restaurants developed and marketed *la cuisine gastronomique*. Parisian gastronomy gradually acquired not only a national but also an international reputation. Gastronomy was not promoted just as good cooking but as the art of the table (eating, drinking, talking), as a theatrical experience involving all of the senses – sight, smell, feel, sound and of course taste.

The national discourse on gastronomy in nineteenth-century France stressed the superiority of Parisian cuisine but it was tinged temptingly with regionalism, drawing on products and dishes from identified regions in the provinces. The high point of this discourse was perhaps at the *Exposition universelle* of 1937 in Paris, at which for the first time in such exhibitions a section on gastronomy was held at the *Centre*

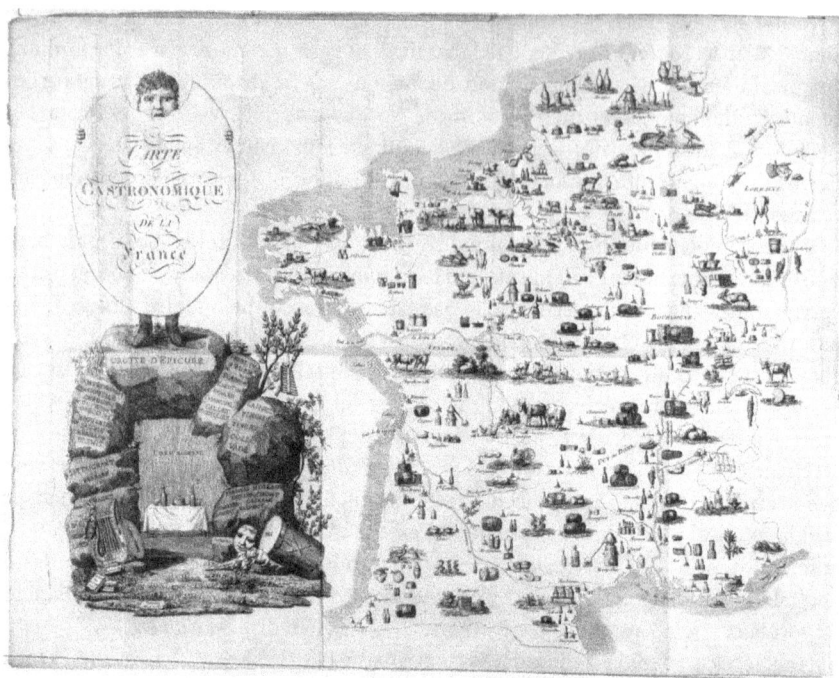

Figure 7.4 Carte Gastronomique de la France 1809.

régional, which displayed products and culinary dishes from each of twenty-five provincial regions of France. Gastronomy came to be seen as a feature of regional and Parisian cultural identities. *Haute cuisine* became an essentially Parisian phenomenon, requiring the meticulous preparation of fresh food beautifully cooked and attractively displayed. It focussed on classical French dishes, unlike the more recent (from 1970s) *nouvelle cuisine* with its non-classical experimental dishes developed in part as a postwar reaction to war-time food rationing and the black market in provisions. *Haute cuisine* was a later development than *haute couture*, another character-forming aspect of the cultured personality of Paris.

Fashion: *haute couture*

Clothing has a dual function: it provides physical protection and it signals social belonging. To its basic functional role is added a symbolic significance, as an act of differentiation indicating, for example, the wearer's gender and generation, economic and social status, marital position and geographical origins and religious and political beliefs. Philippe Perrot has shown how, 'with the acceleration of material progress and social mobility, and with the advent – principally under the Second Empire – of new kinds of consumption by a new strata of consumers, a strict social mechanism began to regulate the relationship between class and dress'. One of the liberating aspects of the Revolution of 1789 was the Convention's decree of 29 October 1793 stating: 'No person of either sex can force any citizen, male or female, to dress in a particular way … everyone is free to wear the garment or garb suitable to his or her sex that he or she pleases.' But a police ordinance of 7 November 1800 expressly forbade Parisian women to wear trousers 'without special dispensation'.

The relationship between class and clothing had deep historical roots. The seventeenth and eighteenth centuries had witnessed an unbridled pursuit of fashion in France, especially in the court at Versailles and in the city of Paris. The notion of Parisian *chic* was developed in those two centuries and attracted clientele from the provinces and from other European countries. An historian of fashion in France, Valerie Steele, has noted that in 1867 a popular French encyclopaedia claimed that 'Paris has been the capital of fashion for three centuries. Since the time of Louis XIV (King of France, 1643–1715), Parisian adornments had as tributaries all the courts of Europe.' Steele (1998, p. 10) identified what she called 'a foundation myth in the process of creation, mixing historical facts with hindsight and hyperbole'. She argued that an assertion that Paris was the centre of fashion ignored the fact that Louis XIV disliked Paris and the Parisians, so much so that in 1682 he moved the royal court to Versailles, where it remained until 1789. Nonetheless, the court at Versailles contributed significantly to the growing reputation of French, and more precisely Parisian, leadership in the world of fashion. In 1789, Fanny de Beauharnais (1737–1813), a Parisian lady of letters, called her city 'the capital of new fashions and love affairs', establishing a link between fashion and sensuality that would become central to the popular image of Paris by 1900. In 1836, the inaugural edition of the *Journal des Coiffures* lauded the fact that it was being published in Paris, 'the capital of fashion' (*capital de la mode*), from where it could diffuse its styles to other places. Fashion was an integral part of Paris as the aspirant cultural capital of Europe because of its long-standing focus on the craft production of high-quality goods for a limited but wealthy market.

By the 1840s, Paris had thousands of anonymous artisanal dressmakers, tailors and mercers and a smaller number of celebrated individuals who, perhaps at first unknowingly, began crafting clothes with what today we call 'designer labels'. The 1840s also saw the take-off of ready-made civilian clothing for men; for women, it came slightly later. A demand for ready-made clothing began among the popular classes first for working clothes (blue overalls or smocks) and for everyday wear, then later for Sunday-best wear. Ready-to-wear clothing gradually caught on with the lower-middle classes. By 1847 Paris had 233 ready-to-wear manufacturers employing about 7,000 workers. Meanwhile, the upper classes continued to rely on 3,013 personal made-to-measure tailors employing about 18,000 workers. In addition, there were many milliners, dressmakers, glovers, shirt makers, shoe makers and corset makers. Philippe Perrot has shown that the production and sale of luxury clothing had a distinctive geography: in the eighteenth century they were focussed on the Rue Saint-Honoré and then spread during the first half of the nineteenth century to the Rue de Richelieu and the surrounding neighbourhood, and in the 1860s to the Rue de la Paix and its neighbourhood. Cheaper ready-made wear became available in the drapery and fancy goods stores (*nouveautés*), selling items mainly for a feminine clientele, which emerged in the early nineteenth century. These came to replace *ancien régime* 'shops', which were often dark, low-ceilinged stores with little if any shopfront glass and with fabrics chaotically piled up inside. By contrast, the fancy goods stores had light from large windows revealing neat displays of goods usually with indicative prices for haggling but in some cases fixed prices. Externally, shopfront signs advertised their commodities, such as silk, cotton and linen goods, hosiery and lingerie. The very name boards of these shops – *Nouveautés* – signalled very clearly to potential customers outside that what was on offer inside included the latest novelties and fashions. They were a step on the way to the department stores which were to replace them.

In 1845, an Englishman, Charles Worth (1825–1895), after an apprenticeship with a textile firm in London, moved to Paris to work in a company selling textiles, shawls and ready-to-wear clothing. He became the firm's principal salesman and set up a fashion department. His designs were modelled at the Great Exhibition in London in 1851 and at the *Exposition universelle* in Paris in 1855. He founded his own company in 1858. Live models exhibited his creations at in-store fashion shows, marking the innovation of fashion parades with models on catwalks. Previously, dresses and suits for the better-off sections of society were made to measure by artisans following the personal instructions of their clients. Worth set in motion a different process whereby clothes were designed and inspired by him and exhibited by him: the role of the client was limited to the choice of material to be used and its colour. Worth created designs which were not unique but were reproduced only in limited numbers and with detailed variations to make them individually distinctive. Collections of his dresses changed styles with the seasons – he promoted spring/summer and autumn/winter collections. This marked the birth of the *couturier* (dressmaker) and of *haute couture* (high fashion) (Figure 7.5). Worth sold his designed garments through Paris's new department stores like *Le Printemps* (founded in 1855) and *La Samaritaine* (founded in 1870). Worth's pioneering provided an example for other fashion design houses to follow, such as that famously established in 1910 by Coco Chanel in Rue Cambon just off the Rue de Rivoli, a wealthy district on the Right Bank in central Paris.

During the nineteenth century, Paris developed and accentuated its reputation for *chic* and good taste, as the favoured place for launching new designs and fashions. Higonnet has asserted that Parisian fashions were blatantly artificial to the point of self-conscious silliness. This aura flourished during the Second Empire, *la fête impériale* of the 1850s and 1860s, when high fashion was ostentatiously displayed by the wealthy to distinguish themselves from the increasingly upwardly mobile and becoming better-dressed bourgeoisie. With its new boulevards, squares and parks, Paris acquired many more public spaces in which the fashion-conscious could promenade, being seen while seeing the styles adopted by others *promenadeurs* – and, of course, it is the essence of fashion that it changes, creating new demands. Fashions for women's clothes changed more often, more rapidly and more subtly than did those for men. In the new Paris, fashion became a lucrative industry and commercial enterprise.

The reputation of Paris for fashion was reinforced by the image of *la Parisienne* cultivated in novels and paintings, in magazines and advertisements, in photographs and in the larger-than-life-sized model placed at the entrance to the 1900 *Exposition universelle*. Fashion is in essence imagery: more and better visual media diffused it to an

Figure 7.5 Fashion plate from *La Mode Illustrée* 20 August 1882.

increasingly wide audience. Debra Mancroft has demonstrated how the Impressionist artists in their Parisian scenes 'expressed the spirit of modernity through the language of fashion'. She comments in turn on groups of paintings portraying, for example, 'the dressmaker and the draper', 'the maison de couture', 'the department store', 'the park' and 'the milliner's'. A significant contribution to the growth of consumerism in general and of fashion in particular was provided by the new phenomenon of department stores.

Department stores: *Grands magasins*

The remodelling of Paris by Haussmann constructed a more extroverted city. The creation of wide arteries for the circulation of both people and commodities encouraged commercial activity and provided access to the city's services for a larger clientele. In

1855, Paris had 347 omnibuses carrying 36 million passengers; in 1865, it had 664 omnibuses carrying 107 million passengers. An increasingly large and increasingly mobile clientele combined to create favourable conditions for the development of *grands magasins*. The new boulevards encouraged movement – unlike the narrow streets they replaced, which had served as *fora* for neighbourhood life, as local street markets. The new boulevards saw the emergence of new centres of exchange, the department stores.

It could be claimed that the department store was essentially a Parisian innovation. In London, Harrods dates from 1849, Gamages from 1878 and Selfridges from 1909; in New York, Stewart's dates from 1846 and Macy's from 1858. The first nascent department store in Paris was founded in 1838 by Aristide Boucicaut. Born in Normandy in 1810, the son of a hatter, he migrated to Paris in 1829 to work in the Rue du Bac as a salesman in a *magasin de nouveautés*. In 1835 he met and cohabited with Marguerite Guérin, not marrying her until 1845 because his parents did not regard her as suitable match for their son. The illegitimate offspring from a seduction in Burgundy in 1816, Marguerite Guérin was an immigrant who ran a small café-restaurant serving a simple *plat du jour* for manual workers and office staff. Boucicaut opened his own small store in Paris in 1838 and significantly upgraded it in 1852 as the Bon Marché, the first department store in Paris, created at the dawn of Haussmann's remodelling of the city's streets (Figure 7.6). A department store relied on a well-developed intra-urban transport system to give access to the store by myriads of customers. The first horse-drawn public tramways in Paris date from the 1850s, travelling along the new boulevards, which – like railways – were straight or slightly sinuous and had only gentle gradients.

Figure 7.6 Le Bon Marché *c.* 1900. Photographer unknown.

A department store had three fundamental differences from traditional boutiques: it made its overall profit from a high turnover of goods at a low rate of profit; its prices were low and fixed, not open to bargaining; and customers were encouraged to enter the store, to browse its vast range of products, with no obligation to buy. This ended the traditional dialogue between shopkeeper and customer: conversation between them was replaced by a fixed price tag. The store also employed a new sales technique of 'panoramic' visual perception which replaced the static and intensive view of merchandise by the customer by one which was a dynamic and extensive relationship. A department store offered a wide and frequently changing consumption landscape, as customers walked through it from section to section (such as from clothing to kitchen wares) and also from one visit to the next (as displays in the store had changed the locations of displayed goods between visits). The department stores worked on a new, modern, selling model. Boucicaut contrived deliberately to orchestrate confusion in the store's layout, in order to oblige shoppers to travel the length and breadth of the store to find items sought, thus exposing them to the spectacle of other items and potentially seducing them into buying additional items they had not planned to acquire. The store functioned as both organized chaos and disorganized purchasing. Émile Zola in his novel *Au Bonheur des Dames* (1883) describes the customer's experience as planned by the department store's owner:

> First, the continual coming and going of the customers disperses them a bit everywhere, increases their number and makes them lose their sense of direction; second, we must be able to lead them from one end of the store to the other; if, for example, they want to buy lining after they've bought a dress, these trips in every direction will make the store seem three times as big; third, because they are forced to go through departments they have never seen before, they will be ensnared as they pass through, and they will succumb.

A department store represented a people's paradise – more specifically, a ladies' paradise, as it is argued that it held more attraction for women than for men. Department stores democratized luxury. They were free and easily accessible centres of luxury and display, providing an ostentatious decor and creating an atmosphere of wealth and well-being conducive to enjoyment and spending. A department store was a permanent exhibition hall in which its goods were not merely displayed but were actually for sale. These buildings made extensive use of the new construction materials, technology and architectural designs of the time. The classic interior form embodied a large sky-lit rotunda in which decorative metal staircases provided access to heavenly upper levels. An open use of metal in the interior would usually be juxtaposed with a sumptuous masonry exterior and an abundant use of colourful ornamentation. The stores were managed by men, with women as shop girls – and Zola's 1883 novel portrays very few sales assistants as having been born in Paris; most were immigrants from the provinces. Similarly, many goods on sale came from the provinces and from the French colonies.

The department stores opened in the mid-nineteenth century (Bon Marché, 1852; Le Printemps, 1865; La Samaritaine, 1870) were a Parisian phenomenon. No provincial town in France offered such a concentration of people and wealth: Paris in 1872 had a population of 1.8 million, almost six times the size of each of the next two largest French towns, Lyon (324,590) and Marseille (312,684). In the windows of the Bon Marché, Le Printemps and La Samaritaine, the Parisian bourgeoisie (and those aspiring to become bourgeois) both saw their own wealth (or their dreams of wealth) and discovered new, unexpected, needs – a store's windows displayed tempting 'bait' to catch customers. Department stores widened the social and cultural gap between Paris and the French provinces and also between its own bourgeoisie and its working class. Window-shopping became one of the city's attractions, part of its offerings of fun.

Fun in *Gai Paris*

In 1836, 55-years-old Fanny Trollope, an experienced traveller in Europe and North America, published an account of her stay during the previous year in Paris. In her book *Paris and the Parisians*, she referred several times to '*la gaieté naturelle*' and '*la joyeuse effervescence*' of Parisians. In 1869, Mark Twain, in his book of travel letters, *The Innocents Abroad*, wrote that as soon as he had set foot in Paris in 1867 he had visited the city's *Exposition universelle*: 'Everything around us was gay and animated.' Whether as a foundation myth or as reality, the concept of a Gay Paris or *Gai Paris* was promoted in tourist guidebooks from the 1850s onwards (especially those for English and American tourists) and by the *Expositions universelles* (especially those of 1889 and 1900). Guides for tourists published in the latter part of the nineteenth century no longer focussed so much on architectural heritage and practical information about public transport and the opening times of museums and art galleries; instead, they became more varied as guides to Paris by day and by night, both above and below ground, in the centre and in the suburbs and on where to walk, dance, eat and find prostitutes. Guides described Paris as being *gai* (gay, lively), *coquin* (mischievous, knavish) and *frondeur* (irreverent, critical of authority) – a reputation that enticed immigrants from the French provinces as well as tourists from abroad, especially England. Thomas Cook had initiated tours to Paris for British travellers in 1861: passports were no longer necessary for such travellers to France, and Cook identified an opportunity to sell excursion tickets to people who had never aspired to foreign travel. The 1861 Cook's tour to Paris was called the 'Working Man's Excursion'. Those who participated were mainly working-class men from the north of England, including 200 employees of Titus Salt's cotton mills in Bradford. By September 1863, Thomas Cook had taken 2,000 visitors to Paris, mostly as conducted parties, although some travelled independently. In the 1865 *Guide to Cook's Excursions to Paris*, the trip was recommended on the grounds that Englishmen could learn 'to emulate its excellences' and 'shun its vices'. It advised gentlemen to 'avoid low neighbourhoods after dark' and ladies that they could 'without impropriety' sit inside or outside the best cafés but that they should 'on no account enter the cafés on the north side of the Boulevards between the Grand Opera and the Place Saint-Denis'. Cook informed travellers that 'the can-can is danced by performers and is altogether of an unnatural and forced abandon'. The 'capital of pleasure' became popularly known as *gai Paris*: it had become the acme of pleasure.

During the Second Empire of the 1850s and 1860s, the Imperial court and opulent members of the Parisian elite – *le tout Paris* – held extravagant balls and masques. Others flocked to the growing number of café-concerts in which to music and singing by performers was added dancing by the customers. Coffee shops 'came out' into the open air as terrace cafés. The renewed, restless, search for freedom of expression challenged France's religious, moral and political traditions. Satirical journals like the *Chat Noir*, the *Courier français* and the *Révue indépendante* challenged prudes, hypocrites and censors. 'Having fun' meant challenging orthodoxy and order – such protests were manifest in journals, magazines, songs and cabarets.

Montmartre became a leading district for light, even lascivious, entertainment, a centre for artists and writers, for drinking and conversing, for listening to singers and witty performers. Le Chat Noir night club was founded in 1881: after a basic start serving poor wine in a drab room to small gatherings of intimate friends, it soon attracted artists, poets and singers and the decor became deliberately dramatic, even Rabelaisian. It gradually acquired a wealthier and famous clientele, including King Edward VII ('Bertie', the playboy and eldest son of Queen Victoria) and the singer and comedian Aristide Bruant, renowned as the man in the red scarf and black cape featured on posters by Henri de Toulouse-Lautrec. When not performing, artists mingled with the customers, producing an informal social mixing not then usual in France. Success for the Chat Noir enabled it to move to larger premises nearby. Its success also led to its being copied: for example, the Moulin Rouge opened in October 1889 initially as a dance hall but soon becoming a cabaret with singers, dancers and variety performers. It rapidly acquired mythical notoriety for its boisterous can-can dancers but that dance in fact dates from 1830s performances of *le chahut* in working-class districts. While the can-can emphasized lifting of the dancers' skirts, the *chahut* was more about the high-kicking of their legs (Figure 7.7). Jacques Offenbach (1819–1880), a German-born French composer who moved to Paris as a music student at the age of fourteen and lived there until his death, gave *le chahut* prominence as an easily recognizable tune in his 1858 operetta *Orphée aux enfers* (*Orpheus in the Underworld*) and in 1866 in his *La Vie Parisienne*. That title – *La Vie Parisienne* – had been given in 1863 to an illustrated magazine which became one of France's famous exports, a patriotic magazine with provocative, and from 1900 onwards even erotic, illustrations which gave it an exotic reputation. During the 1880s and 1890s, Montmartre became a spirited centre of commercial entertainment in Paris. Nonetheless, it retained its village character as a place distinct from Haussmann's modernizing Paris. It was a liberating, culturally transgressive, playground for Parisians, provincials and foreigners.

With the spiralling commercialization of leisure, new places of entertainment flourished. Some catered for working-class labourers as well as for members of the bourgeoisie. Dance halls thrived and some cafés-concerts became akin to English-style music halls with sociable drinking, a pianist or a small band playing light music, a singer and sometimes entertaining turns such as fire-eaters and jugglers. Most successful of the new forms of entertainment was the Folies-Bergère founded in 1869, with its chorus of provocative dancing females flaunting spectacular dresses, feathers and fans, bosoms and bottoms. When Édouard Manet in 1881 painted his *Bar at the Folies Bergère*, beer bottles on the counter have been read as signalling the cabaret's

Figure 7.7 'Le Chahut' 1890 by Georges Seurat.

British clientele, at first the classic aristocratic *milord anglais* but later cross-channel steam ships and trains brought the middle classes to Paris to enjoy all aspects of life thereby escaping the rigours of restrictive Victorian society at home. From the 1890s, venues providing striptease and nude dancers were an added attraction aimed largely, but not exclusively, at tourists.

Posters promoting entertainments and consumer goods were plastered throughout Paris in the 1880s and 1890s. They were mechanically produced colour lithographs. A new liberalizing law of 1881 permitted such postings so that large, bright and startling images covered walls, kiosks for selling newspapers and magazines, public urinals, trams and parading sandwich boards. Hazel Hahn has shown that distinctive and colourful illustrated posters became an integral part of the urban spectacle, especially on the Grands Boulevards, reinforcing the commercial culture of consumption displayed in shop windows. Many fin-de-siècle posters were aimed directly at the relatively few *flâneuses* and the many accompanied women strolling the boulevards, enticing them to consume the newest and fashionable products. Vanessa Schwartz has shown that boulevard activity was a significant feature of the new mass culture of fin-de-siècle Paris in which aspects of quotidian life were transformed into 'spectacular realities'. The landscape of Paris which attracted so many painters now became itself a painted landscape. Buildings along the boulevards were covered with banners and advertisements, many illuminated electrically at night. They added to the theatricality of the boulevards with, as Henry James noted in 1876, their 'long chain of cafés, each one with its little promontory of chairs and tables projecting into the sea of asphalt' and occupied by people seeking and experiencing an ambience which stimulated all of the senses. Those sitting at tables on the terraces of cafés constituted an audience for the dramatic, unrehearsed and unending circulation on the boulevards of traffic and of people (not only pedestrians going about their business or just promenading but also street entertainers, such as musicians, vendors of foods, drinks and trinkets, acrobats, handlers of small performing animals). The boulevards offered constantly changing dramas; they constituted open air and free theatre (free except, perhaps, for the cost of a coffee or glass of wine at a café). Donald Olsen (1987, p. 219) has argued that from the 1860s Paris has used the street 'to blur the distinction between indoors and out. From the dispenser of fresh shellfish outside restaurants to the pavement stalls which the *grand magasins* themselves set up outside their establishments, French life overflows the confines of mere buildings and comes out to mingle with the life of the streets'. Domestic overcrowding might partially account for this development but so too might the growing awareness of the significance of public space as representing egalitarianism: the boulevards were sites where different social classes mingled as one, theatrical stages on which all Parisians could be fraternizing players.

Paris by 1900 had acquired a national and international reputation as the world's capital not only of harmless leisure but also of dubious pleasures. Was this a constructed myth or an historical reality? Prostitution in Paris was probably no more widespread or flagrant than in London or New York. But brothels and streetwalkers did become integral components of the legendary image of Paris in a way that they did not elsewhere. Prostitution, along with gambling and expensive shopping, eating and drinking, was one of the attractions in the district of the Palais-Royal in central Paris in the early nineteenth century. By the late nineteenth century, there were thousands of prostitutes throughout the city.

Alain Corbin has shown that during the nineteenth century prostitution in Paris was both tolerated and regulated by the state. During the first half of the century, brothels were licensed by the police who monitored prostitutes within those *maisons de tolérance*. Other prostitutes were required to register with the police and to report regularly for physical examinations. In practice, such aims to control prostitution were not achievable. By the 1860s, the *maisons de rendezvous* had replaced the brothels, and Corbin judges that clandestine prostitutes outnumbered those registered. Theodore Zeldin has accepted claims that in the 1850s there were an estimated 34,000 prostitutes in Paris and that, in the years 1871–1903, some 155,000 women registered as prostitutes and the police arrested another 725,000 women suspected of prostitution. The police estimated in 1888 that there were 15,000 prostitutes in clandestine brothels in addition to those in the 100 or so official brothels.

Many provincial girls and young women profited commercially from their youth and freedom to slide from their provincial reputations into Parisian anonymity and into respectable work (as, e.g., waitresses, milliners, shop assistants or laundresses) and even into marriage. This was so in the wealthier upper- and middle-class districts on the Right Bank but much less so on the Left Bank where many male students formed temporary associations with young girls and where cafés gave them free meals if they talked to customers and encouraged them to buy more drinks. Many such migrants from the provinces became sex workers.

The number of registered brothels in Paris declined from 145 in 1870 to 125 by 1881 and to 59 by 1892. But this period also saw the growth of unlicensed brothels, often operating from cafés. There were probably about 200 in 1890 while the period 1871–1903 saw 155,000 women registered as prostitutes and another 725,000 arrested on suspicion of working as unlicensed prostitutes. By 1900, far fewer brothels existed than in 1860 and little remained of the initial regulation system, but more and more stringent health checks were required by the government, implemented by closer police surveillance. The nature of the demand for prostitutes changed from the 1860s. As Corbin has argued, until then unassimilated migrants were the main clients, reflecting the fact there were significantly fewer women than men in the city so that some men sought sexual satisfaction in cheap brothels. As the gender balance in Paris improved from the 1860s, more working-class men came to prefer clandestine prostitutes in bars and cafés to visiting cheap brothels. Meanwhile, bourgeois men sought brothels with more domestic comforts and perhaps with more erotic environments. The combined effect of these changes of taste was an increase in unregistered prostitution. The period around 1900 might be considered a golden age for Parisian brothels: although reduced in numbers, they offered more seductive and erotic experiences. The higher-class establishments were opulently decorated and furnished: one such featured rooms in different international styles mimicking the different international pavilions of the *Expositions universelles*. Stephen Clarke has suggested that Parisian brothels attracted almost as many tourists as the Louvre, 'though you weren't allowed to touch the Mona Lisa'. Prostitution also attracted artists like Cézanne, Degas, Manet and Renoir in the 1870s and 1880s. Clayson has highlighted the imagery of prostitution in their paintings, with their dual connotations of disgust and fascination, as well as their portrayal of the vulnerable standing of women in a patriarchal society. She has argued that paintings of prostitution embodied two key elements of modernity, those of commercialization and of ambiguity.

While prostitution – often cited as being 'the oldest profession in the world' – was far from being a Parisian innovation, the city did see the emergence of some much newer forms of commercial leisure. Among them were the Musée Grévin waxworks opened in 1882, inspired by Madame Tussaud's wax museum which had opened in London in 1835. It presented three-dimensional recreations of modern life, ranging from a papal cortege through a scene from Émile Zola's novel *Germinal* (1884) depicting the coalminers' strike in northern France during the 1860s to the elaborate narration of a complete crime story in sequences from a murder through the trial and to the guillotine. In addition to the wax figures, the museum included other attractions, such as magicians, shadow puppets, marionettes and lantern slide shows. Another new visual entertainment was the panorama, a 360-degree viewing room depicting, for example, landscapes of the world and historical dramas, steamship voyages and train rides. Physically rotating canvases on which the scenes were painted created an illusion of movement. But an even more realistic portrayal of places and events came to be provided by moving films, the cinema.

By 1900, new cinemas in Paris had come to compete with its much older theatres. In 1895, Auguste and Louis Lumière organized their first public showing of a moving film for which an admission fee was charged. They used it to illustrate lectures on industrial photography – initially, moving films were seen as a way of popularizing science. The first public cinema in Paris was opened in 1897, showing erotic films of women undressing and preparing for bed. Later, there were films of operas, outdoor scenes and public events. By 1908, Charles Pathé was showing newsreels and the cinema had passed from an artisanal craft to industrial production in just thirteen years. Cinema, unlike opera, rapidly became a popular art form, rather than being appropriated by the élite. Cinema provided for the masses a new and exciting access to culture, escapism and daily events, doing so much more cheaply than could theatre or opera or exhibitions of paintings. Paris was paramount in this new venture: in 1913, cinema ticket sales in Paris amounted to more than half of such sales in the whole of France. By 1914, one in five of the 1,200 cinemas in France were located in Paris. Cinemas in Paris were taking in more money than music halls and more than cafés-concerts. In 1914 for the first time, a cinema in Paris – the *Hippodrome* – earned more than the 1.3 million francs taken that year by the Folies-Bergère, until then the leading, non-subsidized, commercial entertainment venue in Paris.

The democratization of leisure?

To what extent did nineteenth-century Paris witness a democratization of leisure and culture? Alongside *haute cuisine*, *haute couture* and essentially bourgeois 'entertainment' provided by theatres, opera houses, concert halls, art galleries and museums, there emerged a new popular culture, accessible to most people and appealing to basic, simple, tastes for amusement. Fin-de-siècle Paris saw the burgeoning of a mass or popular culture in Paris – such as vaudevilles, cafés-concerts, circuses, cabarets, music halls, cinemas, skating rinks, cycle racing and even horse racing at Longchamp in the Bois de Boulogne which in the 1870s drew attendances of less than 200,000 a year but of 500,000–600,00 in the 1890s (encouraged by a new betting system which allowed those betting small sums without much knowledge and with little expertise a greater chance of winning something). Income from the café-concert and music hall business in Paris between 1893 and 1913 increased from 32.7 million francs to 68.5 million francs, more than doubling while the population of Paris grew by only 18 per cent. Cycle racing provided cheap entertainment on the streets: from the 1870s the *Véloce-club de Paris* staged frequent races in the city, including a *Tour de Paris*. Some major long-distance races, such as the Paris-Brest-Paris race initiated in 1891 and the Paris-Roubaix race in 1896, provided spectacular on-street entertainment for Parisians, and the Tour de France, inaugurated in 1903, started in and, after a gruelling 2,428 km, ended in Paris, in front of an enthusiastic crowd at the Parc des Princes *vélodrome* which had opened in 1897. Christopher Thompson (2002, p. 132) has argued that 'for male workers broadly defined and for the young men filling the growing number of petty white-collar positions in commercial and government bureaucracies, the development of new leisure opportunities, especially new sporting activities such as bicycling, represented a significant improvement in their lives'. But a rift developed between the bourgeois gentlemen-cyclists or cyclo-tourist and the professional racers who almost without exception came from the lower classes. Thompson (2002, p. 134) claims that 'an erect posture distinguished bourgeois cyclists from working-class racers and the working class-youths who sped around town imitating their heroes, as well as from messenger and delivery men who now used the bicycle as a professional tool'. Cycling was perceived as largely a masculine endeavour, in part because of the physical exertion it required, in part because some argued that female attire was unsuited to the activity and in part because some medical men deemed cycling to be potentially harmful to the female reproductive system. Track racing in purpose-built *vélodromes* developed from the 1890s as a commercial spectator sport. The first cycle tracing track in Paris was constructed in 1890 in the Palais des Arts Libéraux which had been built for the 1889 *Exposition universelle*. It was soon followed in 1892 by the Vélodrome de Buffalo and the Vélodrome de la Seine, in 1893 by the Vélodrome d'Hiver in the select Champ-de-Mars district, in 1895 by a track in the Bois de Vincennes and in 1897 by another at the Parc des Princes in the south-western *16ᵉ arrondissement*. Eugen Weber maintains that although cycle track racing was initially merely an 'upper-class fad', both in terms of competitors and spectators, in the 1890s it was taken up by the masses and was to be the earliest popular sporting entertainment of modern times.

Older forms of entertainment evolved to meet the growing demand as working times were reduced and incomes increased. In the 1880s and 1890s, according to Eugen Weber, half a million Parisians went to the theatre once a week and more than twice as many once a month. In the bourgeois theatre the chief topics of the dramas were sex, love and money, social conflict and ambition and domestic crises connecting those themes. These topics were also played less subtly and more directly in the light comedies, usually interspersed with songs, performed in the growing number of vaudevilles. The public flocked to shows that offered colourful and elaborate spectacles, with scenery that was operose, obviously expensive and technically clever. There developed a taste for 'realizing' famous paintings on stage, with actors and scenery producing a 'tableau' or '*tableau vivant*' creating on stage a visual composition familiar to the audience. Plays were sometimes dramatized versions of well-known novels, like Jules Verne's *Around the World in Eighty Days*. Special, startling effects made use of steam, gas, electricity and limelight (produced when calcium oxide is heated to incandescence) at a time when relatively few homes had electric lighting. Staged use of glass and mirrors created reflections and refractions of light, striking metal surfaces such as swords and armour, and shiny fabrics like satins and silks, to produce startling effects. Theatregoers were not only Parisians but also provincials travelling by the capital-focused national train network, using the opportunity to shop in the department stores and in some years to visit the *Exposition universelle*, returning to their homes with vivid memories and with (no doubt exaggerated) stories to recount to family and friends about their adventures in the 'big city', in *gai Paris*.

The growing leisure and entertainment industry encouraged more social mixing but some pursuits were expensively priced: social mixing was theoretically possible but financially restricted. The cost of a theatre or opera ticket in the 1880s was usually between about 16 and 26 francs, the equivalent of several days' wages for the average worker. *Le petit peuple* of Paris tended to relax in their own *quartiers*, in cafés, restaurants, cafés-concerts and in local parks with bandstands. But commercialized leisure of varying forms and costs did make clearer the distinction between work and non-work for many nineteenth-century Parisians. For some, more leisure time provided an opportunity to enjoy its multiplying recreational offerings but also to escape, if only briefly, from the pressures of urban Paris by seeking solace in 'rural' environments both within and without the city.

8

Escaping Paris: (Re-)discovering 'Nature' and the provinces

For much of the first half of the nineteenth century, Paris was dirty, smelly and noisy: it was a maze of narrow, cobbled or unpaved, poorly drained streets, strewn with household refuse, mud and horse dung, and many people urinated and defecated in them. The streets were noisy, echoing to the street cries of hawkers publicizing news and selling merchandise; the bedlam was added to by knife grinders and buskers and the clatter of horses pulling vehicles along cobbled streets. During the second half of the century, a lot of noise and dirt was generated by construction works, notably for Haussmann's rebuilding of large parts of the city. Many Parisians unsurprisingly sought quieter places and calmer atmospheres that provided reassuring echoes of their provincial and often rural origins – they sought to sense again the different feelings of the seasons, the scents of gardens and forests, the movement of light and shade, and the edges of shimmering and reflecting ponds, lakes and rivers. The parks and squares created in Paris during the nineteenth century provided reminders of life in the provinces. Many Parisians searched for rural tranquillity as respite from the commotion of urban life. Some parks and squares were deliberately designed to provide a sense of the non-urban, to re-present Nature or to reinvent Nature. Parks and gardens were culturally constructed Natures.

Parks and gardens in Paris before 1850

Nineteenth-century Paris both inherited parks and gardens from earlier epochs and developed new ones (see Plate 13). The botanical garden, on the Left Bank in the 5e *arrondissement* in eastern Paris, stretched down to the Seine. In the early seventeenth century, it was the royal garden for medicinal plants and from 1634 it was open to the public. With the Revolution of 1789, its title was changed from the Jardin royal des plantes médicinales to the Jardin des plantes de Paris and in 1793 had added to it the National Museum of Natural History, with distinctive collections and a scientific agenda. Visitors observing exotic species travelled in their imaginations to places far away from Paris. During the Bourbon Restoration (1815–30), the garden was again returned to the monarch but in practice it continued to be called by both its royal and its revolutionary names. In 1793, the garden acquired a large menagerie which came to house exotic animals (e.g. a lion, a camel and an elephant), a natural history collection and a collection of human mummies, skeletons and waxworks. From 1827 until 1845 it had a giraffe, which was a diplomatic gift to Charles X from Muhammed Ali, viceroy of Egypt. This public zoo brought many visitors to the garden: it was a novel, very non-Parisian, experience. Additional attractions were the large metal-framed glasshouses displaying plants from contrasting ecological environments around the world. The Jardin des plantes (Figure 8.1) offered to nineteenth-century Parisians not only nostalgic recollections of the supposedly 'natural' world of provincial France but also magical glimpses of foreign places only hitherto portrayed in school geography books and pictured in popular magazines like *Le Monde illustré*, a weekly, first published in 1857.

Some gardens in nineteenth-century Paris evoked the city's history. The Jardin du Palais Royal, located on the Right Bank in the *1er arrondissement*, was created in 1633 as a square to ornament the Palais-Royal. This tranquil and colourful garden was bordered by four *galeries* under arcades where leisurely pursuits prospered and acquired a 'racy' reputation. Here were not only many coffee houses and taverns welcoming journalists and politicians, members of the aristocracy and the bourgeoisie, but also brothels and gambling houses.

Figure 8.1 Le Jardin des Plantes 1905. Wikimedia Creative Commons Licence Ouverte: Séeberger frères/Centre des monuments nationaux

The Jardin des Tuileries was linked to the construction of the Palais des Tuileries in the second half of sixteenth century. The garden had the rigidly rectangular geometric design in the so-called Italian style. It was redesigned in the mid-seventeenth century by André Le Nôtre (designer of the gardens of Versailles) into the form which largely survives today. The large central drive (*allée*) was marked at one end by a circular pond and at the other by an octagonal pond. Although strictly speaking the garden was royal space, it was from the outset accessible to the public. In the nineteenth century, Napoléon III had two identical buildings erected in the western corners of the garden: in the south-western corner in 1852 was added an *orangerie* (today functioning as a museum of modern art); in the north-western corner was added in 1861a *jeu de paume* (an indoor tennis court, functioning today as a museum of contemporary art). The Jardin des Tuileries was a popular place for promenading among the hundreds of trees, colourful flowerbeds, ponds, fountains and statues. Cafés offered shade and refreshments. Musical entertainment on a bandstand was an added occasional attraction, as depicted in Édouard Manet's 1862 painting *Musique au jardin des Tuileries*. The garden's historical connections are legion: in 1572, on 24 August, some of the thousands of Protestants murdered during the Saint Bartholomew's Day Massacre were slaughtered in and around the gardens; in August 1792, Marie Antoinette escaped from the Tuileries palace and for a while hid in the garden before getting lost in (for her) the unfamiliar streets of Paris; in 1871, the Palace of the Tuileries was burned to the ground by the Communards.

Another garden embedded in Parisian history is the Jardin du Luxembourg. Created in 1612 in the geometric Italian style, complete with parterres, terraces and a fountain to set off the Palais du Luxembourg, it was refashioned in 1790 and replanted around 1801 as a picturesque landscape park in the English style. It was one of few public gardens in Paris in first half of the nineteenth century. Napoléon Bonaparte wanted the 23-ha garden to be especially welcoming for children: it provided in due course refreshment kiosks, games such as chess and *boules*, a carousel, a music *kiosque*, a puppet theatre and rides pulled by goats, while the *bassin* was popular for sailing toy boats (Figure 8.2).

A smaller park or garden of 8 ha was the Parc Monceau, in north-western Paris, in the *8ᵉ arrondissement*. Created in 1769–73 by the Duc de Chartres, it featured a two-storey octagonal folly surrounded by a French-style garden that was converted in 1773–9 into an Anglo-Chinese garden supplemented by a 'Swiss' farmhouse, 'Dutch' windmills, a 'Chinese' pagoda, an 'Egyptian' pyramid, some 'medieval 'ruins and a 'Roman' temple. A constructed stream fed into a lake. Artificial caves were built in which games could be played or refreshments taken. In 1787, a tax-collecting pavilion was erected as one of the barrier posts in the wall of the *Fermiers généraux*, with offices on the ground and first floors and, above them, a terrace which permitted visitors a panoramic view of the garden. This park was confiscated during the Revolution but afterwards returned to the Orléans family. The folly was demolished in 1802–6, to be replaced by another pavilion. In 1860, this Parc was expropriated by the state and converted into a public park by Haussmann's engineer at the department of bridges and highways and the man in charge of Paris's *Service des Promenades*, Adolphe Alphand. He added a stream with a bridge, a waterfall and a cave (with artificial stalactites

Figure 8.2 Le Jardin du Luxembourg c. 1905. Wikimedia Creative Commons Attribution Share Alike 4.01

built of cement). The existence and the remodelling of the Parc prompted speculative development in the locality, funded and encouraged by a new financial instrument, the Crédit Mobilier established in 1852 by the Pereire brothers, Isaac and Émile, as an investment bank acting as an intermediary between innumerable small savers and a wide range of economic enterprises, including housing. The Pereires argued that their actions democratized investment and credit. Their funding underpinned high-quality housing developments and even the redevelopment of existing housing into luxury mansions around the Parc Monceau as well as mixed developments around the Opera House and along the Rue de Rivoli, the Champs Élysées and the Boulevard Malesherbes.

Ideas about the reinvention or construction of Nature were debated heatedly in France during 1830s and 1840s. The debate was, Richard Hopkins has argued, a legacy of the discourse on citizens' rights during the French Revolution. The need to provide greenspace was pleaded by hygienists as meeting the 'right' to air and light and to salubrious housing. Children especially had a 'right' to a clean environment. The right to access and use green space underpinned the concept of public parks. One utopian planner, Hippolyte Meynadier, suggested in 1843 that what Paris needed was a public open space the size of London's Hyde Park, 'a real countryside in the town'. Such grand ideas needed money and authority to combine before they could be implemented. There were gardens and squares in Paris before the mid-nineteenth century but, with the exception of a brief interlude during the Revolution of 1789, access to them was generally restricted to local property owners and in some cases to visitors who paid subscription fees or who conformed to a certain dress code. From the mid-nineteenth century, there was a concerted effort to provide a public green space in the form of a municipal park or square in every *arrondissement* of the city.

Parks and gardens in Paris after 1850

The extension or modification of existing green spaces and the creation of new ones was one of the distinctive features of Second Empire Paris. It is essentially a top-down story, initiated by Napoléon III and his team of engineers as the key agents, ambitious to see green public spaces throughout the city as expressions of both French national and municipal Parisian character. They believed that parks and gardens would attract tourists from the provinces and beyond. Manicured landscapes became part of the broader project to put Paris 'on the map' nationally and internationally. But such green spaces were also valued as local improvements within Paris itself. They were seen as fostering urban health and hygiene and enhancing the quality of life for its residents. Green spaces were one way of addressing the issues of urban pollution, disease, foul air and general *insalubrité*. Doctors and hygienists provided strong arguments for more public parks and gardens, especially for the benefits they would bring to the welfare of children. 'A walk in the park', says Christopher Prendergast (1992, p. 165), was 'a manufactured fantasy of release from the strains and tensions of modern city life'.

Landscape gardeners and engineers played crucial roles not only in establishing parks and park gardens but also in managing them. Some park-keepers lodged in the parks, representing the official face of the municipality to members of the visiting public. Many users of the parks and squares were those who lived adjacent or close to them, especially mothers (or nursemaids) and children. Impressively, such groups were able to express their needs and desires in the planning stages for new green spaces. Some other potential users (notably beggars and prostitutes) were not welcome. Some parks became especially popular: open, green, spaces with added attractions of leisure activities, such as musical concerts from bandstands, skating, fishing, cricket and cycling.

Napoléon III's Anglomania drove his ambition to promote green spaces in Paris, which were seriously lacking by comparison with London. During his exile from France from 1836 until 1849, Napoléon spent considerable periods in London, walking frequently in Hyde Park. For Paris, he sought a comprehensive pattern of parks and gardens, linked by tree-lined boulevards. He had some existing parks and gardens remodelled and, more significantly in landscape terms, had some large new ones created. Haussmann and Alphand, knowing that Napoléon III admired the English romantic style as represented by London's Hyde Park, consequently designed and constructed parks with winding paths and streams, with an emphasis on surprise and sinuosity in park views, instead of the rigid geometry of French formal gardens, parks and forests.

A major and enduring achievement during the Second Empire was the conversion of former royal forests to public parks. The Bois de Boulogne along the western edge of the *16ᵉ arrondissement* was a monotonous block of poor woodland traversed by numerous diagonal rides, radiating from two crossroads. The forest had been for centuries a royal hunting ground. When he became emperor in 1852, Napoléon III ceded it to the city of Paris which at that time had only four significant public parks or gardens: the Tuileries Gardens (26 ha), the Luxembourg Gardens (23 ha), the Jardin du Palais-Royal (2 ha) and the Jardin des Plantes (24 ha). All of these were to be dwarfed in size by the remodelled Bois de Boulogne of more than 800 ha.

The new design for the Bois de Boulogne totally changed the former ground plan, destroying the rigid regularity of the forest rides and constructing curving drives and paths. The Bois was extended to include the gardens of the Parc de Bagatelle (a small Anglo-Chinese-style garden created in the late eighteenth century in front of a newly built château) and the plain of Longchamps on which was constructed from 1855 a hippodrome (horse racing course.) On Sunday 27 April 1857, the emperor and his wife Eugénie sailed down the Seine to watch the first day of racing at this new course. Alphand constructed in the Bois de Boulogne two lakes (Figure 8.3) joined by a cascading stream, winding paths, floral gardens, kiosks, pavilions and summer houses – all aimed at achieving a romantic effect. He also laid out a pleasure garden and from 1856 a zoological garden. This new design was a fundamental break from that of traditional French formal gardens and was strongly influenced by English landscape garden designs. It was remodelled between 1853 and 1858 at cost of 14.3 million francs

Figure 8.3 Grand Lac of the Bois de Boulogne *c.* 1860. Wikimedia Creative Commons (public domain)

of which 10.9 million francs were recovered from sales of land for building sites on one side of the park and from a state grant for the racecourse. The actual cost to the city of Paris was only 3.4 million francs, a sum which produced a great park for the western bourgeois district of Paris and one that was not matched at that time in any other world city. As a public park, it was highly valued by many Parisians. An incident in the Bois de Boulogne in the mid-1860s noted by Richard Hopkins (2015, p. 137) illustrates the potential conflict inherent within the concept of a citizen's right to greenspace. An ice-skating club, given a concession to use the lakes, enclosed its clubhouse with a fence, creating a private space within the park, excluding non-members of the club. Such an exclusive enclave was criticized in the press as not being 'in accord with our egalitarian customs … many may wonder by what right the enjoyment of common property is the possession of few certain some-ones'. Park authorities throughout Paris strove to make these green spaces available to the general public while selling time-limited concessions to those providing some form of refreshment or entertainment.

In the eastern working-class district of Paris, another park was created as a result of Napoléon III's wish to create in the city a social balance geographically. Before 1840, the Bois de Vincennes was a large wood, criss-crossed by straight rides. In 1840, it was cut into two so that part could serve as a military training ground; in 1853, remodelling of the remaining area in the English landscape-garden style began and lasted four years. A lake was created and new rides were constructed (Figure 8.4). In 1860, the Bois de Vincennes was ceded to the city, with the boundary of the park extended to the west and another lake constructed. Excavated soil and rocks from the creation of two lakes were used to build a mound, from which visitors could enjoy prospects of the city. Other works included considerable informal tree planting, the construction of sinuous

Figure 8.4 Bois de Vincennes c. 1870. Wikimedia Commons State Library, Victoria (public domain)

rides and a horse racing course. The costs of the works were 24 million francs, none of which could be met from the selling of nearby potential building land because of its situation in a low-value working-class area. The Bois de Vincennes's almost 1000 ha made it the largest public park in Paris, almost 150 ha larger than the Bois de Boulogne.

To these major landscaping ventures for the public good were added other modifications to smaller parks and the creation of other new ones. The Tuileries and the Luxembourg Garden saw minor embellishments while the Parc de Monceau of 8 ha in the *8ᵉ arrondissement* in north-western Paris was remodelled by Alphand away from the formal French style into one of meandering pathways. In addition, two small new parks were constructed: to the south, the Parc Montsouris of 16 ha was constructed between 1875 and 1878 on old stone quarries and piles of rubble resulting from Haussmann's demolitions; to the northeast, the Parc des Buttes-Chaumont of 25 ha, opened in 1867, was a major work by Alphand on a site where public executions by hanging had been performed under the *ancien régime*. The hill had been worked for gypsum, leaving deep excavations, high rock faces and an intractable clay soil. Alphand made skilful use of the site, creating a large lake as a central feature; crowning the surrounding rocky eminence by a rotunda; and within the central eminence a large grotto remaining from the gypsum workings was imaginatively exploited by Alphand by leading a staircase down through it to the level of the lake, while for an alternative approach he provided a light suspension bridge between the lake shore and island. All of which was complemented by a complex network of paths and drives. The Parc des Buttes-Chaumont, located in a relatively deprived industrial and working-class district, came to provide opportunities for cycling, for hiring horse-drawn carriages as well as riding horses, for fishing and boating.

The park's authorities regulated such activities by controlling the concessions given to the providers of such diversions: with the children of working-class Belleville in mind, one of the earliest concessions (beyond those for three restaurants) was for the operation of a small goat cart which could carry up to seven tiny passengers.

The Parc des Buttes-Chaumont stimulated surrealist author Louis Aragon's 'feeling for nature' described poetically in his *Les Paysans de Paris* (1926): it conjured for him 'images that go beyond physical representation', it 'destroyed boredom' and provided 'countless surprises' and it was 'an oasis' in 'a shady, murderous' district of Paris. It could be argued that visitors to this park and others were to a considerable extent deluded. The parks of Paris were historically constructed spaces. In his detailed cultural analysis of the Parc des Buttes-Chaumont, Ulf Strohmayer (2006, p. 565) has suggested that the essence of such a park was the artful construction of a 'natural' scene from which the considerable labour and careful engineering that had produced it were not immediately visible: 'The most prominent feature of the Parc des Buttes-Chaumont, a central "mountain" surrounded by a lake, was not simply a remnant from previous quarrying days; it was technically transformed with the help of recently perfected concrete to appear not as the coupled product of labour and technology that it was but as the natural landform that it was not.' The limestone grotto contained artificial replicas of stalactites and stalagmites; the lake and its imposing waterfall was fed artificially by waters pumped to the heights of the Buttes-Chaumont from the Canal Saint-Martin in an adjacent *arrondissement*. Technological progress had produced the illusion of naturalness. Strohmayer stretches his thesis to the limit of acceptability when he claims that the Parc's suspension bridge, using manufactured steel cables and linking the mountain across the lake to the surrounding landscape, celebrated its construction not as a material product of labour but as a technological advance, an innovation (the bridge was one of the earliest such bridges in France). 'As such', according to Strohmayer (2006, p. 566), 'the disruption of the park's illusions (of naturalness) was seamlessly replaced by another illusion (of national grandeur); crucially, both illusions require neither maintenance not any other input for them to become real'. Nonetheless, parks as highly constructed, seemingly labourless, commodified spaces were also 'moral spaces', where the behaviour of visitors was subjected to regulations enforced by 'guards', whose main purpose was to prevent damage to the fabric of the park and to allow free use of the space as long as that did not hinder another person's enjoyment of the same space. In addition to these park-keepers, employees of the park service engaged in maintenance work undermined the illusion of a labourless 'natural' environment.

The new greening of Paris completed by Napoléon III and Haussmann from 1855 to 1868 was augmented by twenty or so smaller open spaces (*places*), laid out by Alphand following the example of squares in London. One such was the 0.7 ha Place Boucicaut, in the *7ᵉ arrondissement*, constructed on the site of an old hospital adjacent to the Bon Marché department store. It was named after Aristide Boucicaut, founder of the store. At the square's entrance there is a sculpture of his wife, Marguerite Guérin Boucicaut. Another example is the 0.2-ha Square des Batignolles in the *17ᵉ arrondissement*. Here, on what had been a public space (La Place de la Promenade) for the village of Batignolles which was incorporated into the city of Paris in 1860, Alphand created an English-style square, with asymmetrically designed floral beds, sinuous pathways, two small elliptical lakes, a grotto and an *orangerie*. Another but smaller square (actually a rectangle, 130 m by 80 m) was created in 1872 in the centre of the *11ᵉ arrondissement*, on the site of an abattoir demolished in 1867. This Place Parmentier was named after a local 'hero', Antoine Parmentier (1737–1813), a chemist and agronomist who was a powerful advocate for the potato as a human food source: he even persuaded Marie Antoinette to wear a bouquet of potato flowers in her hair to popularize the vegetable. This square was renamed the Place Maurice Gardette after the Second World War, in honour of another local hero, a Communist councillor and member of the Resistance who was executed by a German firing squad in 1941. These tranquil, verdant, squares, many with colourful flower beds, completed Haussmann's attempts to reproduce in Paris the green spaces of London. Some critics have claimed that Haussmann destroyed more private parks and gardens than he constructed public parks. The fact is that by 1870 Paris possessed about 1,800 ha of public parks and open spaces compared to under 20 ha in 1850. A visitor to Paris in 1869 reported that Paris had been developing into an Arcadia. By 1873, even the boulevards and streets of Paris had been embellished with more than 100,000 trees.

The greening or 'wilding' of Paris had not only recreational but also political aims. As Christopher Prendergast has aptly noted, parks 'grafted soothing Nature onto the turbulence of the city'. There were two overlapping images of parks and gardens held by contemporaries. One school of thought saw them as places of sanctuary and retreat, as havens or oases. In the 1890s, a republican politician, freemason and professor of philosophy at the Sorbonne, Jules Simon (1814–1896), said that in the Jardin du Luxembourg you could almost believe yourself to be in the countryside; it was the place, he confessed, that he frequented as a student in the 1840s to find himself hidden among the great trees, to smell the invigorating scents of earth and vegetation and to forget Paris while being in the centre of Paris. It was a space especially for *flâneurs*, for lovers and for mothers and children. Another school of thought envisioned public parks and gardens as spaces of social mixing, of sociability, of informal and spontaneous encounters of city dwellers otherwise separated by class, occupation, gender and residence. Thus, public parks and gardens were integral to the democratization of leisure. They were places open to everybody, thereby potentially encouraging social harmony and defusing social tensions. As uncrowded, tranquil and ordered public spaces, they allowed women to be *flâneuses*, to be themselves subjects and not only objects of male gazing. Public parks and gardens were promoted by some as a kind of egalitarian Arcadia. Open-air activities were deemed to be good for one's health: getting the poor Parisians out of their slums and into public green spaces was both good for the lungs of individuals and good for social order.

To what extent were these utopian, mythical, images rather than delivered realities? Promenading in the Bois de Boulogne on weekday afternoons was favoured by those with more money and more time, and on Sundays (mornings or afternoons) for the rest, *le petit peuple*. This was social separation not in space but in time. The Bois de Vincennes was largely empty during the week but filled with working-class and lower-middle-class people on Sundays; the Jardin du Luxembourg was frequented by many students, *grisettes* (young women of easy virtue) and *vieillards* (old, some homeless, men); it was a space for dreamers and paupers. By contrast, the Jardin des Tuileries was enjoyed mainly by the aristocracy and aspiring upper middle class.

Public parks and gardens attracted Impressionist painters: for example, Claude Monet's *Les Tuileries* (1876) and his *Parc Monceau* (1871 and 1878); Berthe Morisot's *Lady with a Parasol Sitting in a Park* (1872) and *Le Lac du Bois de Boulogne* (1879); and Pierre-Auguste Renoir's *The Bridle Path in the Bois de Boulogne* (1873). It is possible to read such paintings as representing a gendered and class-based use of space in public parks but they may also be read as portraying the connection of Parisians to Nature – even though the Nature being enjoyed was in large measure a cultural construction, it was 'Nature' in the imaginations of Parisians. That culture could dominate Nature is made clear in Édouard Manet's *La Musique aux Tuileries* (1862) which portrays an afternoon concert for the aristocracy or upper middle class, not the full social range of Parisians, even though the gardens were open to all. But the Tuileries also had reputation as a place where gentlemen went in pursuit of the *demi-mondaines*. This is a painting of a thoroughly urban scene; it showcases a dense crowd of urbanites: despite its trees and greenery and its patch of blue sky, it is anti-pastoral, less Nature than City – not a portrayal of people admiring Nature but of people admiring, genuinely or falsely, each other and the cultural landscape they have collectively created. The gardens of the Tuileries provided both recollections of Nature and demonstrations of its appropriation by Culture – many of the individuals in Manet's picture seem more aware of each other than they are of either the garden or the music.

Cemeteries

Not only parks and gardens but also cemeteries offered Parisians an escape from the oppression of the built environment and entry into – at least in imagination – more relaxed, tranquil, rural or quasi-rural landscapes. A law of 1804 prohibited burials in churchyards and required cemeteries to be established outside of towns. Scientific theory current at the time argued that burial places threatened public health because they gave rise to emanations of 'fixed air' released from corpses. Earlier, in 1801, the prefect of Paris called for the closing of burial grounds in favour of new cemetery sites outside the city's walls to the north, east, south and west: thus, in 1804, was created in the east the cemetery of Père-Lachaise; in 1820 in the west that of Passy; in 1824 in the south that of Montparnasse; and in 1825 in the north that of Montmartre (Plate 13). These burial places were primarily for local residents but anyone was able to purchase a concession in perpetuity or for a specific period of years, usually five or thirty. The cost of a concession reflected not only its duration but also the size of the burial plot. Within a few years of the opening, Père-Lachaise had become an attraction for Parisians and for tourists. By the 1860s and 1870s, these four cemeteries collectively had about 70,000 visitors each week – and annually on All Souls' Day (2 November), their number increased to about 400,000 or about one in five of the population of Paris.

A visit to a cemetery was a significant cultural ritual. A cemetery was an enclosed, regulated, social and monumental space. A boundary wall was required by law to contain within the cemetery what were thought to be deathly emanations from the corpses. As the city expanded during the nineteenth century, the cemeteries came to be in close proximity to houses and apartment blocks so that a surrounding wall created a protective space, separating the living from the dead. A cemetery was also a regulated space, with rules intended to ensure that there would be no behaviour likely to be offensive to the dead (or, indeed, to living visitors). A concierge housed in the grounds was responsible for controlling access to the cemetery and for maintaining decorum. Cemeteries were exclusive spaces denying access to unaccompanied children, drunks, smokers, peddlers, students and dogs. Their positive role was to provide a social space, for an intermixing sociability. They were designed as gardens, as tranquil places invoking the beauty of a living Nature as well as remembering generations of the dead. That of Père-Lachaise (Figure 8.5), opened more than fifty years before the Bois de Boulogne became a public park, was in effect a carefully designed public park or garden, constructed on the site of a medieval folly which had then become from the seventeenth century a retreat for Jesuits among whom was François d'Aix de la Chaise (1624–1709), known as Père Lachaise, who was Louis XIV's confessor for thirty-four years. Cemeteries were as much – perhaps more – for the living as for the dead. Over the years since their opening, they have become ecological sanctuaries in the city, harbouring abundant and diverse flora and fauna. Père-Lachaise was gradually expanded from its initial 17 ha to 43 ha by 1850. It acquired thousands of trees, numerous birds as well as rainbows of flowers surrounding the graves and garlanding the many stone tombs and monuments. Cemeteries were also imagined forests of impressive monuments erected by affluent members of the bourgeoisie. In Greek,

Figure 8.5 Entry to the Père-Lachaise Cemetery 1865. Wikimedia Creative Commons (public domain)

Roman and neo-Gothic styles, they reflected the wealth and self-consciousness of the bourgeoisie. Family tombs, columbaria (for storing urns with ashes of the deceased) and chapels were erected as a way of reaffirming family ties in an age when they were being increasingly separated by work and marriage. They signified family solidarity in death, if not in life. Initially, graves of poorer people were marked just by small wooden or metal crosses – but when time-limited concessions expired, those plots were purchased by the bourgeoisie as long-term and even permanent concessions, displacing the dead working class to more remote cemeteries.

Cemeteries were valued as places of remembrance, of collective identity with people in the past. They also brought visitors into imagined contact with famous personages from the past, be they writers, painters, sculptors, musicians, scientists, philosophers or politicians. People strolled the long and winding bucolic paths of Père-Lachaise (see Plate 14), for example, to find themselves encountering the graves and memorials of Camille Corot (1796–1875), Eugène Delacroix (1798–1863), Honoré de Balzac (1799–1850), Frédéric Chopin (1810–1849) and Alfred de Musset (1810–1857). A visit to Père-Lachaise became part of the politics of an anniversary remembrance of the 147 Communards executed there by firing squads on 28 May 1871. In the 1880s, at first small numbers of amnestied Communards marched to lay flowers at the Mur des Fédérés, the execution site. But by the late 1880s these annual marches had become political pilgrimages, major events in the socialist calendar, with thousands participating in the early 1900s, to hear rousing speeches and to sing revolutionary songs. In 1936, the left-wing tabloid *L'Humanité* claimed that the crowd that year numbered 600,000 – very probably an exaggeration but nonetheless indicative of the persistence of strong feelings about an especially turbulent episode in the city's history.

Not all parks and gardens were so politically charged. At the other extreme were enchanted gardens manufactured as commercial entertainment. The *Exposition universelle* of 1889 advertised a children's park as a 'fairy wonderland' (*'un pays des fées'*). Earlier, Alphand, Haussmann's landscape architect, said that the Champs-Élysées had become a supreme example of *'une grande promenade publique'* and that for strollers it had *'un air féerique'* (a fairy-tale air).

In these many ways, nineteenth-century Parisians had reminders of the role of Nature even in an urban setting. An especially powerful lesson about Nature was delivered in 1910 by the Great Flood, when the Seine rose 6 m above its normal level, following months of exceptionally heavy rainfall in the Seine's catchment basin. Many areas in the city were flooded as water backed up through the city's drainage systems and running the Métro was suspended. The basement of the Louvre was inundated. When the flood water eventually receded after a month, it became clear that about 200,000 built structures in the city had been damaged.

Parisians were fortunately able to maintain some contact with Nature within the city itself. But much of that 'Nature' was manufactured and social behaviour in green spaces closely regulated. For those seeking a more relaxed and more authentic – or, at least, a seemingly more genuine – taste of Nature, the siren call of the provinces was irresistible.

In pursuit of 'Nature' away from Paris

Sundays saw a bucolic use of green spaces within Paris itself – strolling in the open air, along boulevards, on riverside quays and in parks and gardens, and might include family picnics and children's games. But increasingly during the nineteenth century, Parisians went beyond the often overcrowded, vice-ridden, sometimes stinking alleys and unhealthy apartments in the city itself in search of the countryside experiences – or imagined benefits – of solitude, security, panoramic views, picnicking in meadows, fields and woods, fresh air, expanding horizons and safe and healthy spaces.

Travelling out of the city for a day or longer, on foot or by horse-drawn coach and from the late 1840s by steam train, from the 1880s by *tramways* (narrow-gauge railways) or by bicycle and from the 1900s by motor bus or (for a few) by car, brought different environmental experiences and a sense of freedom, of escaping from the pressures of city living. There developed a new kind of secular pilgrimage to reputedly 'natural' beauty spots and cultural treasures (such as châteaux and historic sites). This new phenomenon of nature tourism involved extended promenades providing visual, tactile, olfactory and aural sensations of the seasonally changing nature of the countryside which was seen as a much healthier and more stimulating environment than the city.

Travel guides multiplied. By the 1850s brochures, and from 1890 advertisements, of railway companies were promoting tourist attractions at Fontainebleau, Chantilly, Versailles and Saint-Germain-en-Laye . Some writers produced elaborate guides. One such was Claude-François Denecourt (1788–1875), a military veteran from the first Napoleonic era, who became a dynamic entrepreneur of Fontainebleau tourism. His first *Guide* to Fontainebleau and its environs was published in 1839, went through eighteen editions by 1848 and saw its last edition published in 1931. Denecourt invested in Nature not only as a commercial proposition but also to establish his social standing as a writer with great personal knowledge of the area. By the 1850s, a wide range of tourists was visiting Fontainebleau: shopkeepers, clerks and other office workers as well as men of letters and artists. A popular tourist destination for many Parisians was Barbizon, near to Fontainebleau, about 56 km to the south-east of Paris. A key attraction was the château which once belonged to the kings of France and was inhabited by Emperor Napoléon III from time to time between 1856 and1869. The extensive and scenic forest of Fontainebleau was an added attraction. In the 1830s, when some artists started going to Barbizon, it was just a hamlet of about 300 people, mainly families of woodcutters. From the 1850s, a railway provided direct access from Paris to Fontainebleau and to Melun, leaving tourists to travel on foot or horse-drawn cab about a dozen kilometres to Barbizon and its forest (Figure 8.6). In the 1890s, a narrow gauge train (*tramway*) connected Melun to Barbizon (Figure 8.7). Many artists came to stay in the auberge at Barbizon, seeking inspiration from Nature and making Nature the subject of their works. They moved away from the classical symbolism of the Romantic Movement and toward Realism (as pre-Impressionists). Among their leaders were Jean-Baptiste Camille Corot, Théodore Rousseau and Jean-François Millet. Their work attracted the attention of other artists in the 1860s for their promotion of *plein air* painting and of what ultimately became Impressionism. Visitors to Barbizon included Claude Monet, Pierre-Auguste Renoir, Alfred Sisley and Vincent van Gogh. Both Théodore Rousseau and Jean-François Millet died at Barbizon, in 1867 and 1875, respectively. From 1890, this group of painters came to be described by art critics as 'the Barbizon School of Painters'. In addition to Parisians, Barbizon received visits from many painters and writers from throughout Europe, Russia and United States: they included William Morris and Robert Louis Stephenson. From 1867, a hotel keeper in Barbizon initiated an exhibition of works by artists staying there or passing through – it was even visited in 1868 by Napoléon III, an event which enhanced the locale's reputation.

With transportation advances at the end of the nineteenth century and higher wages for workers, Sunday became a day for outings into the countryside. Lenard Berlanstein, an American historian, has argued that for Parisian workers in the late nineteenth century an outing to the countryside for a stroll, a drink or a picnic or a meal was 'the most cherished of family recreations'. Although Paris sprawled increasingly into the surrounding countryside, even the most developed industrial town of the suburbs, Saint-Denis, still had stretches of verdure in the early twentieth century. Workers took cheap trams or trains to pastoral spots along the Seine, such as Billancourt, Bougival, the Île de la Grande Jatte and Argenteuil. These leisurely occasions were beautifully captured in Georges Seurat's paintings *Une baignarde à Asnières* (1883–4) (Figure 8.8) and *Le dimanche après-midi à l'Île la Grande Jatte* (1884–6). The former depicts young, working-class men relaxing on the banks of the Seine in a conflicted environment that is proximately rural and distantly industrial, a world of changing landscapes and values; the latter portrays more self-conscious middle-class men, women and children and their pets. Combined, they suggest very different class values and attitudes. The

Figure 8.6 The artist Jules Le Coeur and his dogs in the forest of Fontainebleau, 1877 painting by Pierre-Auguste Renoir. Wikimedia Commons (public domain)

population of Asnières, on the left bank of the Seine 8 km from Paris, increased from under 2,000 in 1856 to over 30,000 in 1901. It became an attractive recreational centre for Parisians: in addition to water pursuits (sailing, rowing and swimming), it offered pigeon shooting, horse riding, walking and brass band concerts. By 1900, thousands of Parisians were Sunday visitors to Asnières. Among the artists who came – not just on Sundays – were, in addition to Seurat, Van Gogh, Monet and Renoir.

Some working Parisians went further afield, taking advantage of the special excursions to their own *pays* in, for example, Brittany or Limousin, which railway companies were offering at the end of the century. Tourism both benefited from and fed into a developing interest nationally in regionalism and folklore. Tourist activity until 1880 was closely dependent on the main railway lines out of Paris. Completion of the secondary branch lines and of the tertiary narrow-gauge *tramways* in the 1880s and 1890s together with the new modes of transport – bicycles, cars and omnibuses – made

Figure 8.7 The tramway station at Barbizon c. 1900. Photographer unknown

Figure 8.8 *Une baignade à Asnières* 1884 by Georges Seurat (1859–1891).

possible a widening exploration of spaces beyond the city. Guidebooks multiplied after 1900, providing detailed information about local places. From 1889, illustrated postcards of tourist spots proliferated. At Fontainebleau, for example, Parisian publishers dominated the market until 1900 but by 1902 three local publishers were also selling picture postcards portraying almost 400 different subjects. Excluding the 'artistic' cards of scantily clad ladies, they had a strong local focus and fell into three categories: views of Fontainebleau and its monuments and public buildings; depictions of the great social events that happened in local life; and different aspects of the area's local folklore.

Even passing through the spreading suburbs of Paris to reach the countryside meant witnessing the new world of *maisons de campagne* and *pavillons*, detached houses of enormous variety of building styles and garden designs to suit different degrees of wealth and aspiration – and consequently very different from apartment life in Paris. They were products of a utopian idyll of 'imagined' *châteaux* or even just *hôtels de ville* in the countryside, surrounded by trees in a 'natural' environment as opposed to streets of apartments in an 'unnatural', that is to say, cultural, environment. Passing from the city centre through the suburbs into the countryside involved encountering a challenging succession of contrasting landscapes, in imagination perhaps for some a passage from servitude to liberty.

From the 1880s, cycling gained enormous popularity throughout France. It was stimulated by new races like the Paris-Rouen in 1869 and the Paris-Brest-Paris in 1891, and of course the Tour de France in 1903. In addition, touring by cycle became increasingly popular. The Touring Club de France was started in 1890 by group of cyclists in Paris: its aim was '*le développement du tourisme sous toutes ses formes, à la fois par les facilités qu'elle donne à ses adhérents et par la conservation de tout ce qui constitue l'intérêt pittoresque ou artistique des voyages*' (to develop tourism in all its forms, both by the benefits which it provides for its members and by conserving everything of picturesque and artistic interest of its itineraries). There were 257 cycling clubs in Paris in 1909 and perhaps 250,000 cycles in the city in 1914. The Touring Club's membership soon came to include motorists along with its founding cyclists.

Visiting the countryside was for many Parisians a way of keeping faith with their rural roots which for most of them were only a generation or two away. As immigrants from the provinces themselves or as Paris-born descendants of such immigrants, they had not been completely deracinated by living in the capital. Many Parisians had rural roots and retained emotional attachments to their provincial pays.

9

'Assassinating Paris'?: Revolutions, wars and the twentieth century

Processes of urban renewal

The popular and positive image of Paris held by many foreign tourists and by many of the French themselves owes much to the legacy of its nineteenth-century architecture and especially to the imprint of Haussmann on the city. Surprisingly and regrettably, Paris throughout its history has inflicted harm upon itself, destroying some of its own architectural jewels as well as the lives of many of its citizens.

Cities are constantly being redeveloped. Their built forms are never fixed; change is ceaseless. Sometimes structures are deliberately damaged or destroyed for ideological reasons – such activity being described as 'vandalism' by those not subscribing to the ideology in question. Sometimes structures are torn down with the deliberate intention to replace them with what their developers consider to be better buildings, as 'improvements' (aesthetically and/or functionally) – again, such activity being described as 'vandalism' by those not subscribing to the ideology of creative destruction. As geographer David Harvey has asserted: 'The perpetual reshaping of the geographical landscape of capitalism is a process of violence and pain.' The social dislocation and protests characteristic of nineteenth-century Paris were products of – or at least sharpened by – that process of capitalist development. Émile Zola, in his 1871 novel *La Curée*, portrays Saccard, the archetypal speculator of Second Empire Paris, standing on the hill of Montmartre with 'the recumbent giant' of Paris at his feet, smiling into space and 'with his hand spread out, open and sharp-edged as a cutlass', cutting through the space to symbolize Haussmann's wounding slashes through the veins of a living city, wounds that spurt gold and give sustenance 'to a hundred thousand navvies and bricklayers'.

The demolitions necessitated by Haussmann's rebuilding of Paris were hugely extensive and extremely controversial. Some – both contemporaries and later commentators – have argued that his works were acts of vandalism, undertaken as part of a grand project of imperialism sanctioned by Napoléon III's hubris. Some have argued that Haussmann's works contributed to a housing shortage in Paris from the 1850s. But in part that was because of the inevitable time lapse between the demolition of old and the construction of new housing. More significantly, the housing crisis was a consequence of the massive growth of Paris by almost 1 million people between 1851 and 1872. Between 1852 and 1869, 118,000 old housing units were demolished but 215,000 were newly built. Haussmann's works are, in effect, most appropriately described as creative destruction, not as vandalism. But that cannot be said of damage suffered by the fabric of Paris during revolutions and wars.

Revolutions and upheavals

1789 In the eighteenth century, Paris possessed many architectural legacies from its medieval and monarchical past. They were unmistakeable in the maze of narrow streets as monuments, palaces, churches and *hôtels*. The urban fabric itself provided signs of a dislocated social order that the Revolution of 1789 aimed to consign to the past. Transforming the built form of the city would have been an obvious way for revolutionaries to have asserted the arrival of a new social order. Some cultural signs were transformed, including the defacement of royal statues and assaults on the toll gates of the wall of the *Fermiers généraux* in July 1789, but Paris saw less physical destruction during the 1789 Revolution than some had feared and others had wanted. One notable work of vandalism was the demolition in 1797 of the sixteenth-century Church of Saint-Jacques-de-la-Boucherie in the 4e *arrondissement*, leaving only the tower as a monument.

More important than physical damage to the city's physical structure was the French Revolution's bringing the control of France, its seat of government, back to Paris from Versailles where it had been since 1682. The new National Assembly recognized that reconstructing the city wholesale was too expensive and too complex to achieve in the short term. Some buildings were damaged during the insurrection and others destroyed, but not very many. Most famously, 14 July 1789 saw an assault on the Bastille, a fortress and prison, by revolutionaries seeking its stores of arms and gunpowder and in the process releasing the prison's seven detainees, executing the prison's governor and killing or injuring its military guard of thirty-two Swiss soldiers. The building was demolished the following day by a private entrepreneur who sold its stones as souvenirs, some of them carefully sculpted to represent the Bastille in miniature.

Much cheaper and easier than totally remodelling the old pre-Revolutionary city was simply changing the names of some squares and streets. The Revolution and its aftermath literally inscribed the landscape of Paris with a new toponomy. If the layout of streets could not be rapidly altered or 'rationalized' following revolutionary principles, then new street names could easily be used to proclaim the Revolution, to redesignate and thus redesign the city and the mental maps of its citizens. New street names could be used to educate the public about republicanism and revolutionary principles. Such renaming did not take place wholesale as some rationalists wanted: instead, piecemeal changes were made. Streets were politically re-baptized with the names of France's (and especially Napoléon Bonaparte's) military victories and military officers. Following Bonaparte's concordat with the Pope in 1801, the epithets *saint* or *sainte* were restored to old names that had been erased previously by anticlerical revolutionaries. Later regimes also adopted the practice, rewriting the visible history of Paris by changing the names of streets and public spaces. Every revolution in Paris followed this paradigm of renaming the landscape: each of the social upheavals of 1789, 1830, 1848 and 1871 reconfigured to varying extents the toponymic landscape to fit the altered structures of power.

The 1789 Revolutionary process embraced the de-Christianization of Paris. The number of clerics in the city fell from several thousand to a few hundred. Many ancient buildings were damaged because of their religious connections. Many churches were vandalized, their statues damaged or removed and their tombs broken. In 1793, the remaining churches were closed. The tombs of the French kings were desecrated at the cathedral of Saint-Denis, just north of the city. The cathedral of Notre-Dame survived (albeit with twenty-eight decapitated statues of biblical kings mistakenly assumed by the revolutionaries to be French monarchs) as a food depot and also as a building newly designated as a Temple of Reason. In 1802, Bonaparte returned Notre-Dame to the Catholic Church.

1830 During three days of fighting, the most actively involved insurgents were skilled artisans, especially building trades workers (such as stonemasons, locksmiths and carpenters). In general terms, they sought dignity for themselves and glory for France but, in detail, they wanted job security; higher pay; a shorter working day; lower taxes; employment protection from foreign workers, from machines and from the new large-scale methods of production and distribution; government regulation of prices, wages and working rules; and an end, as they saw it, to the hegemony of priests and nobles and a new and aggressive national foreign policy. Additionally, such expectations rested on a persistent anti-monarchism. Street protests were ignited by publication on 26 July 1830 in *Le Moniteur* of ordinances which suspended liberty of the press, excluded the commercial middle class from elections and dissolved the Chamber of Deputies. The 'Three Glorious Days' of 27, 28 and 29 July 1830 saw the regime of Charles X and the Bourbon regime overthrown and replaced by the July Monarchy of Louis Philippe.

The evening of Tuesday 27 July saw rioting in the streets and barricades being erected, national troops were called out and before the tumultuous night was over twenty-one citizens had been killed. Two more days of street fighting ensued. On Wednesday 28 July, the rioters became revolutionaries, fighting for and by the evening taking control of the Hôtel de Ville and demanding the abdication of Charles X. By Thursday 29 July, more than a thousand barricades had been built throughout Paris; that day the Tuileries Palace was sacked, and the Swiss guards of the Louvre abandoned their posts. Most of Paris fell to the insurgents and the army left the city. The crowd sacked the Archbishop's Palace, as a protest against the holding of a Mass there by legitimists (royalists). At least 500 and perhaps almost 3,000 Parisians, mainly labourers and artisans, were killed or wounded: the names of many of the dead were later listed on the July Column inaugurated as a memorial at the Place de la Bastille in 1840. The Archbishop's Palace was sacked again in 1831, after which its site next to Notre-Dame cathedral was turned into a public square, Le Square de l'Archevêché (later renamed Le Square de Jean-XXIII), and the archbishopric moved to the Rue de Grenelle, on the Left Bank.

1832 Paris saw three days of social upheaval during the first week of June. The protests were short-lived, as cholera was spreading in the city, ultimately killing about 18,000 people. The last stand of the rebels on the barricades served as the climactic scene in Victor Hugo's 1862 novel, *Les Misérables*.

1834 In April 1834, there was a brief popular uprising during which an army captain was shot by a sniper from the window of a house in the Rue Transnonain in the 6e and 7e *arrondissements*. As a reprisal, soldiers stormed a house in the street inhabited by thirty artisans and shopkeepers, killing twelve of them and wounding others. Altogether, almost 2,000 people were arrested but only 164 of them were eventually charged with any offences.

1848 The Revolution in 1848 was a response to what contemporary observers called the 'Social Question', by which was meant the perceived gap between, on the one hand, the promises of social equality and better standards of living made by the Revolution of 1789 and by the ongoing Industrial Revolution and, on the other hand, the reality of everyday life in Paris, in which individuals below the middle classes were not seen as active citizens with full citizenship rights and who did not enjoy good or even comfortable living conditions. Mounting public anger at meetings to discuss electoral reform was followed by four days of social protests from 22 to 25 February. On 23 February, troops fired at a crowd on the Boulevard des Capucines, in the 2^e and 9^e *arrondissements*, killing several people. Their bodies were paraded around the city and interpreted by many working-class Parisians and students as evidence of a massacre by military forces. Over the next two days, hundreds of barricades were hastily erected in the narrow streets of central and eastern Paris, manned by armed workers, artisans and students (Figure 9.1). Barricades were made out of the paving stones (*pavés*) easily prized out of the sand that held them in place and to these were added whatever else was at hand (such as carriages, carts, furniture and doors) together with uprooted trees lining the boulevards.

While fighting continued sporadically between the rebels and the Municipal Guard or units of the National Guard, many of whom were more supportive of the rebels than of the government, and although there were numerous, noisy but largely peaceful, street demonstrations, there was some but not much damage to the urban fabric of Paris. Louis Philippe, like Charles X before him, fled to England. Following the departure of the king from the palace of the Tuileries on 24 February, the insurgents forced entry into the palace intent on wreaking havoc on the furniture and its interior but not the building itself. Something similar could have happened to the palace of the Louvre but the insurrectionist students instead acted as guardians of the nation's property. No such caution was exercised at the Palais-Royal, where the contents of the interior were trashed. On 24 February, Louis-Philippe abdicated and in the evening a provisional government was installed in the Hôtel de Ville and the following day it proclaimed the Second Republic.

Frustrations and social unrest simmered in Paris for some months and climaxed between 23 and 26 June when there was an uprising of the working class, taking on the government and its armed forces. But Mark Traugott has carefully calculated from a variety of sources that the *gardes mobiles* were socially indistinguishable from the arrested insurgents, except that the former were significantly younger than the

Figure 9.1 Barricades in Rue Saint-Maur in the *10ᵉ arrondissement*, 25 June 1848. Wikimedia Creative Commons (public domain)

insurgents, and that both sides were dominated by skilled labourers and artisans, not property-less proletarians as Karl Marx had maintained. Traugott rejects a class-based interpretation of the uprising, arguing instead that two armies of workers and artisans confronted each other across the barricades of the Rue Saint-Antoine and its faubourg. More than a thousand street barricades were erected but it is clear from their locations that most fighting took place in the rebels' own neighbourhoods in eastern Paris. The rebels created a ring of barricades to close off a well-defined area in the east of the capital as a challenge to the power of the state. Earlier street barricades in 1830 and 1832 had been distributed more diffusively or had closed off very limited areas of the city. The June Days of 1848 were a key moment in the nineteenth century when men and women armed with rifles at street barricades drew with clarity the boundary between a 'bourgeois' western and a 'proletarian' eastern Paris. Between 1,000 and 2,000 insurrectionists and soldiers were killed during the fighting and almost two thousand were wounded. More than 11,000 people were arrested (mainly males aged eighteen to forty-five, only about 25 per cent of whom had been born in Paris, the others being immigrants, presumably dissatisfied workers who had found that Paris was not living up to their provincial dreams about it).

To the revolutionary vandalism inflicted on Paris periodically between 1789 and 1848 was added damage wrought by both international and civil wars. The 1850s and 1860s, as noted previously, saw considerable destruction of buildings to make way for new ones, a process perceived positively as urban regeneration by supporters of Haussmann's remodelling but by others negatively as devastation of the cityscape.

Wars

1870–1 The Prussians besieged Paris from 20 September 1870 until 28 January 1871. Their artillery heavily bombarded the forts and defensive walls of the city. The Panthéon suffered damage from shelling during the siege and then further damage in May 1871, during fighting between the rebel Communards and the national French army. Three weeks of Prussian bombardment with about 12,000 shells killed 97 people, wounded 278 and damaged 1,400 buildings, including the Luxembourg Palace. But the damage was probably more serious to French morale than to the city's architecture. During the siege of the city, the Prussians occupied the Château of Saint-Cloud, which had served as a royal and an imperial residence to the west of Paris, about 10 km from Notre-Dame: from it had been issued on 15 July the French declaration of war with Prussia but it was taken over by the Prussians in October and held by them during their siege of Paris. The château was destroyed by fire during the siege, the conflagration having been started – according to the Prussians – by a shell fired by the French.

During the Prussian siege, Paris experienced severe food shortages. Most animals in the Jardin des Plantes were slaughtered and eaten, including the elephant and the giraffe, but not, it has been suggested, the monkeys perhaps because Charles Darwin's *Origin of Species* had been published only eleven years previously and monkeys were considered to be near relations of humans. When the siege was lifted and an armistice was agreed with the Germans at the end of January 1871, the French National Assembly (full of conservative politicians from the provinces) took its revenge on the mainly radical Parisian deputies. It ended the moratorium on rents just when the population of the city consisted very largely of ruined tenants, and it terminated payment of the National Guard which had acted as a form of unemployment benefit. Civil unrest led to the proclamation of the Paris Commune on 28 March 1871.

A new siege began but this time imposed by France's national forces that eventually retook the city at the end of May. During the civil war, most productive economic activity ceased in the city. Thousands, possibly tens of thousands, fled (mainly the better-off, abandoning the city to the poorer classes). During the fighting, the Communards vigorously defended their own districts in working-class, eastern, Paris but left the hostile richer, western, districts relatively untouched. Numerous street barricades were built but in response the national forces infiltrated through outlying gardens of properties and over their roofs, to shoot down on the Communards' barricades, so the Communards eventually resorted to setting fire to streets (including some in their own *quartiers*) to drive back the rooftop snipers. In building barricades, the Communards used some of the street furniture of Haussmann's boulevards, such as iron pavement grills designed to protect the roots of trees. Photographs of the men, women and children 'manning' the barricades were taken both as souvenirs, as evidence of their proud role as insurgents (even though the active Communards had to be passive objects for the camera), and as records for the police, as tools of social oversight and regulation. Awareness during the Commune of the value of photography for social surveillance led in 1874 to the creation by the Prefect of Police Léon Renault of a *Service photographique de la Préfecture*, charged with photographing all suspected criminals detained in Paris.

This civil war had disastrous human consequences: exact casualty figures are not known but many Communards and government troops were killed fighting, or died of their wounds, some thousands of Communards were interned at Versailles, many more than a thousand were summarily executed on the spot or after only summary trials. The exact scale of the slaughter has been debated for over a century but describing 21–28 May 1871 as *la semaine sanglante* has been widely accepted – until recently. The number killed during the Commune has been claimed by various historians and commentators to have been between 20,000 and 50,000. Exactitude is impossible for a number of reasons: only few lists of those killed have survived and they probably record only those who were given a summary trial and then executed, not those who were captured carrying arms and shot on the spot. The normal civil registration of deaths was not – could not in the turbulent circumstances be – undertaken. The highways department reported that 5,517 bodies had been removed from public places for burial in the city's cemeteries, but that figure relates explicitly only to ten outer *arrondissements* of the city and is silent about the others. In his 1981 account of the Paris Commune, historian Robert Tombs accepted that the number of deaths could be 'anything between 10,000 and 30,000, with the most probable figure about halfway between'. Further research led Tombs to conclude in 1994 that the total death toll was about 10,000. He argued that the number killed in cold blood by court martial after the fighting accounted for a high proportion of total deaths, 'perhaps half'. Other historians have continued to cling to figures somewhere between 13,000 and 30,000. More recently, in 2011 and 2012, Tombs suggested a revised 'order of magnitude' of the death toll, recognizing that precise figures are impossible to obtain. Detailed work on reports by the police, the highway authority and registers and reports of the cemeteries led him to conclude that the number of Communards killed during *la semaine sanglante* was between 6,000 and 7,500. He extended his argument by concluding – on his own admission, contentiously – that the number executed in cold blood, by order of the military authorities after some sort of trial, was probably around 1,400, far fewer than the number who died in hospital or in the heat of combat. He thus sees the outcome as 'a shocking atrocity' but 'undeniably very different from the "summary mass executions" of tens of thousands of Communards that many historians assume to have been the horrific climax to the cataclysm of 1870–71'. Thus, Tombs claims that *la semaine sanglante* was not marked by 'almost unprecedented violence, but by an almost unprecedentedly traumatic *myth* of violence', 'a traumatic and yet inspiring myth of violence going far beyond reality'. It was, in his view, a myth created by Communards who could not have had any firm evidence of the numbers killed and then diffused in the late nineteenth century and into the twentieth century by communist and left-wing historians of the Commune. Tombs – a right-wing historian – supports his own claim by arguing that there had been bloodier times in French history than the *semaine sanglante* of May 1871: he cites the slaughters of September 1792, the Republican suppression of the counter-revolutionary Vendée 1793–6, the White Terror of 1815, the killing of the Swiss Guards in 1830 and the atrocities of June 1848 and December 1851. Such comparisons qualify but cannot dismiss the horrors of May 1871 in Paris. In 1965, Alastair Horne, an English historian of the Commune, had stated that estimates of the numbers of Parisians killed during the uprising varied between 'the grotesquely wild extremes of 6,500 and 40,000' while 'reliable French historians today seem more or less agreed on a figure of between 20,000 and 25,000'. Horne (1965, p. 418) concluded that 'whichever set of statistics is accepted, the total is still staggering. No single battle of the Franco-Prussian war cost so many French lives'. More recently, in 2014, an American historian of France John Merriman has written a forensically researched book on the Commune, examining it in diurnal and topographical detail. He avoids playing the numbers game – I sense because he knows that direct data does not exist to make it worthwhile – but he has no hesitation in referring to the 'bloody week' in May 1871as a 'massacre'.

Myth or massacre, many – but an uncertain number – Parisians died either fighting or facing a firing squad during that week. By comparing the census of 1861 with that of 1872, it has been established that certain trades in Paris were decimated (50 per cent of plumbers, 35 per cent of roofers and 50 per cent of cobblers). The national troops were victorious and the Communards defeated. Many – more than 4,000 – Communards were deported to the colonies, notably to New Caledonia, an island in the Pacific Ocean, in the belief, according to one historian, Graham Robb, that they were 'terrorists who had turned the City of Light into a beacon of barbarism' and so were removed from Paris and sent to populate the new colony (New Caledonia was used by France as a penal colony from 1864 until 1897).

By the end of the civil war, Paris was a physically battered city. It had also been an attack on the senses of Parisians: the noise of cannon fire and rifle shots combined with the sight, sound and smell of burning buildings and of the barricades produced for activists and spectators new sensory experiences. Substantial parts of Paris were in flames during the *semaine sanglante* in May. The Tuileries Palace, a powerful symbol of imperial and monarchical authority, was totally destroyed and never rebuilt: it had been razed deliberately by the Communards and there is a story (perhaps apocryphal) that one of their commanders left a scribbled note: 'The last relics of Royalty have just vanished.' Another 200 or more buildings were destroyed or badly damaged during the fighting – including some churches, vandalized by anticlericals using the turmoil of the civil war to act on their own beliefs.

Another symbolic structure, the Vendôme Column, was vandalized. It had been erected in 1810 by Napoléon Bonaparte and was destroyed by the Communards with explosives on 16 May 1871. While the insurrectionists in 1793 had attacked symbols of the Catholic Church, those of 1871 attacked symbols of the Napoléonic Empire and of the national government at Versailles. The Vendôme Column was restored in 1873 and still stands. Quite considerable areas of the city were ravaged by artillery assaults and by fire during the Commune: large parts of the Palais-Royal, the Palais de Justice, the Prefecture of Police, the Cour des Comptes, the Conseil d'Etat and the Louvre were badly damaged; some entire streets were destroyed or severely disfigured by fire between the Place de la Concorde and the Hôtel de Ville, notably the Rue de Rivoli. Many streets elsewhere, such as the Rue de Lille in the central 7^e *arrondissement* and the Boulevard Voltaire in the eastern *11ᵉ arrondissement*, were lined with partially or wholly burned-out buildings. Rubble from barricades lay straggled across many streets. The Colonne de Juillet, erected in 1840 in the Place de la Bastille following the Revolution of 1830, was pulled down. The Hôtel de Ville was reduced to rubble and its archives destroyed, having been set on fire by retreating Communards as part of their scorched earth policy (Figure 9.2). Some areas in Montmartre were in ruins. Many fires – but in reality an unknown number – were started by retreating Communards to delay the march of national forces. Such actions spread fear among non-combatant Parisians that, rather than surrender to the national troops, the Communards had a plan to destroy most of the city. A 'myth' of fire-raising *pétroleuses* (female arsonists) fuelled the fear that the Communards were planning deliberately to raze Paris to the ground – it was not entirely a myth, more an exaggeration of the unusual role of women throwing petrol bombs. Women did have active roles in the uprising, helping to build barricades, participating in the fighting and tending to the wounded and dying. The city's firefighting capacity was unable to control the numerous fires, though it did save the Cour des Comptes and the Louvre Museum – it helped that, on what proved to be the penultimate and final days of the civil war, heavy rain dampened down the flames devouring many buildings. And the Venus de Milo, a treasure of the Louvre Museum, housed for safety in the Prefecture of Police, was fortuitously saved from the conflagration by a burst water pipe.

On Saturday 27 May 1871, the last surviving Communards gathered in the Père-Lachaise cemetery, desperately but unsuccessfully fighting national troops among the tombstones. They were defeated and 147 of those who had been captured but not killed in that final battle were executed by firing squads against the wall in the south-eastern corner of the cemetery and buried in a communal grave. For their part, during the

Figure 9.2 The burnt-out Hôtel de Ville 1872. Charles Marville

hostilities the Communards had summarily executed a number of their opponents, including not only soldiers of the national army but also clerics, among them Catholics, including the Archbishop of Paris. The memorial Mur des Fédérés, erected later to honour the executed Communards, was declared a national monument in November 1983, when socialist François Mitterand was the president of France. Next to the wall is a monument dedicated to the Resistance Movement and the deportees of the Second World War. The cemetery soon became a pilgrimage site for left-wing Parisians: on 23 May 1880, two months before an amnesty was declared by the Republican government for the Communards, some 25,000 people wearing red roses in their buttonholes paraded past the wall. Since then, a similar but usually smaller event has become an annual event in the socialists' calendar.

The official inquest into the Commune by the national Republican government blamed socialists, anarchists and the weakening influence of the Catholic Church for this 'moral disorder'. It exuded national and conservative hostility to Paris, claiming that immigration had brought to the city hordes of rootless people ready for revolution; it suggested that Paris should no longer be the capital of France. That suggestion was a step too far from reality; the clock of history could not be turned backwards. But it could be advanced and Paris would not again have the right to have a mayor for over a century, until 1977. The early Third Republic attempted to erase the memory of the Commune through censorship and by promoting Paris as a modern and regenerated metropolis in the 1878 *Exposition universelle*.

Astonishingly, by the beginning of June 1871, Thomas Cook was organizing special excursions for tourists to visit the 'ruins' of Paris. When challenged by a French politician about the propriety of such tours, Cook retorted that the tourists were moved to visit Paris not so much by curiosity as by sympathy. Paradoxically, the Commune renewed intellectual interest in the romance, the poetry, the picturesque nature of ruins which had been debated in European salons since the Renaissance. The ruins produced by the sieges of Paris and the Commune became attractions visited by families promenading on Sundays. Also, many photographers flocked to Paris create the images of a damaged city, some characterizing themselves as auxiliaries of the authorities, by supplying evidence of the Communards' crimes. In 1871, some 18,000 photographs were taken depicting the city's damaged landscape: one album was titled *Ruines de Paris 1871*. Raisa Rexer (2021, p. 306) has argued that 'the city's destroyed landscape presented a unique commercial opportunity' for photographers and that 'the iconography of the ruins developed through photography was also deployed politically, most frequently by those who opposed the Commune'.

The damages inflicted on the landscape of Paris between 1850 and 1871, rising in a crescendo of mutilation from Haussmannization to the '*semaine sanglante*', led Eric Fournier to conclude that Paris had a great – he suggests possibly unique, certainly singular – capacity to produce ruins, which themselves gave rise to a debate about the meaning and value of a materialized past to present-day experience. He claimed, somewhat hyperbolically, that the ruins of Paris defined the nineteenth century as much as did its *Expositions universelles*.

In addition to these major events impacting upon the landscape of Paris in the nineteenth century, there were many other less-damaging incidents of social violence throughout it. Some were related to the growing unionization of the city's labour force and the recognition of street protests and strikes as means towards ends. But more damage was done to the urban fabric of Paris by revolutions and wars in the nineteenth century than by the two world wars of the twentieth century – despite the fact that the armaments then in use were far more powerful.

1914–18 During the Great War, although some skirmishes came within a few kilometres of Paris, the front line was mostly 100 km or more to the north, leaving Paris relatively untouched. A few air raids by German Zeppelins together with shelling from Big Bertha, a powerful howitzer with a range of more than 100 km, killed 500–1,000 Parisians but did little architectural damage other than to the overground Métro station at Corvisart and to the Right Bank church of Saint-Gervais-Saint-Protais, near to the Hôtel de Ville.

1939–45 Direct war-time damage to urban fabric inflicted by military weapons was potentially intensified from one war to the next with increasingly powerful weaponry leading up to devastating aerial bombardment in the Second World War. But Paris suffered only slight physical damage during the Second Word War because early in the war, in 1940, the city was surrendered to the Germans. For much of the war, Paris was occupied by the German military but not attacked by the Allied forces. In 1944, Hitler ordered his appointed governor of Paris, General Dietrich von Cholitz, to destroy the city before it could be liberated by the Allies and German troops forced to withdraw. Hitler instructed that 'Paris must not fall into enemy hands or, if it does so, only as a field of rubble'. The general had his troops set fire to the Grand Palais but disobeyed the order to set off explosives under key Parisian monuments. The Swedish ambassador had persuaded the Nazi commandant not to blow up parts of the city before surrendering it to French forces. The built environment of Paris was saved, fortunately, as part of Europe's cultural heritage.

Paris was largely unchanged structurally during the four years of German occupation during the Second World War. It did not suffer from a bombing blitz as did London. The Allies did not bomb Paris, given that one aim of the war was to liberate the city and to protect French culture and pride. But from 19 to 24 August 1944, the war reverted to its nineteenth-century form: street fighting. Members of the new conservative French national government fought alongside members of the Resistance and Communists to liberate Paris. They built barricades in the streets with sandbags, overturned vehicles, paving stones and branches cut down from roadside trees, to impede the movement of German vehicles and to serve as protective ramparts for street fighting against German troops. Many plaques were later erected on streets to honour and memorialize those French fighters killed during the fight for the liberation of Paris.

Since 1945

The second half of the twentieth century saw many proposals for the development and redevelopment of Paris. In March 1956, an old regulation against building higher than 31 m was revoked and both grandiose schemes for the city as a whole and some for individual *quartiers* were brought forward. The face of the city was to be remade. From the 1950s, various schemes were proposed for the 'renovation' of Paris as a whole, intended to cope with its growing problems of traffic circulation and population pressure. Overarching plans argued the need for redevelopment of Paris. But some saw such plans as ravaging. Donald Olsen, an American architect and author of a brilliant comparative study of London, Paris and Vienna as works of art, was appalled by 'the wrenching changes' that began in late 1950s Paris.

The harshest and most incisive critic of such changes was Louis Chevalier (1911–2001), a history and political science professor at the prestigious Collège de France which dates from 1530 and provides free lectures open to the public. Chevalier argued in his book *L'Assassinat de Paris* (1977, English translation 1994) that Paris was being violated not only by indifferent bureaucrats, by arrogant technocrats and by urban planners – and, of course, by money-grabbing developers and speculators – but also by hubristic politicians and architects seeking to inscribe their own names indelibly in the city's narrative landscape, 'grasping at immortality' – to borrow a telling phrase in Sebastien Faulks's 2018 novel *Paris Echo*.

More recently, in his book *Paris détruit* (2011), Pierre Pinon, an architect and historian, has described as 'architectural vandalism' the transformation of the capital by the combined processes of modernization, speculation, war and a desire by some to efface symbols of power in the cityscape. To gradual and ordinary architectural renewal was sometimes added the rapid, brutal and spectacular impact of revolutions. Pinon narrates the story of city that he considers no longer exists ('*une ville qui n'est plus*'). He also notes the development, alongside the 'vandalism', of the institutions and associations founded to safeguard the city's *patrimoine*: in 1885, the Association des amis des arts parisiens, in 1897 the Comité technique de la ville de Paris and the Commission du Vieux Paris and in 1909 the Commission des perspectives monumentales. Although important in shaping public opinion, these bodies had no formal constraining powers over planned developments. They could check but not prevent acts of architectural 'vandalism', a term first used (as claimed by Sebastian Loew) by the Abbé Grégoire in 1794 when objecting to the damage being inflicted by revolutionaries on religious buildings and monuments. Michael Greenhalgh has explored the 'destruction' of the cultural heritage of nineteenth-century France (not just of Paris) and the connection between heritage and the construction of national identity. Greenhalgh (2015, p. 7) argues that modernization and preservation were irreconcilable opposites, and that there was 'an extended dialogue of the deaf between would-be preservers and much more powerful commercial interests, probably supported by the majority of citizens and go-ahead municipalities'.

That debate had enduring resonance in the second half of the twentieth century. Opposed to those like Chevalier and Pinon who loved the historically constructed townscape of Paris were others who wished to see it renewed as a vibrant and vital world city, not conserved or preserved as a museum piece. Those preferring to look to the future rather than to the past eschewed historically familiar designs, embracing instead 'modern', innovatory, projects. For example, from the 1920s, Le Corbusier (1887–1965), a Swiss-French architect and urban planner, challenged the beauty and variety of Paris, putting forward proposals instead for high-speed expressways cutting through the city east-west and north-south making Paris, in Richard Cobb's description, 'like a hot-cross bun'. Cobb (1985, pp. 188–9) claims that Le Corbusier was 'tireless in his assault on Paris, doggedly determined to line both banks of the river with an aligned barrier of tower blocks like 'dragon's teeth'. He goes further, arguing that twentieth-century architects, planners and public health technocrats collectively shared 'a hatred of a human past and of a human street plan'. A few of the mainly late-twentieth-century developments which appear to – or actually do – go against the grain of the personality, of the elegance and charm, of late-nineteenth-century Paris will be considered here.

A major modernist project – La Défense – launched in the 1950s was named after the statue *La Défense de Paris* erected in 1883 in the commune of Puteaux to the west of the city to commemorate French casualties in the Franco-Prussian War of 1870–1. It is located prominently at the western extremity of the 10-km-long east–west historical axis of Paris which extends from the Louvre, along the Champs-Élysées beyond the Arc de Triomphe and along the Avenue de la Grande Armée (Figure 9.3). This monumental development, built on the outskirts of the city, did not involve destruction of any part of 'Old Paris' but of some factories, farms and fields to create an extension, a 'New Paris'. The first phase of development of this new business district began in 1958. The first new high-rise building was the Esso Tower of eleven storeys built in 1963. The first towers were all restricted to a height of 100 m and each had a footprint 42 m × 20 m. From 1970, a second generation of buildings was started but then halted in 1973 by the economic crisis. The project was enthusiastically supported by Georges Pompidou while he was the president of France (1969–74). He believed that

Figure 9.3 La Défense from the Arc de Triomphe. Wikimedia Creative Commons Attribution Share Alike 4.01 International/Suicsmo

creating a superlative business sector, a centre where all the headquarters of the great corporations would be located, was integral to his endeavour to make France a major economic power and Paris a great commercial capital. From the early 1980s, a third generation of structures was added, including in 1981 a massive shopping mall and in 1989, to mark the bicentenary of the French Revolution, a monumental 110-m-high cube Grande Arche which punctuates the historical east-west axis of Paris. Chevalier objected strongly to what he called 'a monstrous, diabolical arch'. Its construction was promoted by François Mitterand, the president of France from 1981 to 1995. The design competition for the arch was won by a Danish architect and a Danish engineer. In 1993, the thirty-year-old Esso Tower was demolished to be replaced in 2001 by the two towers of the Cœur Défense, each 161 m high, and three eight-storey apartment blocks and business premises.

Given the centuries during which Paris had accumulated its built form, the redevelopment of some dilapidated areas was undoubtedly required by the twentieth century. The need for change was widely acknowledged but the nature of the changes proposed was forcefully contested. A wholesale wine market – Halle aux Vins – had been established in the 1660s on the Left Bank of the Seine, adjacent to the Jardin des Plantes. In 1808, Napoléon Bonaparte decided it needed to be enlarged. Plans for a new building were prepared in 1811 and 70 per cent of it was completed by 1813, the rest not until 1845. The site was taken over by central government in 1958 for the construction of a science campus for the University of Pierre and Marie Curie. The campus was constructed between 1958 and 1972 and included from 1970 the Tour Zamansky (named after a doyen of the Faculty of Science) of twenty-eight storeys at a height of 90 m (Figure 9.4). In the late 1960s, a comprehensive scheme to 'renovate' a large area on the Right Bank involved the demolition in 1971 of the mid-nineteenth-century iron and glass pavilions of Les Halles, the main food market of Paris. They were replaced by an underground shopping mall which included a dozen cinema screens with seating for more than 3,000 filmgoers.

Nearby is the Centre-Pompidou, a hub for modern and contemporary art (Figure 9.5). Named after its initiator, Georges Pompidou (president, 1969–74), it was opened in 1977 by President Valéry Giscard d'Estaing. It was and remains a controversial building. The project was intended to reinstate Paris as a world leader in modern and contemporary art, to promote artistic interdisciplinarity and new forms of artistic expression and to create a monumental building that would demonstrate the best in architecture on the eve of the twentieth century. The project energized a lively debate in France, about the divide between elite and popular culture, and between the centralization of art in Paris and the desirability of decanting it to the provinces. But the controversy was especially heated over the design of the building itself, a product of one Italian (Renzo Piano) and one British architect (Richard Rogers). A renowned British historian of France and lover of Paris Richard Cobb (1985, p. 190) called the Centre-Pompidou 'a strange building that rises above the modest levels of old buildings nearby [and] looks like a *paupiette de veau*, with all its innards displayed on the outside'. Various French commentators have likened the building to an aircraft hangar, a gas works, an oil refinery, a cultural junk room and an avant-garde wart. Some have described it as a toaster or a giant, multicoloured, insect. Jean d'Ormesson, a member

Figure 9.4 La Tour Zamansky and church of Saint-Étienne-du-Mont. Wikimedia Creative Commons Attribution Share Alike 4.0 International/Mbzt

of the exclusive French Academy, said that the Centre-Pompidou raised a fundamental question about the idea of beauty; Jean Baudrillard, philosopher and postmodernist, believed that it marked the first time that the dimension of culture had been raised to that of the commercial hypermarket; Hervé Guibert, a writer and journalist, judged it to be an unfinished work, a place of compromises and confusions, of moving and resting, of wanderings, of apprenticeship, of temporary freedom and of profane prayer. More prosaically, the intellectual newspaper *Le Monde* declared the building to be a powerful blow, a violation, a sort of 'architectural King-Kong'.

To the east of the Centre-Pompidou, a large part of the Marais *quartier* has been transformed. This former 'beehive' of small hotels and craft workshops, many connected to the cloth and garment trade and populated by Algerians and Jews, has been redeveloped as a predominately middle-class district, changed by gentrification. In 1985, Richard Cobb (1985, p. 194) opined: 'The Marais, as an area of social mixture

174   *Personality of Paris*

Figure 9.5 Le Centre Pompidou. Wikimedia Creative Commons Attribution S hare Alike 2.0 Generic/Jeff & Brian

and of varied occupation, is now dead …The Marais has been recovered as a tourists' paradise. But the quarter has lost all warmth and originality.'

In the 1960s, urban motorways were being considered for Paris, to speed traffic through and under the city. A major plan (*Plan autoroutier pour Paris*) proposed not only a *boulevard pérphérique* around the borders of the city and an inner ring of *grands boulevards* but also eight four- or six-lane highways crisscrossing the city, with both banks of the Seine being converted into trunk roads. Most of this brutalizing scheme was abandoned in the 1970s, having encountered strong opposition both from Parisians living near the proposed roads and also more generally from environmentalists.

Proposals for motorways in central Paris were checked but high-rise building continued. The Tour Montparnasse was built on the site of the old Gare Montparnasse, which served as the main railway link between Paris and Brittany (Figure 9.6). This tower, opened in 1973, was the first skyscraper in Paris: 210 m high, it was an architectural cuckoo in its Haussmannian nest. It remained the tallest skyscraper in France until 2011 when it was surpassed by the Tour First at 225 m as part of the development at La Défense. Authorized by André Malraux, minister of culture in General de Gaulle's presidency, the Tour Montparnasse has fifty-nine floors, with, on its fifty-sixth floor, a restaurant called *Le Ciel de Paris* and a terrace on the top floor, both open to the public and providing a panoramic 360-degree view of Paris. Louis Chevalier described this skyscraper as 'a monstrous building'. The tower's simple, almost puritanical, architecture, its large proportions and its monolithic

Figure 9.6 La Tour Montparnasse from the top of the Arc de Triomphe. Wikimedia Creative Commons Attribution Share Alike 3.0/Steven Strehl

appearance have been criticized for being out of place – as 'ghastly' modernity in Paris's Haussmannized landscape. As a result, two years after its completion, the construction of buildings of over seven storeys high in the city centre was banned. An article in the *New York Times* of 26 September 2008 reported that some critics of the Tower claimed its observation deck enjoys the most beautiful view in all of Paris because it is the only place from which the Tower cannot be seen, echoing Maupassant's assessment of the Eiffel Tower in 1889.

Other horrors – or at the very least blots defacing the Parisian landscape – further away from the centre include the conference centre and shopping complex at the Porte Maillot; the immense uniform towers of the new Porte d'Italie, in south-eastern Paris (Figure 9.7); the Boulevard Périphérique; and the huge high-rise complex of shops, offices and flats of Maine-Montparnasse (which includes the Montparnasse Tower and the new railway station).

Figure 9.7 La Porte d'Italie. Wikimedia Creative Commons Attribution Share Alike 3.0/ Thierry Bézecourt

There have been a number of proposals to transform Paris into a version of New York. Georges Pompidou (president, 1969–74) was enthusiastic but died prematurely in 1974. Such grandiose schemes provoked many protests. Pompidou's successor (Valéry Giscard d'Estaing – president, 1974–81) was cautious and decreed that no more skyscrapers could be permitted within the city of Paris, a view which accorded with that of the many Parisians who had been opposing plans for major developments. People had come to love Haussmann's Paris – but we need to recall that many of his contemporaries had opposed his remodelling of the city.

The Pyramide du Louvre is a modernist glass and metal structure erected in 1989, sitting – or rather plonked – uncomfortably and surprisingly in the main courtyard of the Louvre Palace (Figure 9.8). Its architect was I. M. Pei, an American-Chinese, commissioned in 1984 by François Mitterand (president, 1981–95) as one of his *Grands Projets*. Although strikingly beautiful in itself, its modernist juxtaposition with the Renaissance architecture of the Louvre is simply brutal. The charm of the modern pyramid in no way complements its historical context: the architectural contrast is too great. The pyramid provides a startling, visual, distraction from the aesthetic magnificence and cultural significance of the sixteenth-century Louvre. It has created considerable controversy, both admired as a modern technological and geometrical modernist masterpiece and disapproved of as an anachronistic intrusion of an Egyptian death symbol in the living heart of Paris. Political critics caustically termed it the 'Pharaoh François' Pyramid'.

The Opéra Bastille, designed by a Uraguayan/Canadian architect, located at the Place de la Bastille and inaugurated in 1989 on the bicentenary of the storming of the Bastille, was another of François Mitterand's *Grands Projets* (Figure 9.9). Louis Chevalier recounts anecdotes about it which liken this elephantine building to a

'Assassinating Paris'? 177

Figure 9.8 La Pyramide du Louvre. Wikimedia Creative Commons Attribution Share Alike 4.0/SchiDD

Figure 9.9 L'Opéra Bastille. Wikimedia Creative Commons Share Alike 4.0/LPLT

hospital or to a *pissoir* (urinal). In his opinion, the Bastille Opera House 'repels and instils fear' and compares very unfavourably with the nineteenth-century Opéra Garnier. Another of Mitterand's *Grands Projets* was the Bibliothèque Nationale de France or Bibliothèque François Mitterand opened in 1996, the last and most costly

Figure 9.10 La Bibliothèque nationale de France site François-Mitterand. Wikimedia Commons Attribution Share Alike 4.0/Thesupermat

of the works that he had built in Paris (Figure 9.10). Located on the Left Bank of the Seine in the south-eastern *13ᵉ arrondissement*, it consists of four L-shaped towers representing open books, arranged at the corners of a large platform around a sunken garden. Although in the 'minimalist' architectural style, the towers are massive, 79 m high with twenty-two storeys. Construction of the library ran into huge cost overruns and technical difficulties related to its high-rise design, so much so that it was came to be referred to in the media as the '*TGB*' or '*Très Grande Bibliothèque*' ('Very Large Library'), an allusion to France's very successful high-speed rail system, the '*TGV*' ('*Train à Grande Vitesse*').

Paris during the twentieth century witnessed significant changes to the built form it had inherited from the nineteenth century. Professional urbanists argued for major changes to its physical environment which were needed, they judged, especially to address the growing problem of traffic circulation and congestion. Architects sought to improve both the city's built environment and their own reputations. Presidents of France seemed to have been more ambitious for the future of the Parisian landscape than proud of its historical legacy. Aping the first and third Napoléons, many presidents in the twentieth century wrote themselves architecturally, monumentally, into the history and personality of Paris. They promoted hubristic architecture. They have often engaged equally hubristic foreign architects – Danish, British, Italian, American-Chinese and Uraguayan-Canadian – who seem to have had little understanding or appreciation of the harmonious cityscape (if not harmonious society) that had been inherited from the long-nineteenth century. Napoléon III and Baron Haussmann promoted specific individual iconic structures but situated them mellifluously within a general architectural context. The personality of Paris

Figure 9.11 No. 175 Boulevard Haussmann in 2020, redesigned by French architect Phillipe Chiambaretta. Salem Mostefavoui for PCA-Stream Phillipe Chiambaretta architecte

to which they contributed so much has not been 'assassinated' by their successors but it has certainly been changed significantly, for better or worse, according to one's viewpoint 'improved' or 'mutilated'.

That modern developments can be achieved in harmony with the city's architectural traditions have been demonstrated recently with the completion in 2020 of the new investment banking office of the Lazard Bank on a corner site of Boulevard Haussmann in the 8e *arrondissement* (Figure 9.11). This development has redesigned two different buildings: No. 175, a classical Haussmannian residential building from 1863, and No. 173, an office building from the 1920s with Art Déco tones. French architect Phillipe Chiamaretta, sensitive to the historical context of the site, designed a modern building in harmony with its neighbours, retaining key elements of the Haussmannian classical and Art Déco traditions while adding three floors, the top two having a spectacular glass roof which night-time illumination conjures into a startling magic lantern – this modern enhancement of the Parisian street scene by day and night represents rejuvenation rather than assassination or even self-harm.

Epilogue

The personality of Paris was developed on a well-defined topographical structure. The sinuous river Seine and its islands; to the north an abandoned river meander course and gaps between sets of hills; and to the south gentle uplands – these physiographical units influenced powerfully the spatial growth of the city. The trinity of *ville-cité-université* was a positive cultural response to natural guidelines. On the main island in the Seine, a distinctive administrative centre for both the religious and the secular authorities was developed, dominated visually by the cathedral of Notre-Dame for more than eight centuries. To either side, the Left Bank and the Right Bank of the Seine acquired during those centuries differing characteristics while experiencing many of the same or similar influences on their developments. Throughout the medieval and early modern periods, the narrative of Paris was structured by its three distinct components, so obvious to Victor Hugo in the 1830s when portraying the capital's physiognomy in the 1480s. Until the eighteenth century, it would not be inappropriate to narrate Paris as a tale of three cities. But, from around 1789, that story has to be reworked into a tale of two cities and many villages. Victoria Thompson has argued that the social turmoil of the July Revolution of 1830 led to revised descriptions of Paris by contemporary observers, who recognized the existence of two cities: first, a city of the popular classes associated with poverty, vice and revolution, a working-class city that demanded surveillance and control; and second, a middle-class city identified with social mobility and sovereignty, a city that required freedom and mobility. The ancient Rue Saint-Honoré, one of few streets in the 1830s that extended on the Right Bank from east to west, beginning at the Place de la Bastille in the east, the centre of a popular neighbourhood and entrance to the poor *faubourg* Saint-Antoine, and ending in the west in the wealthy and fashionable *faubourg* Saint-Honoré, linked the increasingly distinctive 'two cities'. Victoria Thompson (2003, p. 555) has suggested that it was in the 1830s and 1840s that the image of Paris as comprising many segments combining to form a united whole was replaced by a view of Paris as 'a city divided in two, a city whose populations were depicted as inherently different in their use of urban space'. Paris was lived very differently by the bourgeoisie and by the working class. By 1914, Paris had spread well beyond its medieval and early modern limits so that there was a clear spatial distinction between 'central' Paris, broadly the pre-1860 twelve *arrondissements*, and the expanded 'peripheral' Paris of *faubourgs*, broadly the eight *arrondissements* annexed into the city in 1860. This latter included the Zone, land beyond the 1840s Thiers wall, where many immigrants lived in *bidonvilles* (shanty developments).

In addition to its three key physiographical components, the morphology of Paris was strengthened by enduringly strong historical routes running east-west on the Right Bank and north-south on the Right and Left Banks. Identifiable from the Roman period onwards, what are today the east-west Rue de Rivoli and the Avenue des Champs-Élysées combined with two north-south routes marked today by the Rue St Martin/Rue St-Jacques and the Boulevard Sebastopol/Boulevard St-Michel. These roads are anchored parts of the skeleton around which Paris was spatially structured.

How best, then, to characterize the personality of nineteenth-century Paris? That it had a complex personality was signalled by Walter Benjamin's view that in the nineteenth century there were two versions of the city: 'the real Paris, and Paris the city of dreams'. But it could be argued that different contemporaries and different historians identified for themselves different 'realities' as well as different 'imaginings' of Paris. There are thus multiple versions of Paris, both real and imagined. I have endeavoured here to identify the salient characteristics of the personality of nineteenth-century Paris while acknowledging that it was complex and changed over time. Paris inherited strong topographical and cultural traits from its past but it was transformed during the course of the long-nineteenth century. From 1789, Paris transitioned from its medieval and early modern condition into a modern and in some ways postmodern city. The wheels of capitalism were turning ceaselessly before 1789 but then accelerated markedly, especially from the 1850s. That nineteenth-century Paris had a complex personality is clear from the many histories and myths that have been written and created about it. Patrice Higonnet has meticulously unpacked in turn more than a dozen myths about Paris, starting with an essay on Paris 'City of Myths'. It is not my intention here to interrogate those myths further nor to reproduce them – and certainly not to create a new one. It is instead to consider the making and the meaning of the landscape of the city between 1789 and 1914 and to consider the interaction between the cityscape and its use and understanding by Parisians. Paris was a city of contrasts and conflicts, a city of paradoxes that was simultaneously proud and sordid, temperamental and intellectual, volatile and enduring. It celebrated and worried about its past while dreaming and fretting about its future.

The remodelling of Paris during the 1850s and 1860s by Haussmann produced a distinctive signature landscape which has become legendary and to some extent mythical. Haussmann's elegant landscape – of aesthetically balanced apartment buildings in dressed limestone, flowing along boulevards in harmony and without breaks but decoratively varied in architectural detail, with tree-lined long vistas to monuments or monumental structures – was designed to impress itself on the minds and memories both of Parisians and of visitors. Haussmann's intentionally spectacular streetscape had been preceded by some magnificent individual examples of city architectural embellishment, such as the eighteenth-century Place Vendôme and the seventeenth-century Place des Vosges, but it is the immense geographical scale of Haussmann's work which is remarkable. He placed his imprint over so many parts of the city and to a great extent linked those parts into a better-functioning and more aesthetically pleasing whole. His influence extended directly into the twentieth century. Urban improvements after the Great War included completion in 1927 of the Boulevard Haussmann and in 1936 of the central Halles with the addition of two cast-iron pavilions in the style of original architect, Victor Baltard.

Paris was wholeheartedly and perpetually from the mid-nineteenth century a proudly exhibitionist city which was at its most flamboyant and ostentatious when it hosted five world fairs between 1855 and 1900. Its growing and in some important respects unjustified reputation as a rich and spectacular city, fuelled by the greater connectedness of an increasingly literate French society, powered the flows of provincial migrants to Paris. Control of the society and economy of France by the government in Paris, through its hierarchically nested spatial administrative system of *départements*, *arrondissements*, *cantons* and *communes*, meant that the long arm of Paris – especially in the form of schooling, military service and road and rail communications – reached into even the remotest and isolated parts of the provinces such as the Pyrenees and Languedoc and the Alps and Provence. The reputation of Paris – whether as myth or reality – permeated the French provinces and drew thousands of migrants to the capital.

The exhibitionist character of Paris was also to be seen in the way in which it became a more open and public city. The Second Empire's cleaner, safer, streets and increased number of public spaces brought more people into open circulation as did the windows of department stores and the growing number of cafés which set up their tables on outside terraces. Life in Paris became ever more extrovert and the dramatic, kaleidoscopic, spectacle of daily life on the streets attracted ever larger flows of people. The Second Empire set in motion the *Expositions universelles*, encouraging Paris literally to make an exhibition of itself. Even the ceremonial opening of a new boulevard was deliberately staged as a flamboyant public spectacle. Development of the tourist trade and of commercial leisure attractions brought not only more Parisians but also more provincials and foreigners onto the capital's streets, adding to the cosmopolitan feel of the city. Charles Rearick has argued that 'the fair sex' was to be seen in public places in Paris to a much greater extent than was the case in Victorian London. Paris was more open and liberated than the more disciplined, more prudishly controlled, streets and parks of London. At least, that was an integral part of the image of Paris which brought many foreigners, especially Britons, to it as a city of pleasure, whereas London's image was that of a city of business.

The writer, musicologist and historian Romain Rolland (1904, p. 211) suggested that 'there is not just one Paris, there are three or four – a worldly Paris, a bourgeois Paris, an intellectual Paris, an ordinary people's Paris – living side by side and hardly ever meeting. If you do not know these small cities within the City, you cannot picture the whole, the powerful and often contradictory life of this gigantic organism'. To this litany could readily be added, for example, an artistic Paris, a literary Paris, an aural Paris and an olfactory Paris. That Paris from the Commune to the outbreak of the Great War was a city 'filled with contradictions, energy and a fanatical desire to be entertained' is reflected referentially, Catherine Kautsky has argued, in Claude Debussy's 'astonishing ability to convert social reality into musical paraphrase'. The city's influence on Debussy (born 1862 in St-Germain-en-Laye almost 20 km from Notre-Dame, died 1918 in Paris) was incalculable. He lived in a city of contrasts and contradictions: for example, of old and new, of tradition and revolution, of sobriety and sensuality, of poverty and prosperity, of flocks of people and *flâneurs*, of inhibitions and exhibitions, of a spectrum of artistic, literary and social *-isms*. 'Debussy's music', Kautsky claims, 'embraces both the bustle of the contemporary Parisian music hall and the stillness of classical antiquity'. Given such almost limitless complexity, I instead want to venture a more straightforward simplicity: that Paris between 1789 and 1914 is best understood as a tale of two cities and many villages.

Nineteenth-century Paris had a split personality. It became increasingly two cities, a socially divided city. Writers like Honoré de Balzac, Charles Baudelaire, Gustave Flaubert, Guy de Maupassant and Émile Zola narrated the city as a site of opportunity but also of class conflict and social turbulence. Bourgeois authors broadcast to a wide audience the often-desperate living conditions of the Parisian working class, socially dislocated and geographically separated from wealthier Parisians. Felicity Edlam has highlighted the contrasting experiences of the city by bourgeois men and working-class women, with the former consuming the city 'from above' freely able to enjoy its wonders and spectacle, while the latter viewed it 'from below' constrained by law, social convention and economic vulnerability to the city's central streets and peripheral suburbs. The women who were so crucial to the spectacle and experience of the boulevards were working in spaces controlled by and for bourgeois men.

One of the remarkable features of nineteenth-century Paris is that, although it exploded demographically, it remained small in area. Before 1800, Paris had a radius of less than 4 km so that every part of the city was accessible on foot in about sixty minutes. On 12 April 1803, an Englishman, Bertie Greatheed, took only four and a half hours to walk around the whole of the city's outer wall (and including two ferry trips across the Seine); to walk from the Rue de la Loi (today the Rue de Richelieu) in central Paris where he was staying, near the Palais-Royal, to the Barrière de Mont Martre in the boundary wall took him just fifteen minutes. Even then, he stressed in his diary 'that it must not be imagined that this wall encloses nothing but town, there is empty space without end, fields and vineyards; one might as well enclose Middlesex & call it London'. Even after the expansion of the city's jurisdiction in 1860 by the annexation of some surrounding communes and its administrative reformation into twenty *arrondissements*, the centre of Paris at Notre-Dame was still only about 5 km from the city's southern boundary and about 6 km from its northern boundary, while from the western edge of the city to that on the east was approximately 12 km. It was possible to walk from any *quartier* to the city boundary in about ninety minutes and from many it would have been much quicker. The compact character of Paris helped to conjure its urban identity and an urban consciousness on the part of its residents: as a walled and compact area, Paris provided its citizens with an easily grasped mental map.

The split personality of nineteenth-century Paris was captured by Victor Hugo in 1875 when he stressed that Paris was a totality which accordingly embraced both civilization and barbarism. A different duality has been highlighted by Maurice Agulhon, a leading cultural historian of France, in his 1992 traverse across Paris from east to west. He started by recognizing the long-standing depiction of Paris from north to south, differentiating the Right Bank from the Left Bank, a fundamental legacy from the medieval Paris of *ville* and *université* centred on the island *cité*. Over the years, the Right Bank became identified as the locus of capital and commerce, of elegance and wealth and of the Right politically; by contrast, the Left Bank became a hub of ideas and intellectualism, of radical scholars and rebellious students and on the Left politically. This binary, north-south, Right Bank-Left Bank, characterization of Paris was always a generalization that gained traction only by focusing on central Paris rather than the city as a whole. During the nineteenth century, the population growth and spatial spread of Paris was accompanied by the emergence, building on early modern developments, of a significant contrast between a western *bourgeois* Paris generally voting for the Right and an eastern *populaire* Paris for the Left. Those geographically distinctive electoral patterns were also materially expressed in times of armed civil conflict in June 1848 and in May 1871, when, as Agulhon (1998, p. 526) has argued, 'along a front that ran north to south, popular, working-class eastern Paris, largely in support of a democratic, social republic, faced western Paris, the bastion of legally constituted authority and the party of law and order'. This duality was also, Aguhlon argued, expressed monumentally in the cityscape with, for example, liberal, secular, republican east Paris rooted in the Bastille and the Place de la Bastille and the Panthéon, while the national, military triangle of west Paris was grounded in the Place Vendôme, the Arc de Triomphe and the Invalides. When the Place de la Concorde was equipped with statues representing eight major cities of France, they were located around the periphery in approximately the positions they occupied in reality (e.g. Marseille to the south-east, Strasbourg to the north-east and Bordeaux to the south-west). The Place thus symbolized both the centre of France and the centre of Paris. Agulhon claimed that the east-west, left-right duality of Parisian monumental symbolism was 'an undeniable if somewhat abstract reality that persisted for a century and a half'.

The simplicity of that monumental and political duality is challenged by the findings of a historian of ideas Jean-Pierre Bernard who has investigated forensically in his book *Les Deux Paris* (2001) the representations of Paris during the second half of the nineteenth century in about 700 books and pamphlets published between 1850 and 1914. He concluded that Paris had two fundamental forms of literary representation, one material and the other spiritual. While Paris was perceived as being singular and unique, it was also always represented as being divided in two. There was a Paris by day and a Paris by night; a Paris of opulence and a Paris of poverty; Paris as the capital but also a Paris of revolution; a Paris above ground and a Paris below ground; a masculine Paris and a feminine Paris; a Paris of the living and a Paris of the dead. Mythical Paris, the essence of Paris, Bernard argued, lies in the duality of its representations in late-nineteenth-century writings. His focus is exclusively on literary depictions of Paris, ignoring the potential contributions of painting and photography, of art and architecture, to the imagining of Paris which could have reinforced his case. Kautsky, in her account of Debussy's Paris of the late nineteenth and early twentieth centuries, depicts the city as 'a doppelganger, flaunting the new and secreting itself in the old': crowds flowed through the arcades and department stores; poets sequestered themselves in élite salons and *flâneurs* strolled secure in their anonymity while dancers and entertainers displayed themselves and built a reputation for the city. For Kautsky,

Debussy's music, in turn flamboyant and mysterious, embraced both the bustle and the stillness to be found in Paris.

Bernard and Kautsky both acknowledge that there was a Paris by day and another Paris artificially illuminated by night but Simone Delattre has audaciously and successfully explored with astonishing thoroughness the 'real' character and the 'perceived' or 'mythical' nature of Paris at night during the nineteenth century. For the former, she exploits, both cautiously and provocatively, descriptive and statistical sources compiled by public authorities and, for the latter, private literary accounts of individual and collective nocturnal experiences. She traces, of course, the transition – which she dates as being between 1830 and 1860 – from an old untamed night to a new controlled, artificially illuminated, night with the successive – and dazzling – replacement of oil lamps by gas and then electric lighting of public spaces, a transition from a rarity to a superfluity of illumination. Delattre traces the growth of noctambulism, notably of young bohemians enjoying the enhanced freedom and frisson of Paris by night. These élitist nocturnal *flâneurs* were quite separate from the potentially dangerous night prowlers from lower social groups. Delattre reveals the significant contribution of numerous night workers to the functioning of the city: street cleaners, people emptying cess pits, ragpickers, rubbish collectors, food market workers and bakers (although these were 'troglodytes' tending their ovens indoors, not in full public view). Paris by night had long been the stage for criminal activity, and Delattre reinforces the sombre picture painted by Louis Chevalier in 1958 of the 'labouring and dangerous classes' in Paris during the first half of the nineteenth century. But the artificially illuminated night also came to extend the hours for leisure pursuits and the growth of public entertainments. Many of the pleasures and entertainments of the late nineteenth and early twentieth centuries so vividly described and illustrated by Charles Rearick were nocturnal activities permitted and enhanced by artificial lighting. Paris by day had been extended into the night: for Parisians, the distinction between day and night was much less sharp in 1900 than it had been in 1800.

Paris was indeed a tale of two cities but it was also a tale of many urban villages. Many immigrants from villages with populations of just a few hundred or from provincial towns with populations of a few thousand or even tens of thousands sought to soften the social, economic and psychological challenge of moving to the capital city of more than 1 million people by moving into *quartiers* in which they knew there were already living a large number of people from their own region or *pays* in the provinces. In this way, Paris embraced 'villages' within its walls. Many neighbourhoods had their own subcultures: communities of largely immigrants sharing similar geographical origins, customs and languages or *patois*, and using the same markets and cafés in their own cultivated *quartiers*, such as the Marais and Montparnasse. In his *Paris nouveau et Paris futur* (1865), the journalist and historian Victor Fournel (1829–1894) claimed that 'the capital was nothing but a series of distinct little villages'. Of course, not all new Parisians sought to retain their provinciality: some positively welcomed the deracination and anonymity which the capital offered. Parisian villages were often of relatively poor working-class people, largely dissociated from the grandeur of the city centre. They were comprised of the *petit peuple* in districts just outside the new Grands Boulevards on the Right Bank and in districts to the north and east, such as La Villette, Belleville and Ménilmont. The most iconic of the former villages is Montmartre: not directly impacted by Haussmann's remodelling, it lay immediately outside the boundary of the municipality of Paris until 1860 when it was one of the extramural communes annexed by the city and incorporated into its new *18ᵉ arrondissement*. Montmartre retained until the late nineteenth century something of the atmosphere of a quiet country village, with tree-lined lanes, a few farmhouses and windmills and some basic drinking dens. Gradually, it became a renowned focus for artistic bohemians, for religious pilgrims to the Basilica of the Sacred Heart and for Parisians seeking a change of scene and pace of life – and then also for tourists, French and foreign, seeking to experience its distinctive 'sense of place' and to enjoy from its height a panoramic view of the capital city. Paris was a plurality of villages, of local communities whose life worlds were distinct but nonetheless interacting within the larger body of Paris as a whole. Even today, for Federico Castigliano, a modern *flâneur*, the tiny streets, passages and courtyards that lie along the southern boundary of the *9ᵉ* and *10ᵉ arrondissements* conjure the sensation of being in a village outside the city.

Increasingly during the nineteenth century, social differences came to be magnified spatially as Paris evolved into two cities. David Garrioch has emphasized that pre-Revolutionary literary sources reveal that Paris was already by the 1780s a place of 'contrasting colours, luxury and plenty juxtaposed with poverty and dearth'. That social contrast became also a spatial contrast. In the nineteenth century, central districts experienced much slower population growth than did the peripheries. The historical vertical segregation of households of differing social class on separate floors within the same residential building was gradually replaced by a horizontal social segregation within the city. Studies of the spatial distribution of 'wealth' and of 'poverty' using a range of criteria have revealed the higher levels of 'wealth' in the central and western districts of the city and the higher levels of 'poverty' in the peripheral districts, especially in the eastern and north-eastern *arrondissements*. This social geography of Paris was evident before Haussmann's remodelling of the city but was accentuated by it and continued after it, creating what came to be termed the 'Red Belt' of socialist and communist, working-class, industrial, peripheral, districts ringing the mostly bourgeois, conservative, central city. Extremes of poverty and of wealth, of seemingly limitless luxury and of undoubtedly desperate dearth, were separate but, given the compactness of the city, in close geographical proximity. The beautiful and classical cityscape in the centre, which owed so much to the dreams of Napoléon III and Baron Haussmann, contrasted with the ugly and chaotic, nightmarish, landscapes developed for Parisians living in poor-quality housing amidst industrial developments in the peripheral *banlieues*.

Another aspect of the split personality of Paris was the divide between 'native' Parisians and 'new' Parisians, incomers born in the provinces. A real tension confronted many Parisians who had not been born in the city – they were Parisians in the making but not originally so. They often cultivated dual geopieties, keen to achieve the status of being Parisian but also nostalgic for their former social practices and friendships in the *pays* they had abandoned in the provinces. Nostalgia for 'home' coexisted with the pride of living in the capital city.

Social tensions exploding onto the streets were expressions of the tormented personality of nineteenth-century Paris. A powerful revolutionary tradition dating from 1789 led many Parisians to seek ways of putting into practice, in all aspects of their lives, the principles of liberty, equality and fraternity. Most nineteenth-century Parisians experienced at least one revolution or war during their lifetimes as well as violent street protests and peaceful demonstrations. Paris was a politically turbulent and volatile place. Street barricades became familiar to Parisians: the Revolution of 1830, it is claimed, saw the erection of more than 4,000 barricades built using more than 800,000 cobblestones. Higonnet (2002, p. 60) has argued that after 1830 'the cobblestone, especially the bloody cobblestone, became one of the most eloquent symbols of the Parisian revolutionary spirit'. Frequent street fighting and public executions by guillotining (begun in 1792, briefly abolished in 1848 and continued in public until 1939, although many were held inside as well as outside prison grounds) meant that human blood was all too often splattered across buildings, ponded in public squares and flowed in the gutters of streets where it merged with animal blood from the slaughtering houses or abattoirs (the word dates from 1806) and the premises of butchers. A prolific English writer Edward Lucas (1868–1938) put it succinctly in his book *A Wanderer in Paris* (1909, tenth edition 1913): 'Paris is steeped in blood.'

Paris was excitable, some might say intoxicated, by political turmoil. It often played out its social tensions on the streets. For example, in the summer of 1888, riots erupted in the suburbs when food prices soared and the government refused to remove duties on grain; in 1902, shop clerks in Saint-Denis in northern Paris forcibly escorted customers from stores that did not close at 8 pm as part of their campaign for shorter working hours; in May 1906, 126,000 workers seeking a reduction of the working day to eight hours went on strike in Paris: they included 72,000 construction workers, 20,000 bricklayers and stonemasons, 10,000 housepainters, 8,000 navvies, and 6,000 carpenters; and in 1907, café and restaurant waiters marched on the streets to express their anger about authoritarian managements which denied them the right to grow moustaches.

Militancy, on large and small scales, was part of the personality of Paris. From 1789 until 1914, France moved from regime to regime through revolutions and coups with Paris as the epicentre of its social and political earthquakes. In this turbulent period, thousands of Parisians were killed or wounded during the violent struggles which brought down governments. Many more thousands participated in street protests and strikes. Edward Shorter and Charles Tilly have shown that the bulk of strikes in France between 1830 and 1914 became concentrated in Paris: the metropolis was more conducive to effective organization of workers and to intense social conflict than either the small towns or the isolated clusters of industry in the provinces.

Another fundamental social tension in Paris was that between clerical and secular ideologies, with the former losing out to the latter. This was a conflict that permeated not just Parisian but the whole of French society during the nineteenth century leading to the legal separation of church and state in 1905. The battle for the minds of Parisians was fought monumentally in the religiosity of the Basilica of the Sacred Heart and the modernity of the Eiffel Tower, two buildings intended to impress by the use respectively of traditional and modern materials, by their startling and contrasting designs, and by their domineering stances in the cityscape, both literally looking down on Paris from on high in an attempt to assert individually their religious and secular control of its citizens.

One paradox of the personality of Paris lies in its drawing upon past glories while simultaneously planning a heroic future. Despite – or perhaps because of – the social instability of life in Paris, its residents were remarkably resilient. Revolutions, wars, empires, monarchies and republics ebbed and flowed through the city which coped amazingly well with such vicissitudes. In her delightful book *Hidden Gardens of Paris*, Susan Cahill (2002, p. 44) says that in the Luxembourg Garden, with its statues of artists and statesmen set into deep lawns and its regular visitors for whom the word 'leisure' is not an abstraction, with its chess and *boules* players, with its children's carousel and its many readers of books and newspapers: 'You get a sense of down-to-earth practical wisdom, of the arts of survival that have seen Parisians through centuries of wars and suffering. In the Luxembourg, the tough complex soul of the city comes through.'

Myths about Paris are legion: many of them focus on just one aspect of its history and personality and many of them also tend to freeze the city into a specific time frame. For some, the triumph of Haussmannization has been its defining characteristic and there is no doubt that the picture of the city created by that process has been lodged in people's imaginations from the mid-nineteenth century onwards. But the reshaping and reimagining of Paris in the 1850s and 1860s is best seen as one especially productive phase in the ceaseless process of capitalist construction-destruction-construction. Lovers of Paris and its many myths very probably wish it to be unchanged. But the classic Paris of 1870 was itself a remodelling of a living city, not the construction of a living museum. In its turn, nineteenth-century Paris was always likely to be 'improved' by successive generations of ambitious architects, planners and politicians. 'History', as claimed by Luc Sante, 'is always in the gun sights of planners and developers'. There is a school of thought which considers that the changes made to the landscape of Paris since the end of the nineteenth century have not all been enhancements.

As a virulent critic, Louis Chevalier deplored the late twentieth century's assault on the city's legacy from the nineteenth century, on what he saw as the ruination of the centre of Paris and the destruction of what he believed to be the tranquillity of the city and its human scale. Chevalier referred unhesitatingly to the 'assassination' of Paris, a description adopted readily by Richard Cobb, an eminent British historian of eighteenth- and nineteenth-century France, and by Norma Evenson, a prominent American architectural historian of Paris. Stephen Clarke, a Francophile British author, believes that since the 1789 Revolution Paris has shot itself in the foot 'and elsewhere'. The *bouleversement* of the built environment of Paris during the second half of the twentieth century led Jacques Réda, poet and author, to reflect upon the 'ruins of Paris'. Patrice Higonnet, author in 2002 of an outstanding analysis of the many myths about Paris, considered (p. 210) that during the second half of the twentieth century

> this great city was delivered into the hands of indifferent politicians and avid speculators, whose great collective achievement was the brutalisation of the city, with the banks of the Seine transformed into expressways and the skyline defaced by high-rise office towers at the Gare Montparnasse and the Porte d'Italie. We may

hope, incidentally, that, this sad phase in Parisian history has finally come to an end with the completion of the regrettable, soulless, and depressing Bibliothèque Nationale de France-François Mitterand.

Lovers tend to exaggerate the object of their affections and it might be that some historians and commentators have done so in relation to their beloved Paris. Many physical structures of nineteenth-century Paris have survived into the twenty-first century, although many, it must be conceded, have been lost.

It would be more balanced to say that nineteenth-century Paris has been mutilated rather than assassinated. Fragments of the paradise of Paris 'lost' can in fact be 'rediscovered' by informed explorers, as they have been, for example, by social historian Mary McAuliffein in her delightful book *Paris Discovered: Explorations in the City of Light* (2006). Parts of the Marais, Temple and Saint-Antoine districts in the *3^e and 4^e arrondissements* as well as parts of the Latin Quarter in the *5^e* have retained at least a 'feel' of old, pre-Haussmann, Paris. So, too, do the surviving arcades such as the Passage de l'Industrie, dating from 1827, and the Passage Brady, from 1828, both in the *10^e arrondissement*, the former specializing today in the sale of hair products (such as wigs, hairpieces and perfumes) while the latter includes Asian restaurants and a costumier hiring out a wide range of uniforms and outfits. The golden era of the arcades was the 1830s and 1840s, of the department stores the 1880s, 1890s and 1900s. A nostalgic sense of the latter may be experienced even from the outside of Le Bon Marché on the Left Bank and of Le Printemps on the Right Bank. Despite the changes wrought to the face of Paris by architects, planners and politicians since 1914, the elegant boulevards and parks of Haussmann's city and the picturesque streets and structures which have survived from before 1914 testify to the survival of a maimed city rather than to its assassination. If Paris has lost some of its charm, harmony and uniqueness, it nonetheless retains enough both for visitors and for its residents to appreciate its specific *genus loci* and unique qualities: the poetry of Paris persists for all to enjoy.

A survey conducted by Stanley Milgram and Denise Jodelet in the late 1970s, of the way Parisians drawn from each of its twenty *arrondissements* imagined Paris, confirmed that their mental maps of the city were constructed around many of its historical – and mainly nineteenth-century – features. Their deepest affection was for *le vieux Paris* in the *6^e, 4^e, 1^r* and *5^e arrondissements*, and they feared that urban renewal was destroying much of the city's charm. Tall towers and modern buildings were never going to be readily assimilated into Haussmann's Paris. Nonetheless, the landscape of Paris of the long-nineteenth century has not been erased totally – it has not been assassinated – but it has been significantly modified, in some instances mutilated, losing much of what many would consider to have been its charm and elegance. So, another trait of the personality of Paris must reluctantly be acknowledged: that of a tendency to self-harm, from which it has suffered too frequently since 1789.

Although Paris rejected the damaging plans for 'improvement' proposed in the 1920s by Swiss-French architect and urban planner Le Corbusier, controversial iconic structures promoted by hubristic presidents since the 1960s have notably been designed by equally proud and hubristic foreign (Danish, Italian, British, American-Chinese and Uraguayan-Canadian) architects seemingly insensitive to the charm and elegance of the legacy of the long-nineteenth-century Paris. Together, presidents and architects playing to an international audience have diluted the very Parisian distinctiveness of Paris itself. Its singularity has been diminished. But self-harm is not suicide: the subject survives.

Did the personality of nineteenth-century Paris have a gender base? In some ways it did. But is Paris perhaps more appropriately seen as being binary? The masculine side of Paris found outlets for its forceful nature in vigorous revolutions, wars and street protests. Brutal and even murderous extrajudicial attacks against their presumed adversaries were undertaken by largely masculine mobs and by individual males. Not only other men but also buildings and monuments were targets of their brutalizing anger. Masculinity was paraded in nineteenth-century Paris in an especially aggressive form. The image of an enduringly revolutionary Paris, of the city as a cauldron of insurgency, captures a portentous aspect of its personality which persisted into the twentieth century, for example, surfacing in the student-led protests of May 1968 and in the *Gilets jaunes* demonstrations of recent years. 'Paris' and 'Protest' sit comfortably (or uncomfortably?) side by side. There is also an argument to be made that the reordering of the streets and sewers of Paris in the 1850s and 1860s was a masculine assertion of the power of technology and engineering, indeed of reason, which were considered, at least by (too) many, to be dominantly male domains.

Haussmann's straight boulevards had thrust their way rapaciously through old Paris and the Eiffel Tower was for some a phallic symbol, but a countering balance to that imposition of masculine lines was provided, subtly, by the more feminine sinuosity and curving paths and water features in the newly created parks. There was a feminine side to nineteenth-century Paris. For centuries before 1789 the name 'Paris' was considered to be a feminine noun but thereafter it came increasingly to be viewed as masculine, as in *le vieux Paris* and *le nouveau Paris*. But Hope Mirrlees, in her modernist poem *Paris* (1920), addressed the city as a woman and dedicated it to 'Notre Dame de Paris'. When Paris was portrayed in nineteenth-century satirical journals, it was often as Mademoiselle Lutetia. More prosaically, feminine agency played a notable role in the Revolution when, on 5 October 1789, the market women of Paris marched to Versailles and forcibly brought the royal family back to the city. During the Commune in May 1871, women fought with the Communards as *pétroleuses*, as arsonists throwing petrol bombs to destroy buildings, notably the Hôtel de Ville. But any possible construction of Paris as feminine does not rest on these exceptional and aggressive instances of female power. Women featured largely in both the reality and the myth of nineteenth-century Paris as the capital of leisure and pleasure, with the entertainment industries employing many of them, as singers and dancers in cabarets and as sex workers in brothels. Two other very distinctive feminine images had become current by 1900. One was of the sophisticated and graceful woman of fashion, wedded to *haute couture*, announcing in her clothes her bourgeois or even aristocratic status and wealth – or at least, aspiration. The other image was of *la Parisienne*, a spirited young woman who dressed with a taste and a grace which was coquettish and blatantly 'modern' rather than incorporating any historical signals. Both of these images contained undertones of sensuality and sexuality: they were in effect male constructions, masculine fantasies paraded in erotic, illustrated, magazines such as *La Vie Parisienne*, launched in 1863. Other feminine images of *midinettes* (pretty working-class milliners or dressmakers), *grisettes* (young, supposedly grey-clad, women of easy virtue), demi-mondaines and fashion models also fed masculine fantasies. All of which supports the view that the image of Paris in the late nineteenth and early twentieth century was fundamentally a male construct. A view confirmed, as Charles Rearick has pointed out, by gendered descriptions of *la* Seine as being 'seductive' and 'languorous and curvaceous'. Rearick (2011, p. 34) cited an observation about the Seine made in 1911 by Paul Jarry: 'As it meanders and envelops like an elegant scarf, it gives Paris the attractiveness of a pretty woman.' The feminine identity of Paris was also indicated by the icon selected – by men – to personify Paris at the *Exposition universelle* of 1900: the entrance to the Exposition was dominated by *La Parisienne*, a 5-m-tall model of a woman wearing the latest creations of Parisian *haute couture*. A similar point could be made in relation to some public art. Until the 1850s, the Renaissance emphasis on the male nude as the ideal human form was reflected in its statues and public architecture. But it was then gradually replaced by the nude or semi-nude females embellishing, for example, ornamental public water fountains, lakes and buildings. In sum, in terms of its gender, Paris was androgynous.

My exploration of the personality of Paris in the long-nineteenth century has focussed on its landscape, on its appearance and on the character traits of the city that may be read from the construction and use of its built forms. I have focussed on the changing face of Paris, on the city as spectacle, as a visual experience. I have referred only briefly to the 'tastes' of Paris in a discussion of its *cuisine*. For those who lived in Paris during the nineteenth century, the city was of course experienced through all five senses, not just those of sight and taste.

The relative paucity of histories of the senses has been highlighted by a cultural historian, Alain Corbin. Olfactory and aural histories of Paris are still in their infancy. Corbin has commented briefly on the issue of air pollution and smells in Paris before 1850. The increasing use of coal, the proliferation of cast-iron foundries, the operation of steam engines and the opening of bitumen and rubber factories all added to the noise of Paris and to smoke in its atmosphere – with concern about the latter being not so much because of its smell but because it attacked the lungs, dirtied the facades of buildings and darkened the atmosphere just when people were beginning to develop a concern for cleanliness and light. A survey of industrial establishments in Paris in 1843 revealed that almost two-thirds of them produced olfactory pollution and for another one-fifth smoke was the main concern. Hope Mirrlees in her 1920 poem (2020, pp. 11–12) about Paris wrote:

> It is pleasant to sit on the Grand Boulevards –
>   They smell of
>   Cloacæ
>   Hot indiarubber
>   Poudre de riz
>   Algerian tobacco.

That is to say, of smells emanating from the sewers, from car tyres (by 1914 there were 25,000 cars in Paris), from face powder and from cheap colonial tobacco. Studies of the deodorization of Paris in the nineteenth century by Alain Corbin and by David Barnes have examined the especially noxious odours which emanated from the sewers of Paris in the summer of 1880, putting this 'Great Stink' in the context of the debate during the 1880s and 1890s about environmental pollution and disease and the public health measures needed to deal with them.

Paris provided its residents with distinctive sounds as well as smells. Its soundscape has been addressed by Adrian Rifkin in his book about street noises in Paris from 1900 to 1940 and by Aimée Boutin in her study of nineteenth-century Paris as – in her words – 'the city of noise'. Boutin, arguing that what she terms (mistakenly, in my opinion) 'the myth of Paris as the city of spectacle', has joined with Rifkin in recovering the sounds and noises of Parisian streets and especially those of street traders and musicians. Jann Pasler begins her book on music as a public utility in Third Republic France by examining the semiotics of the Parisian cultural landscape, decoding the city's individual monuments and overall urban design, insisting that the rapid circulation of capital and ideas prevented any stable urban identity from lasting 'very long'. While rapid movement of people and goods as well as capital and ideas undoubtedly underpinned the capitalist development of Paris, as David Harvey has conclusively demonstrated, the significance of large sums invested in many monuments and buildings gave them a greater fixity and longevity than Pasler countenances. She also argues that from the 1870s French republicans of all classes expected music to function as a signifying practice, like public sculpture and architecture. They also, presumably, gained simple enjoyment and sociability from musical performances. Like the cityscape, Parisian music could express many different values, behaviours and actions. Jann describes what she calls 'new promenades in the aural landscapes of Paris' during the Third Republic, emphasizing the broad range within the city of musical performances, from street performers and cafés-concerts to grand opera.

Such sensory histories contribute vividly to our knowledge and understanding of nineteenth-century Paris. More would complement rather than replace the visual paradigm on which my own study of the personality of Paris is based.

Chronology

1785–9	Construction of wall of the *Fermiers généraux*; land area of Paris 2,270 ha
1789	French Revolution begins: 14 July storming of the Bastille
1791	Conversion of the Église Sainte-Geneviève to the Panthéon
1792	Assault on the Tuileries; monarchy overthrown, republic established
1793	Execution of Louis XVI and of Marie-Antoinette; start of the Terror
1795	Paris reorganized into twelve *arrondissements* with forty-eight *quartiers*
1801	First official population census – for Paris 547,756
1804	Construction of Père Lachaise cemetery; in 1820 Passy; in 1824 Montparnasse; in 1825 Montmartre
1805	First consistent naming of streets and numbering of buildings
1806	Construction of Arc de Triomphe begins (completed 1836)
1810	Construction of the Vendôme Column
1814	Occupied by Allied armies
1820	Cholera epidemic killed about 20,000
1820s	Introduction of gas lighting in public places
1823–31	Construction of many glass-roofed *passages couverts* (arcades)
1828	First successful horse-drawn omnibus service
1830	'Three glorious days' and Revolution of 1830
1832	Cholera epidemic *c.* 18,000 killed; June uprising
1833–48	C.-P. Barthelot de Rambuteau prefect of the Seine *département*: environmental improvements (renovation and completion of some squares and monuments, public water fountains and urinals, first tarmac-covered streets)
1834	14 April popular uprising; massacre at 12 Rue Transnonain by the National Guard
1836	Inauguration of the Luxor Obélisque in the Place de la Concorde
1837	First railway station (came to be called the Gare Saint-Lazare)

1840	Gare Montparnasse and Gare Austerlitz; inauguration of the July Column in the Place de la Bastille
1841	Population 935,261; 50 per cent born in Paris
1841–5	"Thiers Wall" built – a ring of fortifications
1844	First public electric lighting, on the Place de la Concorde
1844	Standard street name signs adopted (enamel plaques with white letters on an azure background)
1846	Population 1,053,897; Gare du Nord opened
1848	February Revolution; June repression of popular uprising; Second Republic declared; Louis Napoléon elected president
1848–9	Cholera epidemic: c. 1,800 killed
1849	Garde de l'Est opened
1850	Gare de Lyon opened
1850s	Public horse-drawn omnibuses introduced
1851	December: Louis Napoléon's coup d'état
1852	Louis Napoléon becomes Napoléon III and establishes Second Empire; Bon Marché department store opens
1853	Haussmann appointed prefect of the Seine *département*
1853–70	Remodelling of Paris by Haussmann and his team
1855	First *Exposition universelle*
1857–74	Construction of the pavilions of Les Halles designed by Baltard
1859–60	Annexation of eight suburban *arrondissements*, bringing total to twenty with eighty *quartiers;* land area 8,900 ha. Population in 1856 1,174,346, afterwards in 1861 1,696,141; land area approximately 7,800 ha
1860	Approximately 56,000 gas street lights operating
1867	Second *Exposition universelle*
1850s and 1860s	Department stores: 1852 Bon Marché; 1855 Grands Magasins du Louvre; 1865 Printemps; 1866 Belle Jardinière; 1870 Samaritaine
1860–8	Demolitions on the Île de la Cité, its resident population reduced from 20,000 to 5,000
1869	Folies-Bergère founded
1870–1	Siege of Paris during the Franco-Prussian War
1871	Paris Commune; 'Bloody Week'
1872	Reconstruction of the Hôtel de Ville, burnt down in the Commune

1874	Statue of Joan of Arc erected in the Place des Pyramides
1875	Victor Hugo describes Paris as *la Ville de lumière*
1875	Opening of Opéra Garnier (construction commenced 1862), construction of Sacré-Coeur Basilica begins (completed 1912)
1876	Population 1,988,806
1878	Third *Exposition universelle*; electric lighting of many streets
1880	Monument to the Republic inaugurated in the Place de la République
1881	Le Chat Noir nightclub opened
1882	Musée Grévin wax works museum opened
1884	Introduction of *poubelles* (rubbish bins) by the prefect with that name
1889	Centennial of the French Revolution; fourth *Exposition universelle*; Eiffel Tower opened
1892	Vélodrome de Buffalo and Vélodrome de la Seine opened
1895	First public screening of moving films, by the Lumière brothers at the Grand Café, Boulevard des Capucines
1896	Pont Alexandre III construction (completed 1900)
1900	Fifth *Exposition universelle*; first Métro line opened
1901	Population 2,714,066
1903	First Tour de France cycle race beginning and ending in Paris; fire at the Métro station Couronnes (eighty-four killed)
1910	River Seine floods
1911	Population 2,888,110 (>60 per cent not born in Paris)
1914	Start of the Great War

Sources

A general list of the sources used precedes lists which are specific to each chapter. The date given is that of the edition consulted for writing this book.

General

Agulhon, M. et al. *Histoire de la France urbaine*, vol. 4, *La Ville de l'âge industriel* (Paris, 1983).
Aragon, L. *Le Paysan de Paris* (Paris, 1926; English transln. London, 1971).
Atget, E. *Atget's Paris* (London, 1993).
Baedeker, K. *Paris and Environs: Handbook for Travellers* (London, 15th revised edition, 1904).
Bauer, R. 'Capitale du XIXe siècle. Réflexions sur quelques textes de Walter Benjamin', *Revue d'Allemagne* 4 (1972), 622–37.
Benjamin, W. *Reflections: Essays, Aphorisms, Autobiographical Writings* (New York, 1986).
Bergeron, L. (ed.) *Paris: Genèse d'un paysage* (Paris, 1989).
Bernard, J.-P. A. *Les Deux Paris: Les représentations de Paris dans la seconde moitié du XIXe siècle* (Seyssel, 2001).
Brendon, P. *Thomas Cook: 150 Years of Popular Tourism* (London, 1991).
Brown, F. *For the Soul of France: Culture Wars in the Age of Dreyfus* (New York, 2010).
Burke, E. 'Modernity's Histories: Rethinking the Long-Nineteenth Century, 1750–1950', *UC Berkeley: UC World History Workshop*, 2000. Retrieved from https://escholarship.org/uc/item/2k62f464 (accessed 7 April 2021).
Bury, J. P. T., and J. C. Barry (eds). *An Englishman in Paris: 1803. The Journal of Bertie Greatheed* (London, 1953).
Caillois, R. 'Paris, mythe moderne', *Nouvelle revue française* 284 (1 May 1937), 682–99.
Cannon, J. *The Paris Zone: A Cultural History, 1840–1944* (Farnham, 2015).
Chadych, D., and D. Leborgne. *Paris: The Story of a Great City* (London, 2010).
Christiansen, R. *Tales of the New Babylon: Paris in the Mid-19th Century* (London, 1995).
Christiansen, R. *City of Light: The Reinvention of Paris* (London, 2018).
Churton, T. *Occult Paris: The Lost Magic of the Belle Époque* (Rochester, VT, 2016).
Clark, T. J. *The Image of the People: Gustave Courbet and the 1848 Revolution* (London, 1973).
Clark, T. J. *The Painting of Modern Life: Paris in the Art of Manet and His Followers* (London, 1984).
Clarke, S. *Paris Revealed: The Secret Life of Paris* (London, 2011).
Clayson, H. *Illuminated Paris: Essays on Art and Lighting in the Belle Époque* (Chicago, 2019).
Constantine, H. *Paris Tales* (Oxford, 2004).
Constantine, H. *Paris Metro Tales* (Oxford, 2011).

Corbin, A. '"Public opinion, policy and industrial pollution in the pre-Haussmann town' and 'The blood of Paris: reflections on the genealogy of the image of Paris'", in A. Corbin (ed.), *Time, Desire and Horror: Towards a History of the Senses* (Cambridge, 1995), 146–57, 172–80.
Cosgrove, D., and S. Daniels (eds), *The Iconography of Landscape* (Cambridge, 1988).
Cronin, V. *Paris on the Eve, 1900–1914* (New York, 1989).
Cropper, C., and C. W. Flood (eds), *Mormons in Paris: Polygamy on the French Stage, 1874–1892* (New Brunswick, NJ, 2020).
Dallas, G. *Metrostop Paris: History from the City's Heart* (London, 2008).
DeJean, J. *How Paris Became Paris: The Invention of the Modern City* (London, 2014).
De Planhol, X. *An Historical Geography of France* (Cambridge, 1994).
Dickinson, R. E. *The West European City* (London, 1961), Ch. 12 'Paris', 223–35.
Dupeux, G. *La Société Française 1789–1970* (6th edn, Paris, 1972, English transln., 1976).
Edholm, F. 'The view from below: Paris in the 1880s', in B. Bender (ed.), *Landscape: Politics and Perspectives* (Oxford, 1993), 139–68.
Edwards, H. S. *Old and New Paris: Its History, Its People and Its Places* (London, 1893).
Evenson, N. *Paris: A Century of Change, 1878–1978* (London, 1979).
Evenson, N. 'Paris, 1890–1940', in A. Sutcliffe (ed.), *Metropoles 1890–1940* (London, 1984), 259–87.
Ferguson, P. P. *Paris as Revolution: Writing the Nineteenth-Century City* (Berkeley, 1994).
Fournel, V. *Paris nouveau et Paris futur* (Paris, 1865).
Frascina, F. et al. *Modernity and Modernism: French Painting in the Nineteenth Century* (London, 1993).
Friedrich, O. *Olympia: Paris in the Age of Manet* (London, 1992).
Gaillard, M. *Paris aux XIXe Siècle* (Paris, 1981).
Garrioch, D., *The Making of Revolutionary Paris* (Berkeley, CA, 2002).
George, J. *Paris Province de la Révolution à la Mondialisation* (Paris, 1998).
Gibson, R. *A Social History of French Catholicism 1789–1914* (London, 1989).
Gildea, R. *Children of the Revolution: The French 1799–1914* (London, 2008).
Girouard, M. *Cities and People: A Social and Architectural History* (London, 1985).
Hall, P. *Cities in Civilization* (London, 1998), 201–38, 706–45.
Harison, C. *Paris in Modern Times: From the Old Regime to the Present Day* (London, 2020).
Harvey, D. *Paris: Capital of Modernity* (London, 2003).
Hazan, E. *The Invention of Paris: A History in Footsteps* (London, 2010).
Hazan, E. *A Walk through Paris: A Radical Exploration* (London, 2018).
Hemmings, F. W. J. *Culture and Society in France 1848–1898* (London, 1971).
Higonnet, P. *Paris: Capital of the World* (Cambridge, MA, 2002).
Horne, A. *Seven Ages of Paris: Biography of a City* (London, 2003).
Hugo, V. *Notre-Dame de Paris* (Paris, 1831).
Hussey, A. *Paris: The Secret History* (London, 2006).
Jones, C. *Paris: The Biography of a City* (London, 2004).
Kelly, B. (ed.), *French Music, Culture and National Identity, 1870–1939* (Woodbridge, Suffolk, 2008).
Kranowski, N. *Paris dans les romans d'Émile Zola* (Paris, 1968).
Lavedan, P. *Histoire de Paris* (Paris, 1967).
Lavedan, P. *La question du déplacement de Paris* (Paris, 1969).
Lavedan, P. *Nouvelle histoire de Paris: Histoire de l'urbanisme à Paris* (Paris, 1975).

Lees, L. 'Metropolitan types: London and Paris compared', in H. J. Dyos and M. Wolff (eds), *The Victorian City*, vol. 1 (London, 1973), 413–28.
Loyer, F. *Paris XIXe: L'Immeuble et la rue* (Paris, 1987).
Loyer, F. 'Evolution du paysage de Paris au XIXe siècle', *Franco-British Studies* 18 (1994), 17–26.
Lucas, E. V. *A Wanderer in Paris* (London 1909, 10th edn, 1913).
Mansel, P. *Paris between Empires, 1814–1852* (London, 2001).
Marchand, B. *Paris: Histoire d'une ville XIXe-XXe siècle* (Paris, 1993).
Marrinan, M. *Romantic Paris: Histories of a Romantic Landscape, 1800–1850* (Stanford, 2009).
McAuliffe, M. *Dawn of the Belle Époque: The Paris of Monet, Zola, Bernhardt, Eiffel, Debussy, Clemenceau, and Their Friends* (Lanham, MD, 2011).
McAuliffe, M. *Twilight of the Belle Époque: The Paris of Picasso, Stravinsky, Proust, Renault, Marie Curie, Gertrude Stein and Their Friends through the Great War* (Lanham, MD, 2014).
McAuliffe, M. *Paris, City of Dreams: Napoléon III, Baron Haussmann and the Creation of Paris* (London, 2020).
Meunier, F. *Le Paris du moyen age* (Paris, 2014).
Mirrlees, H. *Paris: A Poem* (London, 1920; reprinted 2020).
National Gallery of Australia. *Paris in the Late-19th Century* (Canberra, 1997).
Noin, D., and P. White, *Paris* (Chichester, 1997).
Nora, P. (ed.), *Realms of Memory: The Construction of the French Past Vol. 1 Conflicts and Divisions; Vol. 2 Traditions; Vol. 3 Symbols* (New York, 1996, 1997, 1998).
Olsen, D. J. *The City as a Work of Art: London, Paris, Vienna* (New Haven, 1986).
Olson, K. *The Cartographic Capital: Mapping Third Republic Paris 1889–1934* (Liverpool, 2018).
Pinon, P. *Paris: Biographie d'une capitale* (Paris, 1999).
Pitte, J.-R. *Histoire du paysage français*, 2 vols. (Paris, 1983).
Pitte, J.-R. *Paris: Histoire d'une ville* (Paris, 1993).
Pitte, J.-R. 'Paris et l'État: violence et passion', *Franco-British Studies* 18 (1994), 97–104.
Prendergast, C. *Paris and the Nineteenth Century* (Oxford, 1992).
Price, R. *Revolution and Reaction: 1848 and the Second French Republic* (London, 1975).
Price, R. *A Social History of Nineteenth-Century France* (London, 1987).
Rabinow, P. *French Modern: Norms and Forms of the Social Environment* (Chicago, 1995).
Rearick C. *Paris Dreams, Paris Memories: The City and Its Mystique* (Stanford, CA, 2011).
Robb, G. *The Discovery of France* (London, 2007).
Robb, G. *Parisians: An Adventure History of Paris* (London, 2010).
Rosanvallon, P. *The Demands of Liberty: Civil Society in France since the Revolution* (Cambridge, MA, 2007).
Rouleau, B. *Paris: Histoire d'une espace* (Paris, 1997).
Russell, J. *Paris* (New York, 1983).
Saalman, H. *Haussmann: Paris Transformed* (New York, 1971).
Sante, L. *The Other Paris: An Illustrated Journey through a City's Poor and Bohemian Past* (London, 2015).
Schama, S. *Citizens: A Chronicle of the French Revolution* (London, 1985).
Stovall, T. *The Rise of the Paris Red Belt* (Berkeley, CA, 1990).
Sue, Eugène. *Les Mystères de Paris* (Paris, 1842–3).

Sutcliffe, A. *London and Paris: Capitals of the Nineteenth Century* (Chichester, 1983).
Sutcliffe, A. *Paris: An Architectural History* (New Haven, CT, 1993).
Thorold, P. *The British in France: Visitors and Residents since the Revolution* (London, 2008).
Trollope, F. *Paris and the Parisians* (London, 1836; reprinted 1985).
Van Zanten, D. *Building Paris: Architectural Institutions and the Transformation of the French Capital, 1830–1870* (Cambridge, 1994).
Weber, E. *France: Fin de Siècle* (London, 1986).
Weiss, L. *Writing Paris: Transformations of Urban Geography from Haussmann to the Medina*, PhD dissertation, University of California, Santa Cruz (ProQuest Dissertations Publishing, 2007).
Willms, J. *Paris: Capital of Europe* (New York, 1997).
Zeldin, T. *France 1848–1945*, vol.1 (Oxford, 1973); vol. 2 (Oxford, 1977).

Prologue

Baker, A. R. H. *Geography and History: Bridging the Divide* (Cambridge, 2003), 163–5.
Braudel, F. *L'identité de la France* (Paris, 1986).
Brettell, R. R., and J. Pissarro. *The Impressionist and the City: Pissarro's Series Paintings* (London, 1992).
Clark, A. 'Geographical diversity and the personality of Canada', in M. McCaskill (ed.), *Land and Livelihood: Geographical Essays in Honour of George Jobberns* (Christchurch, 1962), 23–47.
Claval, P. 'From Michelet to Braudel: Personality, identity and organization of France', in D. Hooson (ed.), *Geography and National Identity* (Oxford, 1994), 39–57.
Domosh, M., Heffernan, M., and Withers, C. W. J. (eds), *The Sage Handbook of Historical Geography* (Newbury Park, CA, 2020).
Dunbar, G. 'Geographical personality', in H. J. Walker and W. G. Haag (eds), *Man and Cultural Heritage: Papers in Honor of Fred B. Kniffen* (BatonRouge, LA, 1974), 25–33.
Ferguson, P. P. *Paris as Revolution: Writing the Nineteenth-Century City* (Berkeley, CA, 1994).
Fox, C. *The Personality of Britain: Its Influence on Inhabitant and Invader in Prehistoric and Early Historic Times* (Cardiff, 1932).
Michelet, J. *Histoire de France* (Paris, 1833), 1–128.
Stanislawski, D. *The Individuality of Portugal* (Austin, TX, 1959).
Vidal de la Blache, P. *Tableau de la géographie de la France'*, in E. Lavisse (ed.), *Histoire de France vol. 1 Part 1* (Paris, 1903). Translation published as *The Personality of France* (London, 1928).

1 Beginnings: The founding of Paris and Its growth to 1789

Couperie, P. *Paris through the Ages* (London, 1970).
Crone, G. R. 'The site and growth of Paris', *The Geographical Journal* 98 (1941), 35–47.

De Planhol, X. *An Historical Geography of France* (Cambridge, 1994), especially 245-75.
Dion, R. '2ᵉ millénaire de Paris: Paris dans la géographie: le site et la croissance de la ville', *Revue des Deux Mondes* (1 January 1951), 5-30
Gallois, L. 'The origin and growth of Paris', *The Geographical Journal* 13 (1923), 345-67.
Leith, J. A. *Space and Revolution: Projects for Monuments, Squares and Public Buildings in France, 1789-1799* (Montreal, 1991).
Meunier, F. *Le Paris du moyen age* (Paris, 2014).
Rice, H. C. *Thomas Jefferson's Paris* (Princeton, NJ, 1976).

2 The peopling of Paris: The making of 'Parisians'

Aragon *Paris Peasant* (Paris, 1926, London; transln. 1971).
Ackerman, E. B. *Village on the Seine: Tradition and Change in Bonnières, 1815-1914* (Ithaca, NY, 1978).
Anderson, R. T., and B. G. Anderson, *Bus Stop for Paris* (New York, 1965).
Bastié, J. *La Croissance de la banlieue parisien* (Paris, 1964).
Berlanstein, L. R. *The Working People of Paris 1871-1914* (Baltimore, MD, 1984).
Chevalier, L. *La Formation de la population Parisienne au XIXᵉ siècle* (Paris, 1950).
Chevalier, L. *Labouring Classes and Dangerous Classes in Paris during the First Half of the Nineteenth Century* (London, 1973).
Corbin, A. 'The peasants of Paris', in his *Time, Desire and Horror: Towards a History of the Senses* (Cambridge, 1995), 158-71.
Daumard, A. *Les Bourgeois de Paris au XIXᵉ Siècle* (Paris, 1970).
Delaporte, F. *Disease and Civilisation: The Cholera in Paris, 1832* (Cambridge, MA, 1986).
Frey, M. 'Du mariage et du concubinage dans les classes populaires à Paris (1846-1847)', *Annales Économies Sociétés Civilisations* 33 (1978), 803-29.
Gaillard, J. *Paris, La Ville 1852-1870* (Paris, 1977).
Garrioch, D. *Neighbourhood and Community in Paris 1740-1790* (Cambridge, 1986).
Harison, C. *The Stonemasons of the Creuse in Nineteenth-Century Paris* (Newark, 2008).
Kramer, L. S. *Threshold of a New World: Intellectuals and the Exile Experience in Paris, 1830-1848* (Ithaca, NY, 1988).
Kudlick, C. J. *Cholera in Post-Revolutionary Paris: A Cultural History* (Berkeley, CA, 1996).
Lees, A. *Cities Perceived: Urban Society in Europe and American through 1820-1940* (Manchester, 1985), 69-83.
Moch, L. P. 'Networks among Bretons? The evidence of Paris, 1875-1925', *Continuity and Change* 18 (2003), 431-55.
Moch, L. P. *The Pariahs of Yesterday: Breton Migrants in Paris* (Durham, NC, 2012).
Ogden, P. E. 'Foreigners in Paris: Residential segregation in the nineteenth and twentieth centuries', *Dept. of Geography Queen Mary College Occasional Papers*, no. 11 (1977).
Ogden, P. E., and P. E. White (eds). *Migrants in Modern France* (London, 1989).
Ogden, P. E., and S. W. C Winchester. 'The residential segregation of provincial migrants in Paris in 1901', *Transactions of the Institute of British Geographers* 65 (1975), 413-28.
Piette, P., and B. M. Ratcliffe. 'Les migrants et la ville: un nouveau regard sur le Paris de la première moitié du XIXᵉ siècle', *Annales de démographiehistorique* 115 (1993), 263-302.
Pinkney, D. H. 'Migrations to Paris in the Second Empire', *Journal of Modern History* 25 (1953), 1-12.

Pourcher, G. *Le Peuplement de Paris* (Paris, 1964).
Raison-Jourde, F. *La Colonie auvergnate de Paris au XIXe siècle* (Paris, 1976).
Ratcliffe, B. M. 'Classes laboreuses et classes dangereuses à Paris, pendant la première moitié du XIXe siècle? The Chevalier thesis re-examined', *French Historical Studies* 17 (1991), 542–74.
Ratcliffe, B. M. 'Popular classes and cohabitation in mid-nineteenth-century Paris', *Journal of Family History* 21 (1996), 316–50.
Ratcliffe, B. M., and C. Piette. 'Immigration into Paris in the first half of the nineteenth century: A reassessment', *Proceedings of the Annual Meeting of the Western Society for French History* 18 (1991), 283–91.
Roche, D. *Le Peuple de Paris* (Paris, 1981).
Shapiro, A.-L. *Housing the Poor of Paris 1850–1902* (Madison, WI, 1985).
Tindall, G. *The Journey of Martin Nadaud: A Life in Turbulent Times* (London, 1999).
Tindall, G. *Footprints in Paris: A Few Streets, a Few Lives* (London, 2009).
Trollope, F. *Paris and the Parisians* (1836; reprinted Gloucester, 1985).
Williams, R. 'The metropolis and the emergence of modernism', in E. Timmsand and D. Kelly (eds), *Unreal City: Urban Experiences in Modern European Literature and Art* (Manchester, 1985), 13–24.

3 Monumentalizing Paris: Commemorating its past

Aldrich, R. 'Putting the colonies on the map: Colonial names in Paris streets', in T. Chafer and A. Sackur (eds), *Promoting the Colonial Idea: Propaganda and Visions of Empire in France* (Basingstoke, 2002), 211–23.
Agulhon, M. 'La statuomanie et l'histoire', *Ethnologie française* 3–4 (1978), 145–72.
Agulhon, M. 'Paris: A traversal from East to West', in P. Nora (ed.), *Realms of Memory: The Construction of the French Past, Vol. 3, Symbols* (New York, 1998), 523–52.
Barrès, M. *Les Déracinés* (Paris, 1897).
Ben-Amos, A. 'Les funérailles de Victor Hugo', in P. Nora (ed.), *Les Lieux de mémoire t.1 La République* (Paris, 1984).
Cahill, S. *The Streets of Paris* (New York, 2017).
Cassagne, J.-M. *Paris: dictionnaire du nom des rues* (Paris, 2012).
Garval, M. '"A dream of stone". Fame, vision and the monument in nineteenth-century French literary culture', *College Literature West Chester* 30, no. 2 (2003), 82–119.
Hargrove, J. 'Les Statues de Paris', in P. Nora (ed.), *Les Lieux de mémoire vol. 2 La Nation* (Paris, 1986).
Hargrove, J. *The Statues of Paris: An Open-Air Panthéon* (New York, 1990).
Lalouette, J. *Une Peuple de statues: La célébration sculptée des grandes hommes, 1804–2018* (Paris, 2018).
Lanfranchi, J. *Les Statuts des héros de Paris* (Paris, 2013).
McWilliam, N. 'Conflicting manifestations of Parisian commemorations of Joan of Arc and Étienne Dolet in the early Third Republic', *French Historical Studies* 27 (2004), 381–418.
Milo, D. 'Street names', in P. Nora (ed.), *Realms of Memory: The Construction of the French Past*, vol. 2 (New York, 1997), 363–89.
Therborn, G. 'Monumental Europe: The national years. On the iconography of European capital cities', *Housing, Theory and Society* 19, no. 1 (2002), 26–47.

Thomazo, R. *L'Histoire de France racontée par les monuments* (Paris, 2018).
Tindall, G. *Footsteps in Paris: A Few Streets, a Few Lives* (London, 2009).
Winock, M. 'Joan of Arc', in P. Nora (ed.), *Realms of Memory: The Construction of the French Past Vol. 3 Symbols* (New York, 1998), 433–80.

4 Modernizing Paris: Rebuilding the city

Bédarida, F., and A. Sutcliffe. 'The street in the structure and life of the city: Reflections on nineteenth-century London and Paris', *Journal of Urban History* 6 (1980), 379–96.
Benjamin, W. *The Arcades Project*. Transln. H. Eiland and K. McLaughlin (Cambridge, MA, 1999).
Bowie, K. (ed.). *La Modernité avant Haussmann: formes de l'espace urbain à Paris, 1801–1853* (Paris, 2001).
Brettell, R., and J. Pissaro. *The Impressionist and the City: Pissarro's Series Paintings* (London, 1992).
Carmona, M. *Haussmann* (Paris, 2000). English edn *Haussmann: His Life and Times and the Making of Modern Paris* (Chicago, 2002).
Chapman, B. 'Baron Haussmann and the planning of Paris', *Town Planning Review* 24 (1953), 177–92.
Chapman, J. M., and B. Chapman. *The Life and Times of Baron Haussmann: Paris in the Second Empire* (London, 1957).
Christiansen, R. *City of Light: The Reinvention of Paris* (London, 2018).
Clark, C. E. *Paris and the Cliché of History: The City and Photographs, 1860–1970* (Oxford, 2018).
Daniel, M. *The Photographs of Édouard Baldus* (New York, 1994).
Daumard, A. *Maisons de Paris et propriétaires Parisiens au XIXème Siècle* (Paris, 1965)
Des Cars, J., and P. Pinon. *Paris-Haussmann: 'Le Paris d'Haussmann'* (Paris, 1991).
Fraser, J. 'Atget and the city', *The Cambridge Quarterly* 3, no. 3 (1968), 199–233.
Friedrich, O. *Olympia: Paris in the Age of Manet* (London, 1992).
Gaillard, J. *Paris, La Ville (1852–1870)* (Paris, 1977).
Gandy, M. 'The Paris sewers and the rationalisation of urban space', *Transactions of the Institute of British Geographers* 24 (1999), 23–44.
Gregory, D. *Geographical Imaginations* (Oxford, 1994), 'Walter Benjamin and the Arcades Project', 227–41.
Harvey, D. *Consciousness and the Urban Experience* (Oxford, 1985), Ch. 3.
Hughes, S. 'Imag(in)ing Paris for posterity', *Future Anterior: Journal of Historic Preservation, History, Theory, and Criticism* 10, no. 2 (2013), 1–15.
Hovey, T. *Paris Underground* (New York, 1991).
Jordan, D. P. *Transforming Paris: The Life and Labors of Baron Haussmann* (New York, 1995).
Kirkland, S. *Paris Reborn: Napoleon III, Baron Haussmann, and the Quest to Build a Modern City* (New York, 2014).
Loua, T. 'Pompes funèbres et distribution de richesses dans Paris', *Journal de la Société de Statistique de Paris* 23 (1882), 157–62.
Loyer, F. *Paris XIXe siècle: L'immeuble et la rue* (Paris, 1987).
Loyer, F. *Paris Nineteenth Century: Architecture and Urbanism* (New York, 1988).

Marrinan, M. *Romantic Paris: Histories of a Cultural Landscape, 1800-1850* (Stanford, CA, 2009).
McAuliffe, M. *Paris, City of Dreams: Napoléon III, Baron Haussmann and the Creation of Paris* (Lanham, MD, 2020).
Maneglier, H. *Paris impériale: La vie quotidienne sous le Second Empire* (Paris, 1990).
National Gallery of Art, USA. *Charles Marville: Photographer of Paris*, www.nga.gov (accessed 16 March 2021).
Papayanis, N. *Planning Paris before Haussmann* (Baltimore, MD, 2004).
Pinkney, D. H. *Napoleon III and the Rebuilding of Paris* (Princeton, NJ, 1972).
Pinon, P. *Paris pour mémoire: Le livre noir des destructions haussmanniennes* (Paris, 2012).
Pinon, P. *Atlas du Paris Haussmannien: La Ville en heritage du Second Empire à nos jours* (Paris, 2016).
Przyblyski, J. M. 'Revolution at a standstill: Photography and the Paris Commune', *Yale French Studies* 101 (2001), 54-78.
Reid, D. *Paris Sewers and Sewermen: Realities and Representations* (Cambridge, MA, 1991).
Rizov, V. 'Eugène Atget and documentary photography of the city', *Theory, Culture and Society* 38, no. 3 (2021), 141-63.
Saalman, H. *Paris Transformed* (New York, 1971).
Sartre, J. *Atget: Paris in Detail* (Paris, 2002).
Shapiro, A.-L. *Housing the Poor of Paris 1859-1902* (London, 1985).
Smith, W. H. C. *Napoleon III: The Pursuit of Prestige* (London, 1991).
Sutcliffe, A. *The Autumn of Central Paris: The Defeat of Town Planning 1850-1970* (London, 1970).
Sutcliffe, A. *Towards the Planned City: Germany, Britain, the United States and France, 1780-1914* (Oxford, 1981).
Sweeney, N. 'Fictitious capital: Haussmannisation and the (un-)making of Second Empire Paris', *Esprit Créatur* 55, no. 3 (2015), 100-13.
Thompson, V. E. 'Telling "spatial stories": Urban space and bourgeois identity in early nineteenth-century Paris', *Journal of Modern History* 75 (2003), 523-56.
Van Zanten, D. *Building Paris: Architectural Institutions and the Transformation of the French Capital, 1830-1870* (Cambridge, 1994).
Vigier, P. *Nouvelle histoire de Paris: Paris pendant la Monarchie de Juillet 1830-1848* (Paris, 1991).
Weeks, W. *The Man Who Made Paris Paris: The Illustrated Biography of Georges Eugène Haussmann* (London, 1999).
Yates, A. M. *Selling Paris: Property and Commercial Culture in the Fin-de-Siècle Capital* (Cambridge, MA, 2015).
Zola, É. *Le Ventre de Paris* (Paris, 1873; English translation Oxford, 2007).

5 Symbolizing Paris: Architectural icons

Barthes, R. *La Tour Eiffel* (Paris, 1964).
Barthes, R. *The Eiffel Tower and Other Mythologies* (Berkeley, CA, 1979).
Bolloch, J. *The Eiffel Tower* (Woodbridge, 2005).
Braibant, C. M. *Histoire de la Tour Eiffel* (Paris, 1964).
Gaillard, M. *Paris: Les Expositions universelles de 1855 à 1937* (Paris, 2003).

Harris, J. *The Eiffel Tower: Symbol of an Age* (London, 1976).
Harvey, D. 'Monument and myth', *Annals of the Association of American Geographers* 69 (1979), 362–81.
Harvey, D. *Consciousness and the Urban Experience* (Oxford, 1985), Ch. 4 on the Basilica of the Sacred Heart.
Harvie, D. I. *Eiffel: The Genius Who Reinvented Himself* (Stroud, 2004).
Jonas, R. 'Constructing the moral order: The Sacré-Cœur as an exercise in national regeneration', *Proceedings of the Western Society for French History* 19 (1992), 191–9.
Jonas, R. 'Sacred mysteries and holy memories: Counter-revolutionary France and the Sacré-Coeur', *Canadian Journal of History* 32 (1997), 347–59.
Jonnes, J. *Eiffel's Tower and the World's Fair Where Buffalo Bill Beguiled Paris, the Artists Quarrelled and Thomas Edison Became a Count* (New York, 2009).
Lemoine, B. *Architecture in France 1800–1900* (New York, 1988).
Levin, M. 'The Eiffel Tower revisited', *French Review* 62 (1989), 1052–64.
Loyer, F. 'Sacré Cœur of Montmartre', in P. Nora (ed.), *Rethinking France: Les Lieux de Mémoire*, vol. 3 (Chicago, 2004), 419–42.
Loyrette, H. Gustave *Eiffel* (Paris, 1986).
Loyrette, H. (1998), 'The Eiffel Tower', in P. Nora (ed.), *Realms of Memory: The Construction of the French Past*, vol. 3 (New York, 1998), 349–76.
Ozouf, M. 'The Panthéon: The École Normale of the Dead', in P. Nora (ed.), *Realms of Memory: The Construction of the French Past*, vol. 3 Symbols (New York, 1998), 325–46.
Peyrel, B. *The Eiffel Tower: Timeless Monument, Universal Monument* (New York, 2020).
Rivière, H. *Trente-six vues de la Tour Eiffel* (Paris, 1902).
Woolf, P. 'Symbol of the Second Empire: Cultural Politics and the Paris Opera House', in D. Cosgrove and S. Daniels (eds), *The Iconography of Landscape* (Cambridge, 1988), 214–35.

6 Projecting Paris: World fairs 1855–1900

Allwood, J. *The Great Exhibitions: 150 Years* (London, 2001).
Clayson, H. (ed.). *Is Paris Still the Capital of the Nineteenth Century? Essays on Art and Modernity, 1850–1900* (Abingdon, 2016).
Fraser, A. *Musical Encounters at the 1889 Paris World's Fair* (Rochester, NY, 2005).
Gaillard, M. *Paris: Les Expositions universelles de 1855 à 1937* (Paris, 2003).
Greenhalgh, P. *Ephemeral Vistas: The Expositions Universelles, Great Exhibitions and World's Fairs, 1851–1939* (Manchester, 1988).
Hall, J. H. 'Sheetiron, syphilis, and the Second International: The Paris International Exposition of 1889', *Proceedings of the Eleventh Annual Meeting of the Western Society for French History* (1984), 244–54.
Jonnes, J. *Eiffel's Tower and the World's Fair Where Buffalo Bill Beguiled Paris, the Artists Quarrelled and Thomas Edison Became a Count* (New York, 2009).
Kalifa, D. *La Véritable histoire de la Belle Époque* (Paris, 2018).
Lebovics, H. *True France: The Wars over Cultural Identity 1900–1945* (Ithaca, NY, 1992).
Mainardi, P. *Art and Politics of the Second Empire: The Universal Exhibitions of 1855 and 1867* (New Haven, CT, 1987).
Mandell, R. D. *Paris 1900: The Great World's Fair* (Toronto, 1967).

Peer, S. *France on Display: Peasants, Provincials and Folklore in the 1937 Paris World's Fair* (Albany, NY, 1998).
Prochasson, C. *Paris 1900: Essai d'histoire culturelle* (Paris, 1999).
Roos, J. M. *Early Impressionism and the French State (1866–1874)* (Cambridge, 1996).
Strohmayer, U. 'Pictorial symbolism in the age of innocence: Material geographies at the Paris World's Fair of 1937', *Ecumene* 3 (1996), 282–304.

7 Enjoying Paris: Food, Fashion and Fun

Baker, A. R. H. *Amateur Musical Societies and Sports Clubs in Provincial France,1848–1914* (Cham, 2017).
Berlanstein, L. R. *The Working People of Paris, 1871–1914* (Baltimore, CA, 1984).
Brassaï, *The Secret Paris* (New York, 1976).
Castigliano, F. *Flâneur: The Art of Wandering the Streets of Paris* (North Charleston, SC, 2016).
Churton, T. *Occult Paris: The Lost Magic of La Belle Époque* (Rochester, VT, 2016).
Clark, R. 'Threading the maze: Nineteenth-century guides for British travellers to Paris', in M. Sheringham (ed.), *Parisian Fields* (London 1996), 8–28.
Clark, T. J. *The Painting of Modern Life: Paris in the Art of Manet and His Followers* (London, 1985).
Claval, P. 'Space and creativity. *Belle Époque* Paris: Genesis of a world-class artistic centre', in G. B. Benko and U. Strohmayer (eds), *Geography, History and Social Sciences* (Dordrecht, 1995), 133–42.
Clayson, H. *Painted Love: Prostitution in French Art of the Impressionist Era* (London, 1992).
Clayson, H. *Illuminated Paris: Essays on Art and Lighting in the Belle Époque* (Chicago, 2019).
Cobb, R. *People and Places* (Oxford, 1985).
Collier, P. 'Nineteenth-century Paris: Vision and nightmare', in E. Timms and D. Kelly (eds), *Unreal City: Urban Experience in Modern European Literature and Art* (Manchester, 1985), 25–44.
Corbin, A. *Women for Hire: Prostitution and Sexuality in France after 1850* (London, 1990).
Csergo, J. 'Extension et mutation du loisir citadin', in A. Corbin (ed.), *L'Avènement des Loisirs* (Paris, 1995), 121–68.
Dauncey, H. *French Cycling: A Social and Cultural History* (Liverpool, 2012).
Defrance, E. *Histoire de l'éclairage des rues de Paris* (Paris, 1904).
DeJean, J. *The Essence of Style: How the French Invented High Fashion, Fine Food, Chic Cafés, Sophistication and Glamour* (London, 2005).
D'Souza, A., and T. McDonough (eds). *The Invisible Flâneuse? Gender, Public Space and Visual Culture in Nineteenth-Century Paris* (Manchester, 2006).
Edholm, F. 'The view from below: Paris in the 1880s', in B. Bender (ed.), *Landscape, Politics and Perspectives* (Oxford, 1993), 139–68.
Evenson, N. 'Paris 1890–1940', in A. Sutcliffe (ed.), *Metropolis 1890–1940* (London, 1984), 259–87.
Ferguson, P. P. 'The *flâneur* on and off the streets of Paris', in K. Tester (ed.), *The Flâneur* (London, 1994), 22–82.

Forgione, N. 'Everyday life in motion: The art of walking in late-nineteenth century Paris', *The Art Bulletin* 87 (2005), 664–87.
Fulcher, J. *The Nation's Image: French Grand Opera as Politics and Politicised Art* (Cambridge, 1987).
Gaillard, M. *Paris Ville lumière* (Amiens, 1994).
Girot, G. 'Histoire des brasseries du XIXe et XXe siècles', in A. Huetz de Lemps and J.-R. Pitte (eds), *Les Restaurants dans le Monde et à travers les âges* (Grenoble 1990), 31–7.
Gosling, N. *Paris 1900–1914: The Miraculous Years* (London, 1978).
Hahn, H. 'Boulevard culture and advertising as spectacle in nineteenth-century Paris', in J. Steward and A. Cowan (eds), *The City and the Senses: Urban Culture since 1500* (London, 2007), 156–75.
Hahn, H. *Scenes of Parisian Modernity: Culture and Consumption in the Nineteenth Century* (Basingstoke, 2009).
Haine, S. C. '"Café Friend": Friendship and fraternity in Parisian working-class cafés, 1850–1914', *Journal of Contemporary History* 27 (1992), 607–26.
Haine, W. S. *The World of the Paris Café: Sociability among the French Working Class, 1789–1914* (Baltimore, MD, 1996).
Hancock, C. '*Capitale du plaisir*: The remaking of imperial Paris', in F. Driver and D. Gilbert (eds), *Imperial Cities* (Manchester, 1999), 64–77.
Harsin, J. *Policing Prostitution in Nineteenth-Century Paris* (Princeton, NJ, 1985).
Herbert, R. *Impressionism: Art, Leisure and Parisian Society* (New Haven, CT, 1988).
Huetz de Lemps, A., and J.-R. Pitte (eds). *Les Restaurants dans le Monde et à travers les âges* (Grenoble, 1990).
James, H. *Parisian Sketches: Letters to the New York Tribune 1875–1876* (London, 1856).
Kautsky, C. *Debussy's Paris: Piano Portraits of the Belle Epoque* (Lanham, MD, 2017).
Kete, K. *The Beast in the Boudoir: Pet-Keeping in 19th-Century Paris* (Berkeley, CA, 1994).
Leslie, E. '*Flâneurs* in Paris and Berlin', in R. Koshar (ed.), *Histories of Leisure* (Oxford, 2002), 61–77.
Mancoff, D. *Fashion in Impressionist Paris* (London, 2012).
Marrus, M. 'Social Drinking in the Belle Époque', *Journal of Social History* 7, no. 2 (1974), 115–41.
Miller, M. B. *The Bon Marché: Bourgeois Culture and the Department Store, 1869–1920* (London, 1981).
Mitchell, A. 'The Paris morgue as a social institution in the nineteenth century', *Francia* 4 (1974), 581–96.
Moon, I., and R. Tawn (eds). *Time, Media and Visuality in Post-Revolutionary France* (New York, 2021).
Moret, F. 'Image et réalité de la restauration parisienne à travers les guides touristiques 1855–1889', in A. de Lamp and J.-R. Pitte (eds), *Les Restaurants dans le Monde et à travers les âges* (Grenoble, 1990), 27–30.
Muehlig, L. *Debussy's Paris: Art, Music and Sounds of the City* (Northampton, MA, 2012).
Nelson, B. 'Zola and the counter revolution: *"Au bonheur des dames"*', *Australian Journal of French Studies* 30 (1993), 233–40.
Nesci, C. *Le flâneur et les flâneuses. Les femmes et la ville à l'époque romantique* (Grenoble, 2007).

Ortoli-Denoix, V. 'Géographie des restaurants de Paris au cours des deux derniers siècles', in A. Huetz de Lamp and J.-R. Pitte (eds), *Les Restaurants dans le Monde et à travers les âges* (Grenoble, 1990), 17–25.
Ory, P. (1997), 'Gastronomy', in P. Nora (ed.), *Realms of Memory: The Construction of the French Past* (New York, 1997), vol. 2, 443–68.
Perrot, P. *Fashioning the Bourgeoisie: A History of Clothing in the Nineteenth Century* (Princeton, NJ, 1994).
Perutz, V. *Édouard Manet* (London, 1993).
Pitte, J.-R. 'Les espaces de la bonne chère à Paris à la fin du XVIIIe siècle', in I. S. Black and R. A. Butlin (eds), *Place, Culture and Identity: Essays in Honour of Alan R. H. Baker* (Laval, 2001), 133–42.
Pitte, J.-R. *French Gastronomy: The History and Geography of a Passion* (New York, 2002).
Rearick, C. *Pleasures of the Belle Époque* (New Haven, CT, 1985).
Rearick, C. *The French in Love and War: Popular Culture in the Era of the World Wars* (New Haven, CT, 1997).
Rudorff, R. *Belle Époque: Paris in the Nineties* (London, 1972).
Schwartz, V. *Spectacular Realities: Early Mass Culture in Fin-de-Siècle Paris* (Berkeley, CA, 1998).
Skinner, C. O. *Elegant Wits and Grand Horizontals: La Belle Époque* (London, 1963).
Spang, R. L. *The Invention of the Restaurant: Paris and Modern Gastronomic Culture* (Cambridge, MA, 2000).
Steele, V. *Paris Fashion: A Cultural History* (London, 2017).
Steele, V. (ed.). *Paris: Capital of Fashion* (London, 2019).
Tester, K. (ed.). *The Flâneur* (London, 1994).
Thompson, C. 'Bicycling, class and the politics of labour in Belle Époque France', in R. Koshar (ed.), *Histories of Leisure* (Oxford, 2002), 131–46.
Tiersten, L. *Marianne in the Market: Envisioning Consumer Society in Fin-de-Siècle France* (Berkeley, CA, 2001).
Weber, E. *France: Fin de Siècle* (Cambridge, MA, 1986).
White, E. *The Flâneur: A Stroll through the Paradoxes of Paris* (London, 2016).
Wolff, J. 'The invisible *flâneuse*: Women and the literature of modernity', *Theory, Culture and Society* 2, no. 3 (1985), 37–46.

8 Escaping Paris: (Re-)discovering 'Nature' and the provinces

Cahill, S. *Hidden Gardens of Paris* (New York, 2012).
Chadwick, G. F. 'The parks of Paris', in G. F. Chadwick (ed.), *The Park and the Town: Public Landscape in the 19th and 20th Centuries* (London, 1966), 152–62.
Corbin, A. 'Paris-Province', in P. Nora (ed.), *Realms of Memory: The Construction of the French Past*, vol. 1 (New York, 1996), 427–64.
George, J. *Paris Province de la Révolution à la Mondialisation* (Paris, 1998).
Green, N. *The Spectacle of Nature: Landscape and Bourgeois Culture in Nineteenth-Century France* (Manchester, 1990).
Green, N. 'Rustic retreats: Visions of the countryside in mid-nineteenth-century France', in S. Pugh (ed.), *Reading Landscapes: Capital-Country-City* (Manchester, 1990), 161–76.

Herbert, R. *Impressionism: Art, Leisure and Parisian Society* (London, 1988).
Hopkins, R. S. *Planning the Green Spaces of Nineteenth-Century Paris* (Baton Rouge, LA, 2015).
Kselman, T. A. *Death and the Afterlife in Modern France* (Princeton, NJ, 1993).
Nourry, L.-M. *Les Jardins publics en province: Espace et politique au XIXe siècle* (Rennes, 1997).
Vigarello, G. 'The Tour de France', in P. Nora (ed.), *Realms of Memory: The Construction of the French Past*, vol. 2 (New York, 1996), 469–500.

9 Assassinating Paris?: Revolutions, wars and the twentieth century

'18 mars-28 mai 1871: la Commune', *Herodote.net 17 mars 2021* (accessed 18 March 2021).
Agulhon, M. 'Guerres et après guerres', in M. Agulhon et al. (eds), *Histoire de la France urbaine*, vol. 4 *La Ville de l'âge Industriel* (Paris, 1983), 625–32.
Bergdoll, B. 'A matter of time: Architects and photographers in Second Empire France', in M. Daniel (ed.), *The Photographs of Édouard Baldus* (New York, 1994).
Boyer, M. C. '*La Mission héliographique*: Architectural photography, collective memory and the patrimony of France, 1851', in J. M. Schwartz and J. R. Ryan (eds), *Picturing Place: Photography and the Geographical Imagination* (New York, 2003).
Chevalier, L. *L'Assassinat de Paris* (Paris, 1977); English transln. with an added 'Epilogue' *The Assassination of Paris* (Chicago, 1994).
Clarke, S. *Paris Revealed: The Secret Life of a City* (London, 2011).
Clay, R. *Iconoclasm in Revolutionary Paris: The Transformation of Signs* (Oxford, 2012).
Clayson, H. *Paris in Despair: Art and Everyday Life under Siege, 1870–71* (London, 2002).
Cobb, R. *People and Places* (Oxford, 1985), 'The assassination of Paris', 187–99.
Edwards, S. *The Paris Commune 1871* (London, 1971).
Edwards, S (ed.), *The Communards of Paris, 1871* (London, 1973).
Fiori, R. *L'Invention du Vieux Paris: Naissance d'une conscience patrimoniale dans la capital* (Wavre, 2012).
Foss, C. *The Culture of War: Literature on the Siege of Paris 1870–1871* (Liverpool, 2020).
Fournier, E. 'Les photographies des ruines de Paris en 1871 ou les faux-semblants de l'image', *Revue d'histoire di XIXe siècle* 32 (2006), 137–51.
Fournier, E. *Paris en ruines: du Paris haussmannien au Paris communard* (Paris, 2008).
Gallaher, J. G. *The Students of Paris and the Revolution of 1848* (Carbondale, IL, 1980).
Gildea, R. *Children of the Revolution: The French, 1799–1914* (London, 2008), 'War and Commune 1870–1871', 229–45.
Gould, R. V. *Insurgent Identities: Class, Community and Protest in Paris from 1848 to the Commune* (Chicago, 1995).
Greenhalgh, M. *Destruction of Cultural Heritage in 19th-Century France: Old Stones Versus Modern Identities* (Leiden, 2015).
Harsin, J. *Barricades: The War of the Streets in Revolutionary Paris, 1830–1848* (New York, 2002).
Hazan, E. *The Invention of Paris: A History in Footsteps* (London, 2010).
Horne, A. *The Fall of Paris: The Siege and the Commune 1870–71* (London, 1965).
Hughes, S. 'Imag[in]ing Paris for posterity', *Journal of Historic Preservation, History, Theory and Criticism* 10, no. 2 (2013), 1–15.

Jackson, J. H. *Paris under Water: How the City of Light Survived the Great Flood of 1910* (Basingstoke, 2010).
Kennel, S. et al. *Charles Marville, Photographer of Paris* (Washington, 2013).
Loew, S. *Modern Architecture in Historic Cities: Policy, Planning and Building in Contemporary France* (London, 1998).
Luxenberg, A. 'Creating *désastres*: Andrieu's photographs of urban ruins in the Paris of 1871', *The Art Bulletin* 80, no. 1 (1998), 113–37.
Merriman, J. *1830 in France* (New York, 1975).
Merriman, J. *Massacre: The Life and Death of the Paris Commune of 1871* (New Haven, CT, 2014).
Monier-Vinard, B. 'À Paris, le couronnement d'Haussmann', *Le Point* 2513 (22 October 2020), 24.
Pinkney, D. H. *The French Revolution of 1830* (Princeton, NJ, 1972).
Pinon, P. *Paris détruit: du vandalisme architectural aux grandes opérations d'urbanisme* (Paris, 2011).
Prendergast, C. *Paris in the Nineteenth Century* (Oxford, 1992), Ch. 3 'The High View: Three Cityscapes', 46–73, and Ch. 5 'Insurrection', 102–25.
Price, R. *Revolution and Reaction: 1848 and the Second French Republic* (London, 1975).
Réda, J. *Les Ruines de Paris* (Paris, 1993).
Rexer, R. 'On seeing and believing: The ruins of Paris, national identity and experiential photography', *Nineteenth-Century French Studies* 49, nos. 3 and 4 (2021), 305–28.
Ross, K. *The Emergence of Social Space: Rimbaud and the Paris Commune* (London, 2008).
Shorter, E., and C. Tilly. *Strikes in France, 1830–1968* (Cambridge, 1974).
Stovall, T. *The Rise of the Paris Red Belt* (Berkeley, CA, 1990).
Sutcliffe, A. *The Autumn of Central Paris: The Defeat of Town Planning 1850–1970* (London, 1970).
Tilly, C., L. Tilly and R. Tilly. *The Rebellious Century 1830–1930* (Cambridge, MA, 1975).
Tombs, R. *The War against Paris 1871* (Cambridge, 1981).
Tombs, R. *France 1814–1914* (London, 1996), 'Paris: Seat of Power', 185–92.
Tombs, R. *The Paris Commune 1871* (London, 1999).
Tombs, R. 'How bloody was la Semaine Sanglante? A revision', *H-France Salon* 3 (2011), 1–13.
Tombs R. 'How bloody was *la Semaine Sanglante* of 1871? A revision', *Historical Journal* 55 (2012), 679–704.
Traugott, M. *Armies of the Poor: Determinants of Working-Class Participation in the Parisian Insurrection of June 1848* (New Brunswick, NJ, 2005).
Traugott, M. *The Insurgent Barricade* (Berkeley, CA, 2010).
Wawro, G. *The Franco-Prussian War: The German Conquest of France* (Cambridge, 2003).
Wilson, C. E. *Paris and the Commune 1871–78: The Politics of Forgetting* (Manchester, 2007).

Epilogue

Barnes, D. S. *The Great Stink of Paris and the Nineteenth-Century Struggle against Filth and Germs* (Baltimore, MD, 2006).
Boutin, A. *City of Noise: Sound in Nineteenth-Century Paris* (Urbana, IL, 2015).

Corbin, A. *The Foul and the Fragrant: Odor and the French Social Imagination* (Leamington Spa, 1986).
Corbin, A. 'The blood of Paris: Reflections on the genealogy of the image of Paris', in A. Corbin (ed.), *Time, Desire and Horror: Towards a History of the Senses* (Cambridge, 1995), 172–80.
McAuliffe, M. *Paris Discovered: Explorations in the City of Light* (Hightstown, NJ, 2006).
Milgram, S., and Jodelet, D. 'The way Parisians see Paris', *New Society* 42 (3 November 1977), 234–7.
Pasler, J. *Composing the Citizen: Music as Public Utility in Third Republic France* (Berkeley, CA, 2009).
Rifkin, A. *Street Noises: Studies in Parisian Pleasures 1900–1940* (Manchester, 1993).

Index

Abattoirs de la Villette 121
Abbé Grégoire 85
Abbey of Sainte-Geneviève 84
About Paris (Davis) 121
Académie des Beaux Arts/Academy of Fine Arts 99, 101
Ackerman, Evelyn 22
Admission Ticket for the Exposition universelle 1900 112
Age of Capital 1848–1875, The (Hobsbawm) 3
Age of Empire 1875–1914, The (Hobsbawm) 3
Age of Revolution 1789–1848, The (Hobsbawm) 3
Agulhon, Maurice 38, 48, 184–5
Album de Vieux Paris 64
Alexandre III 97
Algeria 104, 107, 173
Ali, Muhammed 41, 142
Alphand, Adolphe 62, 143, 145, 153
Ancien Régime 23
André Le Nôtre 143
Anglomania 69, 79, 145
Antoinette, Marie 103, 143, 149
Aragon, Louis 58, 148
Arcades Project, The (Benjamin) 58
Arc de Triomphe 33–4, 39–41, 52, 92, 94, 102, 120, 171, 175, 185
Archbishop of Paris 35, 88, 168
architecture 83–100
  Basilica of the Sacred Heart 88–90
  Eiffel Tower 90–6
  heritage 132
  hubristic 178
  Le Pont Alexandre III (bridge) 96–7
  Métro of Paris 98–100
  Middle Ages 14
  Opéra Garnier 86–8
  Panthéon 83–6
  Petit Palais 113
  Place des Vosges 16
  public 33, 192
  Renaissance 176
  urban 61, 119
  vandalism/damage 169–70
Around the World in Eighty Days (Verne) 138
arrondissements 19
  1er *arrondissement* 49, 51, 142
  1^r *arrondissement* 56
  2e *arrondissement* 25, 162
  3e *arrondissement* 51, 190
  4^e *arrondissement* 51, 160, 190
  5^e *arrondissement* 57, 141
  6^e *arrondissement* 162
  7^e *arrondissement* 149, 162, 166
  8^e *arrondissement* 44, 59, 143, 148, 179, 181
  8e^e *arrondissement* 79
  9^e *arrondissement* 27, 59, 162, 187
  9e^e *arrondissement* 79
  10^e *arrondissement* 27, 163, 187, 190
  10e^e *arrondissement* 79
  11^e *arrondissement* 33, 46, 149, 167
  12e *arrondissement* 46, 181
  13e *arrondissement* 28, 178
  14e *arrondissement* 27, 121
  15e *arrondissement* 27, 30, 52
  16e *arrondissement* 46, 51–2, 138, 146
  17e *arrondissement* 149
  18e *arrondissement* 187
  19e *arrondissement* 51, 68
  20e *arrondissement* 27, 48
Atget, Eugène 74
Au Bonheur des Dames (Zola) 131
Australia 116
Austria 38, 40, 51, 105, 116
Avenue de la Grande Armée 171
Avenue de la République 80
Avenue de l'Opéra 66, 80
Avenue de Nicolas II 97

Avenue des Champs-Élysées 182
Avenue des Gobelins. *See* Saint-Marcel

Baedeker, Karl 122
Baldus, Édouard 74
Baltard, Victor 183
banlieues (suburbs) 10, 15, 22–3, 28,
    46, 64, 73, 79, 90, 132, 154, 157,
    184, 187–8
Bar at the Folies Bergère (Manet) 133
Barnes, David 193
Barthes, Roland 94
Bartholdi, Frédéric Auguste 46–7
Basilica of the Sacred Heart 88–90
Bastille Day 120
Bastille Opera House 177
Battle of Austerlitz 39
Baudelaire, Charles 7, 49, 119, 184
Beaux Art 108
Bédarida, François 64
Belgium 104, 116
Belgrand, Eugène 62
Belle Époque 115, 118
Belleville 70
Benjamin, Walter 58, 182
Berger, Jean-Jacques 80
Bergeron, Louis 2
Berlanstein, Lenard 154
Berlioz, Hector 103
Bernard, Jean-Pierre 185–6
Bibliothèque François Mitterand 177–8
bidonville (shanty town) 28, 182
Bois de Boulogne 146, 150
Bois de Vincennes 69, 147–8
Bonnières, Seine 22
Boulevard des Capucines 162
Boulevard des Maréchaux 27
Boulevard Haussmann 80, 179, 183
Boulevard Malesherbes 144
Boulevard Montmartre: Nuit (Pissarro) 5
Boulevard Périphérique 175
Boulevard Poissonnière 124
Boulevard Raspail 80
Boulevard Saint-Germain 80
Boulevard Saint-Marcel 44
Boulevard Saint-Michel 64, 66
Boulevard Sebastopol/Boulevard St
    Michel 121, 182
Boulevard Voltaire 167

Bourbon Restoration 141
Boutin, Aimée 193
Braille, Louis 85
brasseries 30, 125
Braudel, Fernand 1–2
Brettell, Richard 7
bridges 10–11, 14, 90, 121
    ceremony on 47
    construction 34, 60
    Pont Neuf 17
    stone and iron 97
    suspension 148–9
    wooden 9, 15
Bridle Path in the Bois de Boulogne
    (Renoir) 150
brothels 59, 135–6, 142, 191
Bruant, Aristide 133
Burial at Ornans, A (Courbet) 104
Butte de Chaillot 40

Cadolle, Herminie 110
Café de la Régence 31
cafés 29, 58, 118, 125, 130, 132–3, 135–7,
    139, 143, 183, 186, 188, 193
    1789 Revolution 122
    bars and 108
    bazaars and 109
    Café de la Régence 31
    defined 122
    Le Café Procope 123
    North African 105
    primitive 27
Caillois, Roger 4
Cambridge University Library 7
Canal de l'Ourcq 122
Canal Saint-Martin 148
Carte Gastronomique de la France 126
Cartier, Jacques 51
Castigliano, Federico 187
casual labourers 33–4, 61
catacombes (ossuaries) 102
Catharine de Médicis 103
cathedrals of capitalism 64
Catholic Church 4, 43, 86, 88, 90, 161,
    166, 168
cemeteries 151–3
Centre-Pompidou 172–3
Chabrol, Gilbert-Joseph-Gaspard 80
Chaillot Hill 106–7, 110–11

Champ-de-Mars 55, 104, 106, 108, 110–11, 138
Champs-Élysées 16, 27, 33–4, 40, 55, 97, 102, 113, 144, 153, 171
charcutiers (pork butchers) 29, 50, 123
Charles V 12, 59
Charles X 40, 42, 142, 161–2
Château de Saint-Cloud 103, 164
Château (or Palais) des Tuileries 15
Chat Noir 133
Chaussée-d'Antin 27
Chevalier, Louis 19, 25, 57, 170, 174, 186
Chiamaretta, Phillipe 179
chiffoniers (ragpickers) 28, 34
Chopin, Frédéric 152
cinema 112, 137, 172
City of Light 4–6, 63, 117, 166
Clark, Andrew 2
Clark, Timothy James 7
Clarke, Stephen 63, 136
Clayson, Hollis 5–6, 116–17
clothing. *See* fashion *(haute couture)*
Cobb, Richard 21, 170–3
Cochin-China 110
Cocteau, Jean 93
cohabitation 25–6, 60
Collège de France 170
Colline de Chaillot 27
colonies provinciales 29
Colonne de Juillet 167
Column in Rome 38
Communards 39, 85, 90, 143, 152, 164–8, 191
Commune 46, 81, 89, 106, 110, 114 165–6, 168, 183, 191
concubinage 25, 56
Conseil d'Etat 166
Corbin, Alain 28, 114, 135, 192–3
Corbusier, Le 170–1, 190
Corot, Camille 152, 154
Cosgove, Dennis 3
Côtes-du-Nord 22
Courbet, Gustave 104
Cour des Comptes 166–7
Courier français 133
Coutant Forges of Ivry 28
Curie, Pierre 85

Curie, Marie 85
Curran, Charles Courtney 118
cycling 112, 122, 138, 145, 148, 157

Daniels, Stephen 3
Darwin, Charles 164
Davioud, Gabriel 62–4
Davis, Richard 121
Death of the Stag, The (Courbet) 104
de Balzac, Honoré 7, 49, 56, 152, 184
de Beauharnais, Fanny 127
Debussy, Claude 183, 185–6
de-Christianization 161
de Conty, H. A. 121
Degas, Edgar 118
DeJean, Joan 16–17
de Jouy, Victor-Joseph-Étienne 26
de la Blache, Paul Vidal 1
Delacroix, Eugène 152
de La Reynie, Gabriel Nicolas 5
de la Reynière, Alexandre Grimod 125
Delattre, Simone 186
de Maupassant, Guy 92, 184
democratization of leisure 137–9
de Musset, Alfred 152
Denecourt, Claude-François 153–4
department stores *(Grands magasins)* 24, 58, 112, 119, 128, 129–32, 138, 149, 183, 185, 190
de Planhol, Xavier 2
député (member of parliament) 30, 61, 123, 161, 164
de Rambuteau, Claude-Philippe-Berthelot 80
de Sorbon, Robert 11
d'Estaing, Valéry Giscard 172, 176
de Toulouse-Lautrec, Henri 118, 133
Dolet, Étienne 48
Dominique Halifa 115
d'Ormesson, Jean 172
dormitories *(chambrées)* 28
Drames de Paris (du Terrail) 4
Dreyfus Affair 111
Duc de Chartres 143
Duke of Angoulême 40
Duke of Luxembourg 16
Dumas, Alexandre 49, 92
du Terrail, Pierre Ponson 4
Duveyrier, Charles 35

Early modern Paris 13–18
early settlement in Paris 9–10
École des Beaux-Arts of Paris 113
École Militaire 104
École Normale Supérieure 62
Edlam, Felicity 184
Edward VII 133
Eiffel, Gustave 104, 108
Eiffel Tower 81, 90–6, 108–9, 115, 120, 175, 191
electricity 5–6, 92, 109, 115, 138
Élysée Palace 100
embourgeoisement 31
Engels, Friedrich 31
England 5, 107, 111, 114, 132, 162
Enlightenment 6–7, 79
epidemic 32, 34, 56, 61, 63, 68, 111
Europe 3–6, 16, 30, 38, 50, 72–3, 87, 90, 97, 99–101, 106, 123, 125, 127, 132, 154, 168, 169
expansion of Paris 11–13
Exposition universelle 6, 67, 75, 92–3, 96–8, 100, 102–16, 120–1, 124–5, 128, 132, 138, 153, 168

fashion *(haute couture)* 126–9
Faulks, Sebastien 170
Ferguson, Priscilla 7, 119
Fermiers généraux 58–9
Fiori, Ruth 74
Flâneur: A Stroll through the Paradoxes of Paris, The (White) 119
flâneuses 119, 134, 150
Flaubert, Gustave 7, 49, 184
food *(haute cuisine)* 122–6
Forgione, Nancy 119
Fournel, Victor 186
Fournier, Eric 78, 168
Fox, Cyril 2
francization 19
François I 13
Franco-Prussian War of 1870–1 120, 124
Fraser, John 74
Frémiet, Emmanuel 43
French National Assembly 164
French Revolution of 1789 3, 6, 46, 51, 90, 100, 107, 144, 160, 172
Frey, Michel 25

Friedrich, Otto 7
fun 132–7

gai Paris 132–7
Galerie des Machines 108–9, 115
Galeries de Bois 58
Gandy, Matthew 76
Gare d'Austerlitz 28–9
Gare de Lyon 29
Gare Montparnasse 29
Garnier, Charles 86, 92, 110
Garrioch, David 187
Garval, Michael 49
gastronomy 4, 125–6
Gauguin, Paul 108
Gaul (tribe) 9–10
Geography and History 2
Germinal (Zola) 136
Global Positioning System (GPS) 51
Gomboust, Jacques 15
Gothic Paris 14
Gounod, Charles 92
Grand Lac of the Bois de Boulogne 146
Grand Palais 113, 115
Grands Boulevards 58
grands hommes 38, 84
Grands Projets (Mitterand) 176–7
Great Britain 116
Great Depression 115
Great Exhibition of 1851 101
Great Exhibition of the Works of Industry of all Nations 101
Great Flood 153
Greatheed, Bertie 184
Great War 3, 49, 115–16, 169, 183
Greenhalgh, Michael 170
Greenhalgh, Paul 113
Grégoire, Abbé 170
grisettes 31, 150, 192
Guérin, Marguerite 130
Guernsey 6
Guibert, Hervé 173
Guibert, Joseph-Hippolyte 88
Guide to Cook's Excursions to Paris 132
guignettes (primitive cafés) 27
Guimard, Hector 98

Hahn, Hazel 134
Hall, Peter 19

Halle aux Vins 172
Hancock, Claire 33
Hardouin-Mansart, Jules 17
Harper's Weekly 121
Harris, Joseph 91
Harvey, David 3, 34, 81, 90, 159, 193
Haussmann, Baron 8, 35, 62, 86, 105, 117, 121, 129, 133, 145, 149, 153, 159–60, 164, 176, 178, 182, 187
  transformation of Paris 63–72
  work by his contemporaries 73–6
  work by historians 76–81
Haussmannization 80–1, 98–9, 168, 189
haute couture 114, 126–9, 137, 191–2
Hazan, Eric 27
health and disease 32–3
Henri II 13
Henry IV 16–18
Herbert, Robert 118
Higonnet, Patrice 4, 7, 182, 188–9
Histoire de France (Michelet) 1
Hitler, Adolf 169
Hobsbawm, Eric 3
Hokusai 92
Hopkins, Richard 144, 147
Horne, Alastair 166
Hôtel Carnavalet 75
Hôtel de la Marine 41
Hôtel des Invalides 16, 40, 97
Hôtel de Ville 28, 32, 40–1, 56, 63, 74, 79, 162, 166–7, 169, 181
Huart, Louis 119
Hughes, Sabrina 74
Hugo, Victor 6, 43, 49, 67, 74, 85, 162, 184
Hundred Years War with the English 13
Hyde Park, London 144–5

idleness 117–22
Île-aux-Cygnes 47
Île de la Cité 9–11, 15, 17, 28, 34, 72, 121
Île Saint-Louis 15
Illuminated Paris: Essays on Art and Lighting in the Belle Époque (Clayson) 5, 117
immigration 20–4, 31, 168
Imperial École des Beaux-Arts 40
Imperial Rome 37
Impressionists 5, 7, 20, 108, 113, 118, 129, 150, 154

Index-Atlas of France 52
Industrial Enquiry of 1847–8 23
industrialization 22, 24
Industrial Revolution 3, 90, 100, 108, 162
Innocents Abroad, The (Twain) 132
Italy 51, 84, 108, 116

James, Henry 135
Jardin des Plantes (Botanical Garden) 41, 77, 141–2, 146, 164, 172
Jardin des Tuileries 143, 150
Jardin du Luxembourg 47, 150
Jardin du Palais Royal 142
Java 109–10
Jeu des Monuments de Paris (board game) 37
Joan of Arc in the Place des Pyramides 43–5
Jodelet, Denise 190
Jones, Colin 2, 55, 77–8
Joséphine 40
Journal des Coiffures 127
July Column 42–3, 161
July Monarchy 48, 161
July Revolution of 1830 181

Kaempfen, Albert 4–5
Kautsky, Catherine 183–5
Kourakine, Alexandre 125
Kudlick, Catherine 32

La barrière des Fermiers généraux 18
La Bastille 60
labourers
  casual 33–4, 61
  demand 22, 73
  manual 11
  market 31
  shortages 23
  skilled 163
  working-class 133
La Curée (Zola) 159
La Défense 171, 174
La Défense de Paris 171
Lady with a Parasol Sitting in a Park (Morisot) 150
Lafargue, Paul 120
La France distribuant des couronnes au Commerce et à l'Industrie 102

La Liberté éclairant le monde 46
L'Almanach des Gourmets (de la Reynière) 125
Lalouette, Jaqueline 48
La Marseillaise (Rude) 40
La Mode Illustrée 129
La Musique aux Tuileries (Manet) 150
Lanfranchi, Jacques 49
L'Angélus (Millet) 106
La Parisienne 114, 192
la petite Pologne 44
La Porte d'Italie 176, 189
La Pyramide du Louvre 177
L'Assassinat de Paris (Chevalier) 170
La Tour Montparnasse 175
La Tour Zamansky 173
La Vague (Courbet) 106
Lavedan, Pierre 34
La Vie Parisienne 133, 192
La Villette 70
La vision de Paris dans l'exil (Hugo) 6
Lavisse, Ernest 1
Le Bon Marché 130
Le Café Procope 123
Le Centre Pompidou 174
Le Chahut 134
Le Chat Noir night club 133
Le Ciel de Paris 174
Le Coeur, Jules 155
Le dimanche après-midi à l'Île la Grande Jatte (Seurat) 154
Le Droit à la paresse 121
Left Bank 136, 181, 184–5
Le Grand Cerf 58
Le Grand Palais 112
Le Guide Michelin 125
leisure 7–8, 24, 115–16, 118–22, 133, 135, 136, 137–9, 142, 145, 154, 183, 186, 189, 191
Le Jardin des Plantes 142
Le Jardin du Luxembourg 144
Le Lac du Bois de Boulogne (Morisot) 150
Le Louvre (fortress) 13
Le Marais 34
Le Monde illustré 142
Le Monomane (Duveyrier) 35
Le Nouveau Paris (Mercier) 17
Le Palais de l'Industrie 103
Le Palais du Louvre (royal palace) 13

Le Paysan de Paris (Aragon) 58
Le Petit Palais 112, 114
Le petit peuple 139
Le Pont Alexandre III (bridge) 96–7
Le Printemps 128
Le Procope (café) 122
Les Deux Paris (Bernard) 185
Le Secq, Henri 74
Les Enfants du Nord 29
Les Fleurs du Mal (Baudelaire) 119
Les Glaneuses 106
Les Halles 60, 70
Les Mariés de la Tour Eiffel (Cocteau) 93
Les Misérables (Hugo) 6, 43, 67, 162
Les Mystères de Paris (Sue) 35
Les Paysans de Paris (Aragon) 148
Le Spleen de Paris (Baudelaire) 119
Le Square de l'Archevêché 161
Les Tuileries (Monet) 150
Le Tableau de Paris (Mercier) 17
Le Ventre de Paris (Zola) 68, 98
Levin, Miriam 93
lighting 5–6, 33, 63, 67, 76, 85, 117–18, 138, 186
Limoges 36
Limousin 28–9
L'Opéra Bastille 177
Loubet, Émile 98
Louis IX 51
Louis XIII 13, 15, 17, 59
Louis XIV 15–17, 97, 127, 151
Louis XV 41, 55, 84
Louis XVI 41, 103
Louis XVIII 40, 51, 86
Louvre Museum 167
Louvre Palace 176
Loyer, François 80, 85, 89
Loyrette, Henri 92
Lozère 29–30
Lucas, Edward 122
Lumière, Auguste 137
Lumière, Louis 137
Lutetia Parisiorum, Parisii 9–10
Luxembourg Gardens 146
Luxembourg Palace 16, 100, 164
Lyon 35, 132

Madeleine, La 34
Mademoiselle Lutetia 191

madras (a knotted headscarf) 30
Malraux, André 174
Mancroft, Debra 129
Manet, Édouard 7, 104, 118, 133, 143, 150
Marchand, Bernard 34
Marie-Louise of Austria 40
Marrinan, Michael 2
Marrus, Michael 125
Marseille 132
Marville, Charles 64, 74, 106
Marx, Karl 31, 163
Marx, Roger 112–13
Massenet, Jules 92
McAuliffe, Mary 2, 190
McWilliam, Neil 48
Medieval Paris 10–11
Mediterranean 3, 41
Mercier, Louis-Sébastien 17
Mérian, Matthäus 14
Merriman, John 166
Métro of Paris 98–100
metropolis 19–20, 79, 168, 188
Mexico 1–2
Meynadier, Hippolyte 61, 144
Michelet, Jules 1, 43
Middle Ages 14, 55
Milgram, Stanley 190
Millet, Jean-François 106, 154
Milo, Daniel 52
Mirrlees, Hope 27, 191–2
Mitterand, François 168, 172, 176
modernism 19, 55–81
    context for change 62–3
    Haussmann's transformation of Paris 63–72
    Haussmann's work by his contemporaries 73–6
    Haussmann's work by historians 76–81
modernization 6, 8, 19, 72–4, 76–7, 79–80, 86, 170
Monet, Claude 150, 154
Monge, Gaspard 85
Montagne Sainte-Geneviève 11, 75
Montmartre 9, 17, 27, 76, 88–90, 133, 151, 159, 167, 187
Montparnasse Cemetery 46
    (See also cemeteries)
Monument à la République, Place de la République 45–6
monuments 37–53
    Arc de Triomphe 39–41
    collective memory 52–3
    history 52–3
    meanings of 48–50
    national 90
    Place de la Bastille 42–3
    Place de la Concorde 41–2
    Place Vendôme 38–9
    Republic 45–6
    statue of Joan of Arc in the Place des Pyramides 43–5
    Statue of Liberty 46–7
    street names 50–2
morgue 121
Morisot, Berthe 150
Morocco 104
Morris, William 154
Municipal Guard 162
Mur des Fédérés 152, 168
Mur d'octroi 18
Musée Carnavalet 75
Musée des Beaux Arts de la Ville de Paris 113
Music in the Tuileries (Manet) 104
Musique au jardin des Tuileries (Manet) 143
myths 4, 7, 29, 58, 79, 127, 132–3, 135, 150, 165–7, 182–3, 185–6, 189, 191, 193

Napoléon III 6, 8, 16, 23, 36–8, 41, 51, 62–4, 68–9, 72, 75, 79–80, 85–6, 101–5, 114, 143, 145, 154, 159–61, 166, 172, 178, 187
National Assembly 42, 84, 123, 160
National Guard 162, 164
National Museum of Natural History 141
nature and the provinces 141–57
    away from Paris 153–7
    cemeteries 151–3
    parks and gardens after 1850 145–50
    parks and gardens before 1850 141–5
New Caledonia 166
New York 19
Nile 41
No. 175 Boulevard Haussmann 179
noise(s) 74, 141, 166, 192–3

Notre-Dame 11, 37, 72, 92, 121, 161, 164, 181, 184
Notre-Dame de Paris (Hugo) 6, 13, 74
Nouveautés 127–8
Nymphs of the Seine 97

Oakley, Annie 110
Obélisque de Luxor 41
Offenbach, Jacques 133
Old Montmartre Society 75
Olsen, Donald 53, 100, 135, 170
Olympia (Manet) 104
Opéra Bastille 176
Opéra Garnier 80, 86–8
Origin of Species (Darwin) 164
Orphée aux enfers (Orpheus in the Underworld) 133
Otis, Charles 104
Otis, Norton 104
Ozouf, Mona 86

Painter's Studio, The (Courbet) 104
Palais de Justice 166
Palais de l'Industrie 96, 102–3, 112, 115
Palais des Beaux Arts 102, 108
Palais des Industries 108
Palais des Tuileries 15, 40, 143
Palais de Trocadéro 106, 115
Palais du Louvre 15
Palais du Luxembourg 143
Palais du Trocadéro 107
Palais-Royal 117, 123–4, 135, 142, 146, 162, 166
Panthéon 83–6, 185
Papayanis, Nicholas 80
Parc de Bagatelle 146
Parc de Monceau 148
Parc de Saint-Cloud 103
Parc des Buttes-Chaumont 148
Parc des Princes 138
Parc Monceau (Monet) 150
Parc Montsouris 69
Paris (Mirrlees) 191
Paris, Capitale du Monde (Kaempfen) 5
Paris, Capital of the Nineteenth Century (Benjamin) 58
Paris and its Environs (Baedeker) 122
Paris and the Parisians (Trollope) 132
Paris-Brest-Paris race 137

Paris: Capital of the World (Higonnet) 4
Paris détruit (Pinon) 170
Paris Discovered: Explorations in the City of Light (McAuliff) 190
Paris Echo (Faulks) 170
Paris en ruines (Fournier) 78
Paris: Genèse d'un Paysage (Bergeron) 2
Parisianization 19, 28
Paris nouveau et Paris futur (Fournel) 186
Paris Pittoresque et Monumentale (Meynadier) 61
Paris-Roubaix race 137
parks and gardens
    before 1850 141–5
    after 1850 145–50
Parmentier, Antoine 149
Pasler, Jann 193
Passage de l'Opéra 59
Passage du Grand Cerf 58
Passage Feydeau 58
Pasteur, Louis 62
Pathé, Charles 137
Pei, I. M. 176
people/peopling 19–36
    health and disease 32–3
    immigration 21–4
    metropolis 19–20
    Parisians 25–31
    population growth 20–1
    town planning 33–6
    urbanism 33–6
Père-Lachaise Cemetery 151–2, 167
Perrot, Philippe 126
Personality of Britain, The (Fox) 2
Perutz, Vivien 7
Petit Palais 113, 115
pétroleuses (female arsonists) 167, 191
Philip II 3
Philippe, Louis 38, 41, 86, 161–2
Physiologie du flâneur (Huart) 119
Piano, Renzo 172
Picard, Alfred 91
Piette, Christine 26
Pinkney, David 81
Pinon, Pierre 2, 170
Pissaro, Joachim 7
Pissarro, Camille 5, 7, 108, 118
Pitte, Jean-Robert 2, 123
Place Dauphine 17

Place de Grève 79
Place de la Bastille 42–3, 181, 185
Place de la Concorde 33, 40, 41–2, 94, 117, 185
Place des Conquêtes 17
Place des États-Unis 46
Place des Pyramides 43–5
Place des Victoires 17
Place des Vosges 10, 16, 29, 38, 77, 182
Place du Château d'Eau 45
Place du Palais-Royal 31
Place Louis XV 17–18, 41
Place Royale 16–17
Place Vendôme 17, 27, 38–9, 182, 185
Plan autoroutier pour Paris 174
Planning Paris before Haussmann (Papayanis) 80
Pompidou, Georges 171–2, 176
Pont Louis XVI (bridge) 55
Pont Marie (bridge) 15
Pont Neuf (bridge) 14–15, 17–18
Pont Rouge (bridge) 15
Pont Royal (bridge) 15
Pont Saint-Michel (bridge) 121
population growth 10, 13, 20–1
Porte d'Italie 189
Porte Saint-Denis 16, 37
Porte Saint-Martin 16
Poubelle, Eugène 33
Prefect of Police 165–7
Prendergast, Christopher 7, 145, 149
preservation 74–6, 170
Procopio, Francesco 122
prostitution 31, 56, 135–6
Prudhomme, Louis 26
Prussia 27, 40, 43, 61, 81, 89, 93, 105–6, 125, 164
Pyramide du Louvre 176
Pyrenees 36, 183

Quai de l'Archevêché 121
Quai du Marché-Neuf 121
quartiers 24, 27–8, 34, 44, 46, 50, 55, 59, 68, 73–4, 79, 123, 139, 164, 169, 173, 184, 186
Queen Victoria 108

railway stations 27, 64, 78, 86, 98, 113, 175
  Gare d'Austerlitz 28, 29, 64
  de l'Est 64
  de Lyon 29, 64
  d'Orsay 112
  du Nord 64, 67
  Montparnasse 29, 64, 174–5, 189
  Saint-Lazare 64
Rambuteau, prefect 34
Ratcliffe, Barrie 26
Rearick, Charles 58, 118, 183, 186, 192
Renaissance Paris 14
Renoir, Pierre-Auguste 150, 154
Republic 38, 45–6, 50, 52, 85
Resistance Movement 168
restaurants 30, 92, 94, 108, 122–5, 130, 135, 139, 148, 174, 188, 190
Revolution of 1789 51, 83, 92, 103, 120, 125, 145, 160, 162
Revolution of 1830 188
Revolution of 1848 36, 61, 76, 162
revolutions and upheavals 160–4
Révue indépendante 133
Rexer, Raisa 168
Rhine 10, 38
Rifk, Adrian 193
Right Bank 25, 136, 142, 181, 184–5
River Bièvre 68
Rivière, Henri 92
Robb, Graham 96, 166
Rogers, Richard 172
Rolland, Romain 183
Romania 109–10
Roman Paris 14
Romantic Paris 2
Rousseau, Théodore 85, 122, 154
Royal Library 38
Rude, François 40
Rue de la Loi 184
Rue de l'Ancienne-Comédie 122
Rue de Lille 166
Rue de Rivoli 182
Rue de Saint-Denis 49
Rue des Nations 107, 112
Rue du Bourdonnais 56
Rue du Louvre 80
Rue du Pont-Neuf 64
Rue Estienne 65
Rue Rambuteau 60
Rue Saint-Antoine 39, 163
Rue Saint-Denis 58

Rue Saint-Honoré 38, 181
Rue Saint-Maur 163
Rue Soufflot 71
Rue St Martin/Rue St-Jacques 182

Saint Bartholomew 143
Saint-Denis 27, 161
Sainte-Chapelle 11, 92
Sainte-Geneviève 50, 84
Saint-Étienne-du-Mont 173
Saint Germain (bishop of Paris) 10, 24, 27
Saint-Germain-des-Prés (abbey) 10–11
Saint-Germain-l'Auxerrois 34
Saint-Gervais-Saint-Protais 169
Saint-Honoré 55
Saint-Leu-Saint-Gilles 49
Saint Marcel (bishop of Paris) 10, 28
Saint-Martin-des-Champs 11
Saint Monday 120
Saint-Simon, Claude-Henri 62
Saint Victor (abbey) 11
Sand, George 119
Sante, Luc 27
Sargent, John Singer 118
Sauer, Carl 1–2
Schwartz, Vanessa 135
Sébastopol, Boulevard 64
Second Empire 48, 81, 105, 126, 133, 145–6, 183
Second Olympic Games 111, 112
Second Republic 86, 162
Second World War 94, 149, 168–9
Seine 9–10, 14–15
Service des Promenades 143
Service photographique de la Préfecture 165
Seurat, Georges 154
sewers 32–3, 56, 65, 67–8, 72, 74, 76, 121, 191, 193
Simon, Sorbonne Jules 150
Sisley, Alfred 154
smells 17, 32, 109, 115, 125, 141, 150, 166, 192–3
Société générale des téléphones 109
Soufflot, Jacques-Germain 84
sounds 4, 88, 109, 115, 125, 166, 193
Spain 40, 108, 116
Stanislawski, Dan 2
Statue of Liberty 46–7
statuomania 48–9, 100

Steele, Valerie 127
Stephenson, Robert Louis 154
street names 50–2
Strohmayer, Ulf 148–9
Sue, Eugène 32, 35
Sutcliffe, Anthony 64, 75
Swiss Guards 166

'*Taxe des boues et lanternes*' ('Tax on mud and lights') 5
Texier, Edmond 4
theatres 9, 37, 58, 88, 94, 100, 118, 124, 135, 137–9, 143
Therborn, Göran 99–100
Thiers Wall 61
Third Republic 39, 43–4, 48–9, 52, 78, 85–6, 90, 168, 193
Thomas Cook & Son 105, 107, 111, 132, 168
Thompson, Christopher 138
Thompson, Victoria 26–7, 35, 60, 181
Thompson, William 94
Tombs, Robert 165
Tour de France 113, 137, 157
Touring Club de France 157
Tour Montgomery, Rue des Jardins-Saint-Paul 12
Tour Montparnasse 174
'*tout à l'égout*' (everything to the sewers) 33
town planning 33–6
tramways 130, 153–6
Traugott, Mark 162–3
Trente-six vues de la Tour Eiffel (Rivière) 92
'*Très Grande Bibliothèque*' ('Very Large Library') 178
Trocadéro Palace 108
Trollope, Anthony 5
Trollope, Fanny 5, 132
Tuileries Gardens 113, 146
Tuileries Palace 161, 166
Tunisia 104–5
Twain, Mark 132

Une baignarde à Asnières (Seurat) 154, 156
Union des Femmes pour la défense de Paris et les soins aux blessées 110

University of Paris 11
University of Pierre and Marie Curie 172
urbanism 16, 18, 33–6, 60–1, 72, 80
urban renewal 159–60, 190

Vallès, Jules 7
vandalism 75, 159–60, 163, 170
van Gogh, Vincent 154
Van Zanten, David 80
vaudevilles 137–8
Véloceclub de Paris 137
Vendôme Column 33, 38–9, 166
Venus de Milo 167
Verne, Jules 110, 138
Viennet, Jean-Pons-Guillaume 48
Vigier, Philippe 34
Ville lumière 6
von Cholitz, Dietrich 169

Wanderer in Paris, A (Lucas) 122
wars 164–9
  civil 38, 88, 90, 120, 164–7
  France losing war with Prussia 48, 164
  veterans 16
  (*See also* Great War)
Waterloo 40
Weber, Eugen 138

Weiss, Lisa 7
White, Edmund 119
White, Paul 24
Wild West Show (Buffalo Bill) 110
Wolff, Janet 119
Woolf, Penelope 86, 88
World Fairs 5, 8, 101–16
  1855 *Exposition universelle de Paris* 102–3
  1867 *Exposition universelle de Paris* 104–5
  1878 *Exposition universelle de Paris* 106–7
  1889 *Exposition universelle de Paris* 107–11
  1900 *Exposition universelle de Paris* 111–13
Worth, Charles 128

Young Flautist, The (Manet) 104

Zeldin, Theodore 125, 135
Zola, Émile 7, 49, 52, 68, 85, 98, 131, 136, 159, 184
the Zone 27–8, 181–2
zone non aedificandi ('not to be built on') 27

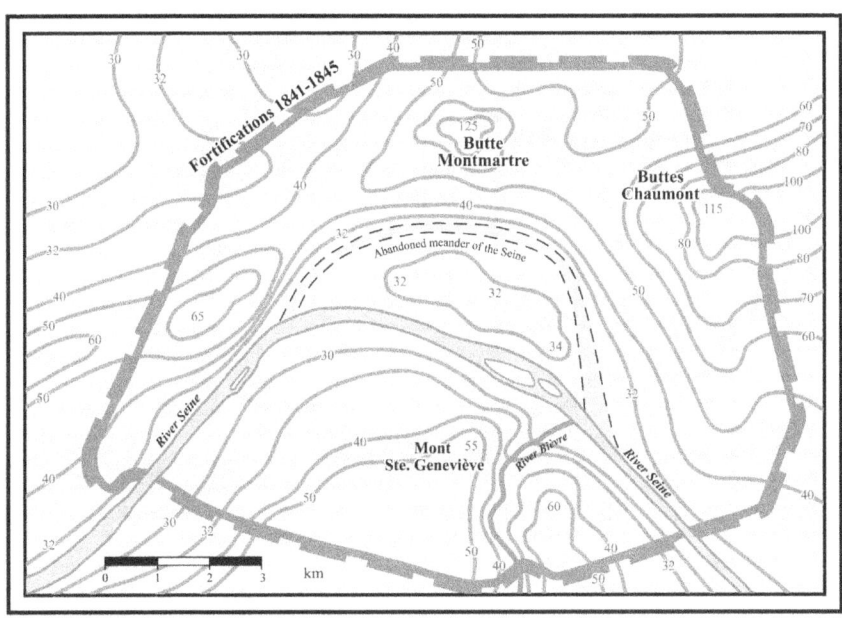

Plate 1 The site and situation of Paris. After Crone 1941, p. 37 and Gallois 1923, p. 439. © Alan R. H. Baker

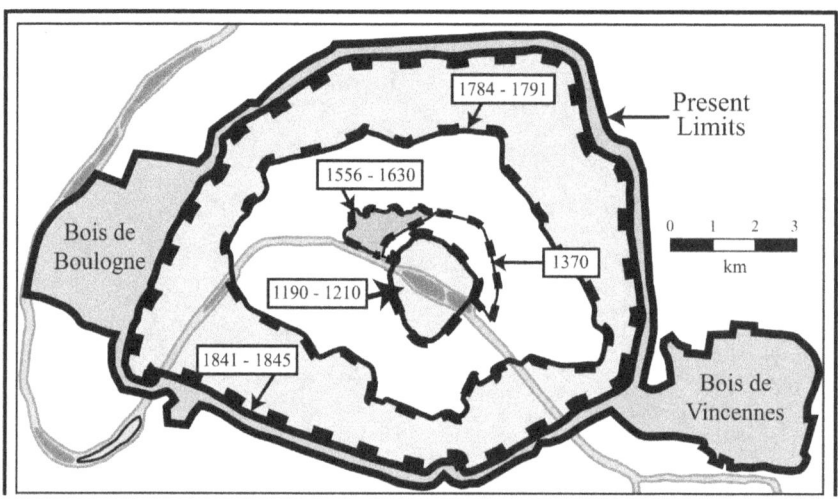

Plate 2 The walls of Paris 1190–1845. After Dickinson 1961, p. 226. © Alan R. H. Baker.

Plate 3 The *départements* of France in 1790. After Dupeux 1976, p. 9. © Alan R. H. Baker.

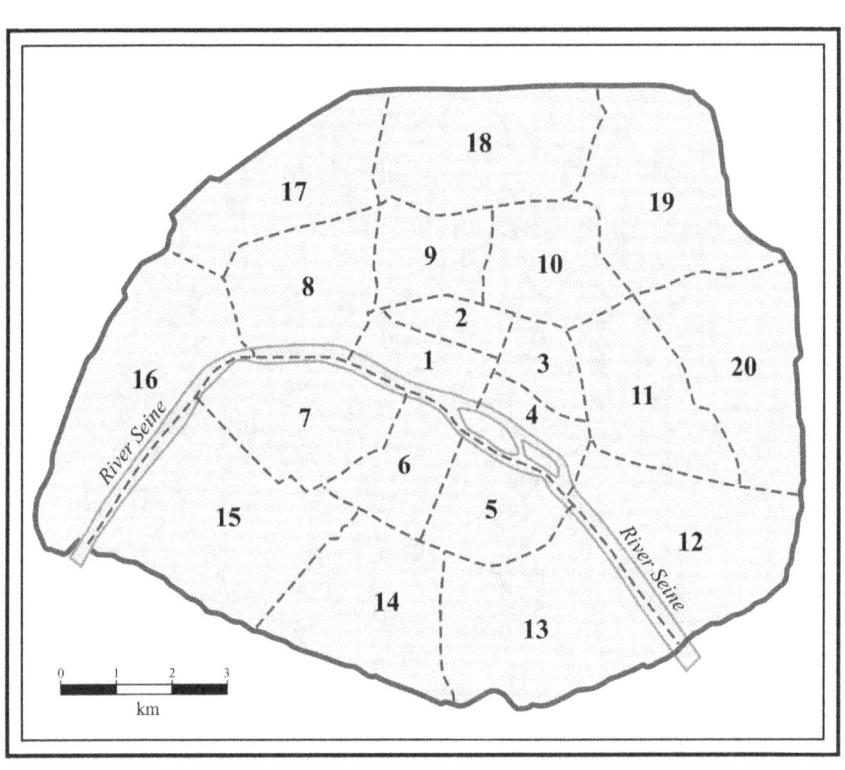

Plate 4 The *arrondissements* of Paris in 1870. After Pitte 1993, p. 101. © Alan R. H. Baker.

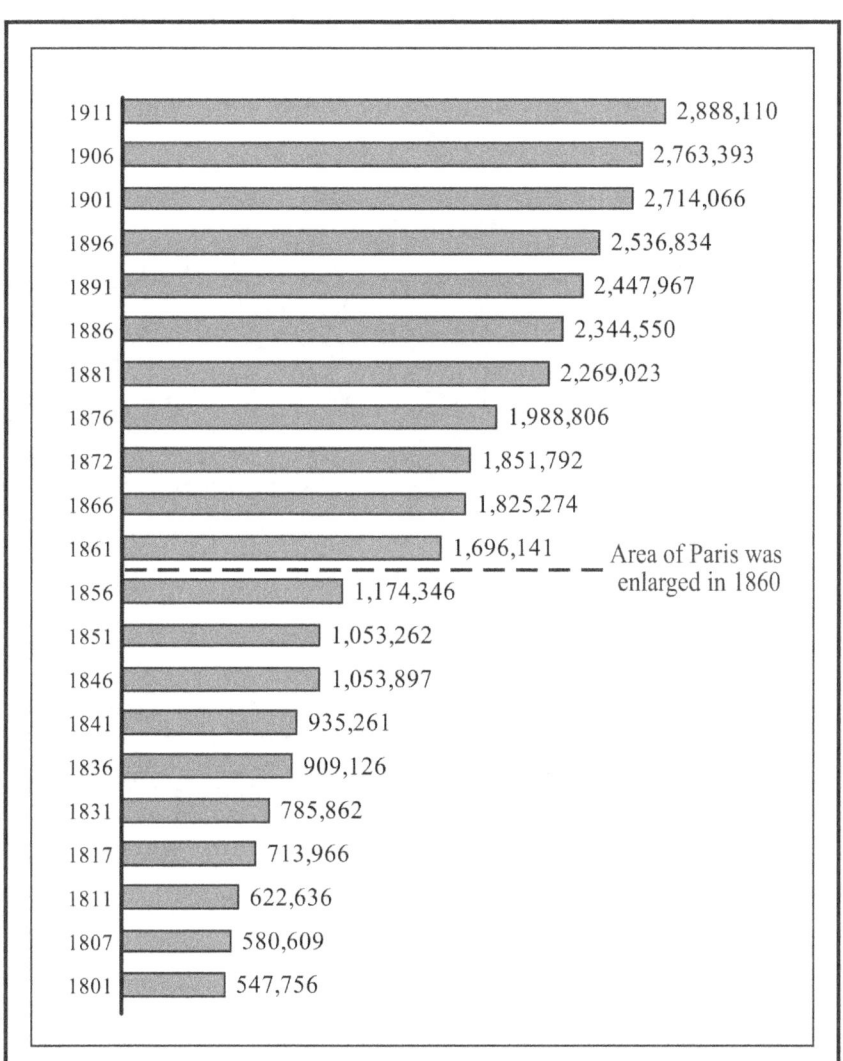

Plate 5 Population of Paris 1801–1911. Data from official French Census: fr.wikipedia.org/Paris/7.1.1. © Alan R. H. Baker.

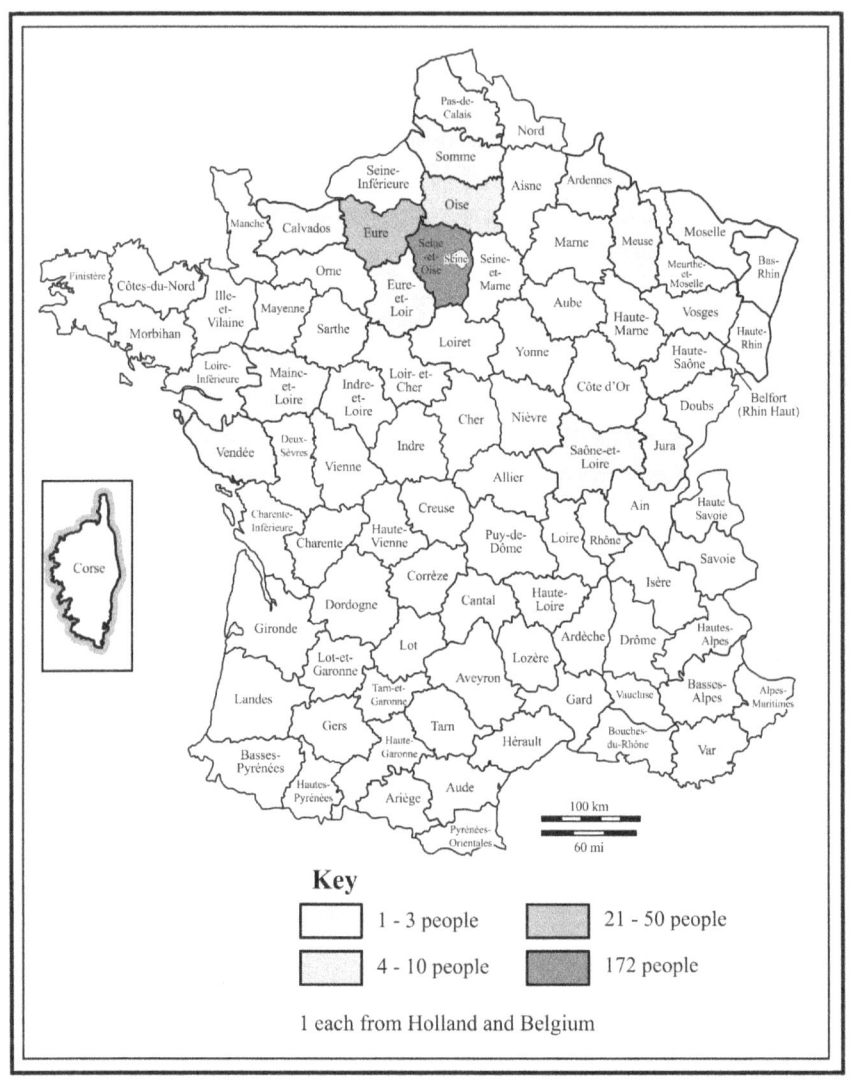

Plate 6 Geographical origins of immigrants in Bonnières 1817–46. After Ackerman 1978, p. 121. © Alan R. H. Baker.

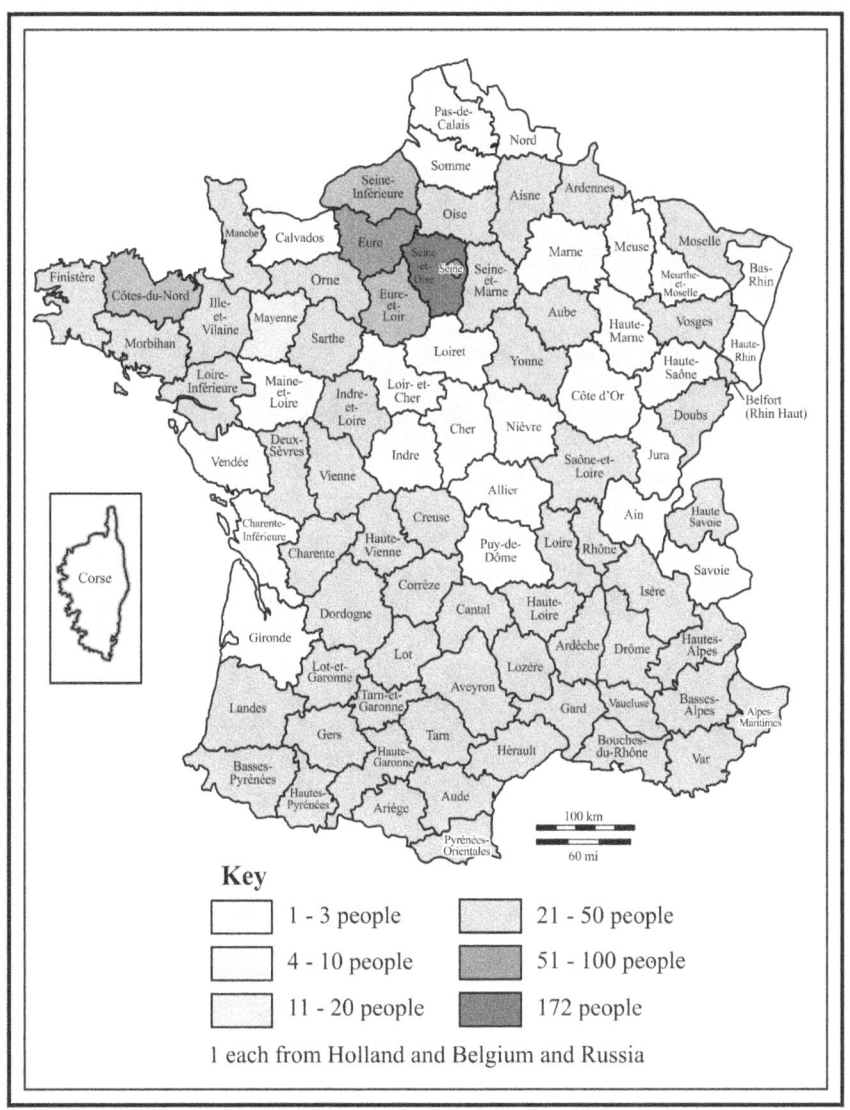

Plate 7 Geographical origins of immigrants in Bonnières 1896–1906. After Ackerman 1978, p. 122. © Alan R. H. Baker.

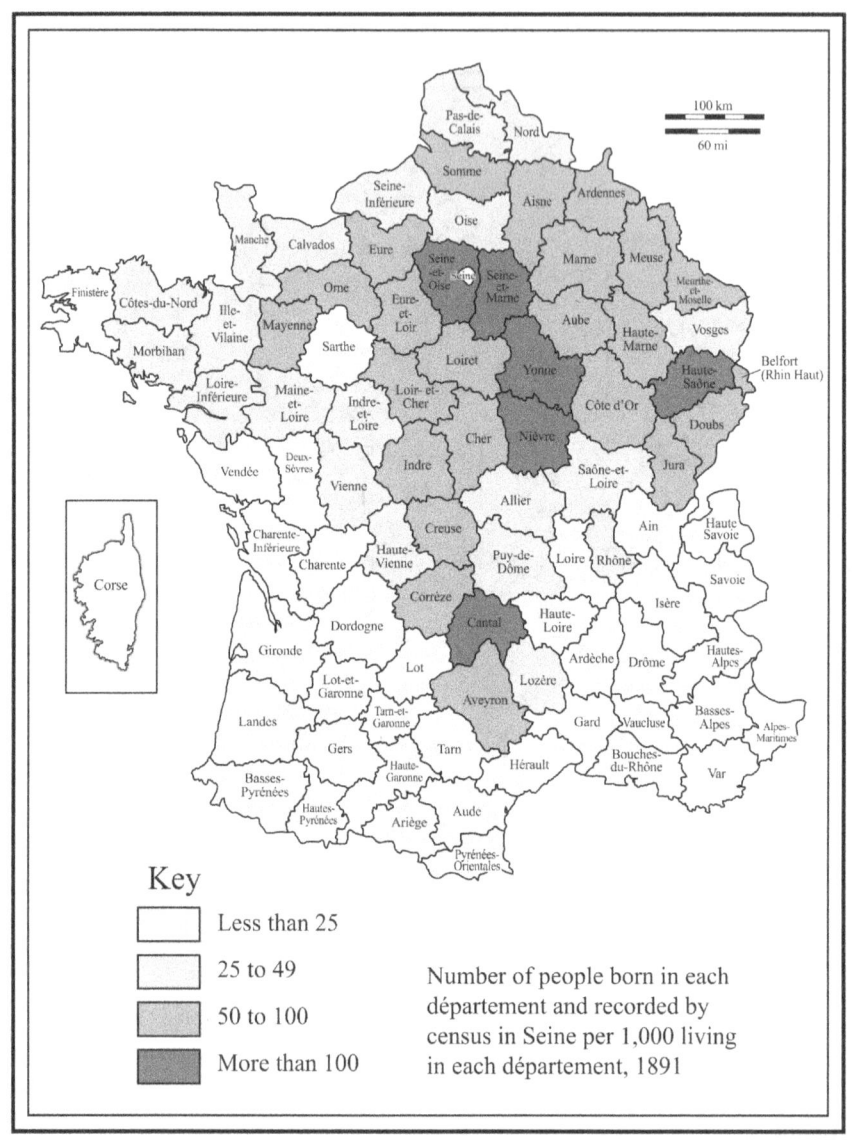

Plate 8 Geographical origins of immigrants living in Paris in 1891. After Dupeux 1976, p. 43. © Alan R. H. Baker.

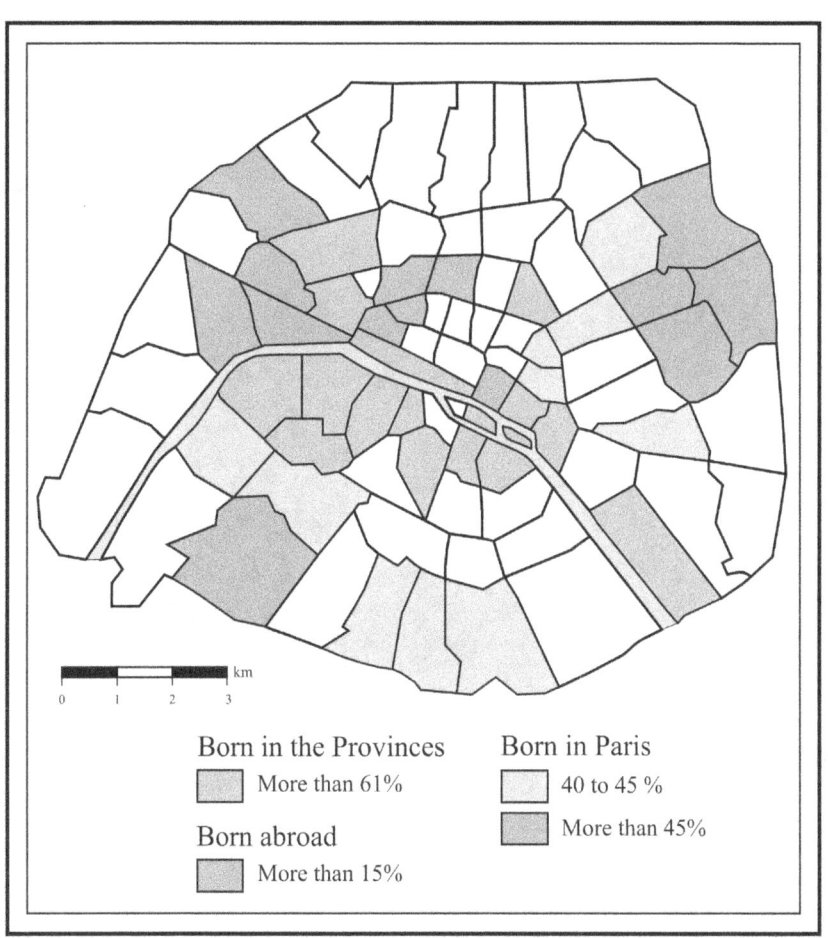

Plate 9 Foreign, provincial and Parisian origins of residents of the *quartiers* of Paris in 1886. After Marchand 1993, p. 135. © Alan R. H. Baker.

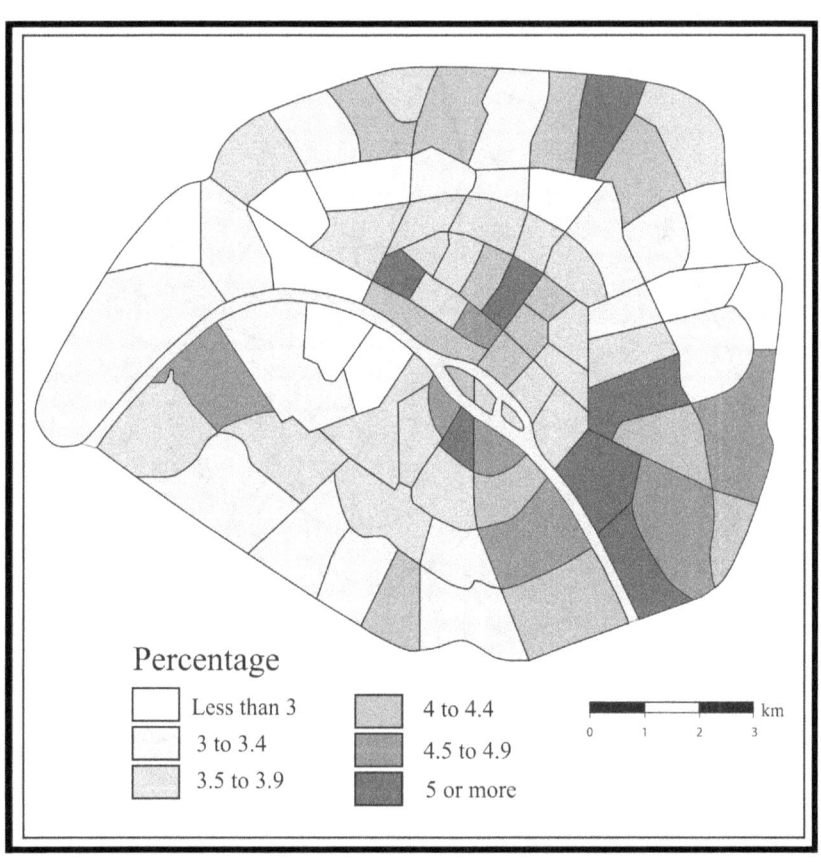

Plate 10 Auvergnats in Paris in 1911. After Agulhon 1983, p. 384. © Alan R. H. Baker.

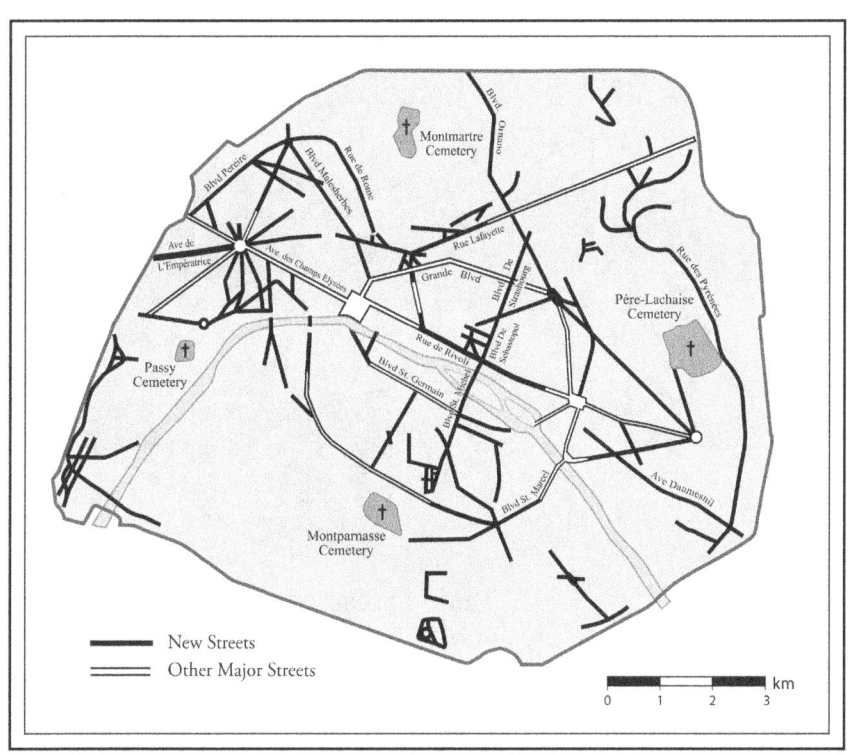

Plate 11 New streets in Paris constructed 1850–70. After Pinkney 1958, p. 73. © Alan R. H. Baker

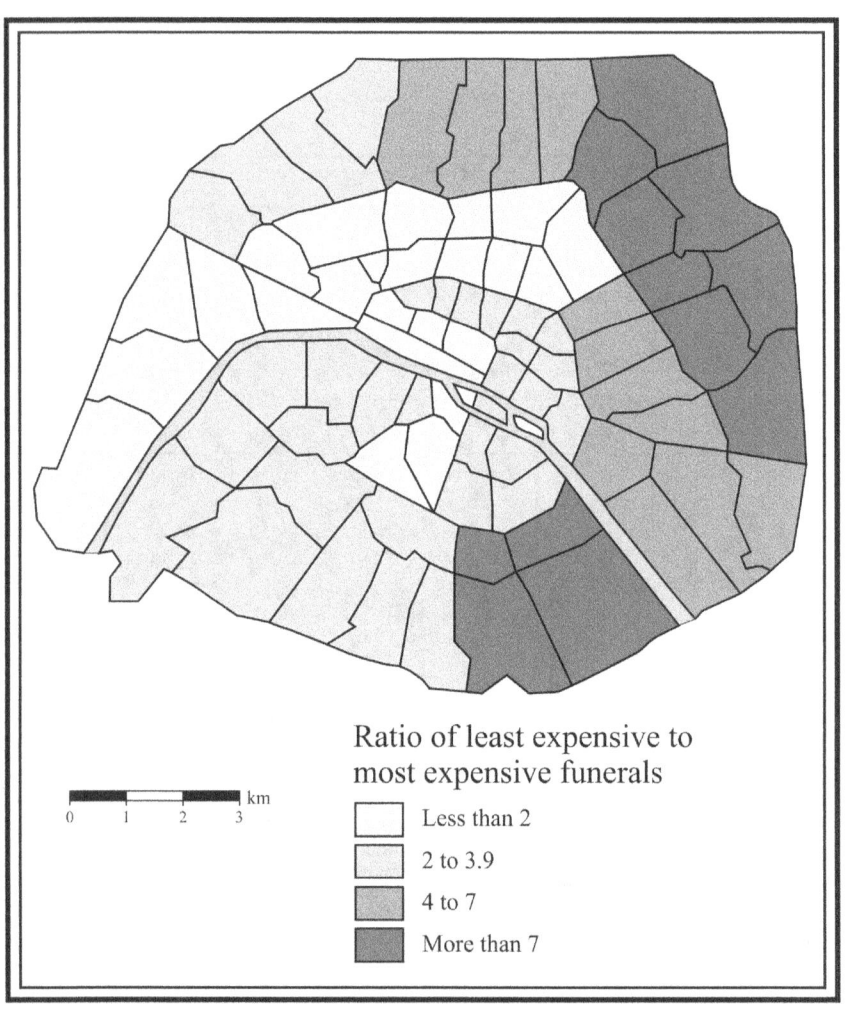

Plate 12 The geography of 'poverty' and 'wealth' in Paris in 1880. After Marchand 1993, p. 139. © Alan R. H. Baker.

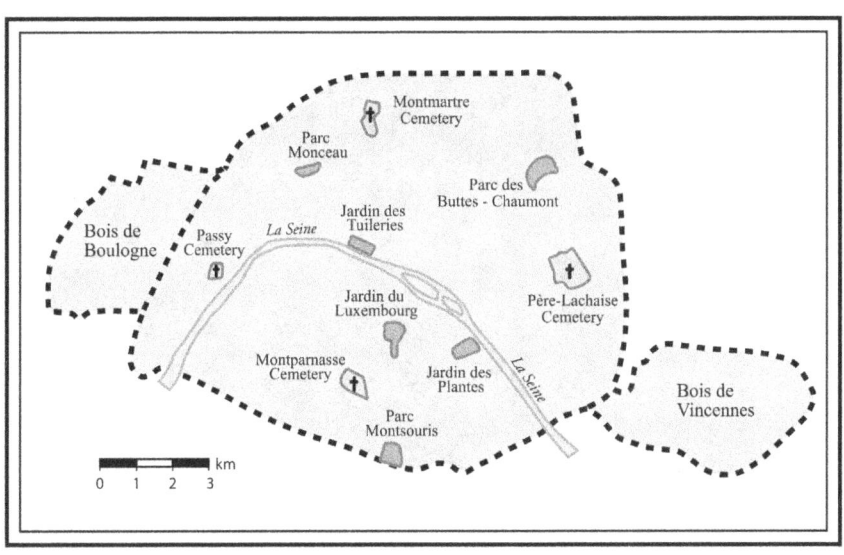

Plate 13 Principal parks, gardens and cemeteries in Paris 1870. © Alan R. H. Baker.

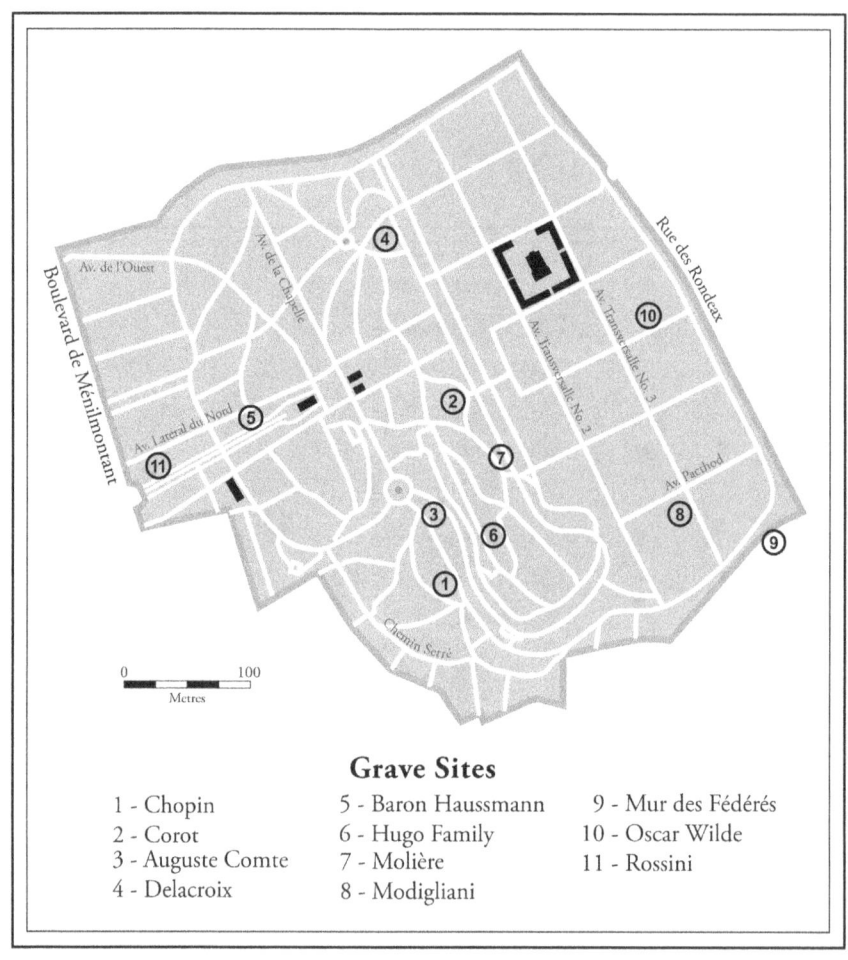

Plate 14 Plan of Père-Lachaise Cemetery indicating the burial sites of some famous individuals. After *Paris: Michelin* (Greenville, SC, 2007), pp. 286–7. © Alan R. H. Baker.

www.ingramcontent.com/pod-product-compliance
Lightning Source LLC
Chambersburg PA
CBHW062135300426
44115CB00012BA/1940